Happy Birthday
Bill

for your own paradise.
Love

Fred & Mary te

The Heavenly Food
of Sicily

Clifford A. Wright

SIMON & SCHUSTER
NEW YORK • LONDON • TORONTO
SYDNEY • TOKYO • SINGAPORE

Cucina Paradiso

For my children ALI, DYALA, *and* SERI

 SIMON & SCHUSTER
Simon & Schuster Building
Rockefeller Center
1230 Avenue of the Americas
New York, New York 10020

Copyright © 1992 by Clifford A. Wright
All rights reserved including the right of reproduction in whole or in part in any
form. SIMON & SCHUSTER *and colophon are registered trademarks of Simon &*
Schuster Inc. Designed by Edith Fowler. Manufactured in the United States of
America. Title art and map by Laurie Davis.

10 9 8 7 6 5 4 3 2 1

Grateful acknowledgment is made to the following for permission to reprint or
adapt previously published material:

William Morrow & Company, Inc.: Adaptations of the Basic Bread Dough,
Pomegranate Quail, and Roast Onion recipes from The Food of Southern
Italy, *by Carlo Middione © 1987.*

Barron's Educational Series, Inc.: Adaptation of the Involtini di Pesce Spada
recipe from The Best of Southern Italian Cooking, *by J. C. Grasso ©*
1984.

Library of Congress Cataloging-in-Publication Data

Wright, Clifford A.
  Cucina paradiso : the heavenly food of Sicily /
Clifford A. Wright.
    p.   cm.
Includes bibliographical references and index.
1. Cookery, Italian—Sicilian style.   2. Cookery,
Arab.   3. Sicily (Italy)—History.
I. Title.
TX723.2.S55W75   1992
641.5945′8—dc20   *92-20611*
                                         CIP
ISBN: 0-671-76926-X

ACKNOWLEDGMENTS

First and foremost I must thank Nancy Harmon Jenkins, whose enthusiasm for my project provided the opportunity to write this book, and my agent, Doe Coover, who guided me.

Without the enormous assistance of Paula Wolfert and Carlo Middione in helping me contact people in Sicily and generally providing sound tips and advice during the course of my research and cooking, I would have been the much poorer and I am deeply grateful to them both.

I am especially grateful to several new friends in Sicily who helped me find recipes and provided extraordinary assistance. First my greatest thanks and gratitude go to Pino Correnti, the doyen of Sicilian culinary authorities, for his invaluable assistance in providing commentary and recipes; to Enzo Siena, of the Accademia Italiana della Cucina, who went far out of his way to help me with my research; to Tommaso d'Alba, with whom I discussed the Arab influence on Sicilian cuisine, about which he has written extensively; to Fiammetta di Napoli Oliver, her husband, Arthur, and her son Carlo for their hospitality and assistance; to Michele Papa, president of the Associazione Siculo-Araba in Catania, who provided me with resources and contacts in Sicily.

I very much want to acknowledge the help of three people who have written in English on Sicilian cuisine: Mary Taylor Simeti, Nick Malgieri, and Mimmetta Lo Monte.

I also owe a debt to several restaurateurs who assisted me in my research and provided contacts and recipes. Thanks to Tony May, owner of Sandomenico in New York; Giuseppe Stancampiano, owner of La Scuderia in Palermo; Felice Piacentino, owner of Trattoria del Porto in Trapani; the proprietor of La Galleria Ristorante in Caltagirone; and Pasqualino Giudice, owner and chef of Jonico 'a Rutta e' Ciauli in Syracuse. I must especially thank Pasqualino, who not only provided recipes and prepared dishes from *cucina arabo-sicula* but also spent hours talking with me about food and listening to my painfully slow Italian.

Thanks too to Franco Marenghi, Accademia Italiana della Cucina; Count Giovanni Nuvoletti Perdomini, president of the Accademia; Monsignor Rino Passigato, Apostolic Nunciature, Washington, D.C.; Cynthia Salvato, pastry teacher, Johnson and Wales College, Providence, Rhode Island; Michele Topor, L'Arte di Cucinare, Boston; Eleonora Consoli, food journalist, *La Sicilia*, Catania; Domenico Vittorio Bruno, Centro di Cultura Siciliana "G. Pitrè," Palermo; Lucio Messina, director, Azienda Autonoma Provinciale per l'Incremento Turistico, Palermo; Domenico Manzon, a journalist based in Naples; Dr. Salvatore Impaglione, director, Azienda Autonoma Provinciale per l'Incremento Turistico, Catania; Clarice Florence, Trapani-born Sicilian cook, Long Island, New York; Sorella Margherita, librarian, Pio Istituto Educativo San Benedetto; Jan Longone and Dalia Goldstein, cookbook researchers; Charles Perry, restaurant critic, *Los Angeles Times*; Professor Bert Gordon, Mills College, California.

Thanks also go to several scholars whose conversations, correspondence, and research have helped me, especially Professor Andrew Watson, whose research and discussions with me about the Arab Agricultural Revolution are the basis of much of my thinking about the link between Arab agriculture in Sicily and Sicilian cuisine. I would also like to thank Professor Santi Correnti, University of Catania, Sicily; Professor Bernard Lewis, Princeton University; Professors James Reilly and Jon Cohen, University of Toronto; Professor Zachary Lockman, Harvard University; Dr. Gaetano Cipolla, president, Arba Sicula, Brooklyn, New York; Dr. Rudolf Grewe, New York; and Professor John Rosser, Boston College.

I would especially like to acknowledge several scholars and writers whose work I found indispensable: Professor Giovan Battista Pellegrini, the world's foremost scholar of Arabisms in Neo-Latin languages; Professor Henri Bresc, Université Paris-Nanterre, and the Sicilian food writers Giuseppe Coria, Anna Pomar, N. Sapio Bartelletti, Baldo Russo, and Antonio Cardella.

Finally I would like to thank my former wife, Najwa al-Qattan, who not only helped in some Arabic translation but years ago casually suggested that I write this book. For the help I often needed with translation in at least six languages I would especially like to thank Kristina Hmeljak, Anna Gandini, Anahi Pari, Leena and Najwa al-Qattan, Nora Rossi, Laura Pizer, and Mimmetta Lo Monte.

Special thanks go to my fishmonger, Salvatore Fantasia, who every Monday devoted hours of talking with me about fish. And to a wonderful gentleman, Francesco Quinci, of Mazara del Vallo, who along with the renowned Professor Giorgio Bini, represented Italy in joint Arab-Sicilian fishing cooperation talks, and who talked with me about the Sicilian use of fish.

Thanks to my very good friend Boyd Grove, who accompanied me on one of my research trips to Sicily, and to Kate and Nadim Rouhana, Stephan Haggard, Nancy Gilson, Ronnie Littenberg, Phil Brown, Omar al-Qattan, Susan Rashid Horn and Richard Horn, Sarah and Sam Thayer, and Niki Gilsdorf. I also want to thank my friend Ameena Ghattas, an Egyptian cook from whom I learned much and who has cared for my children on occasion with love and affection. Very special thanks go to Harry Irwin, Pam Haltom, David Forbes, Virginia Sherwood, Marsha Gordon, Nancy Campbell, and Beth Brownlow, who all gladly lent me their kitchens and gave me their advice and smiled politely through recipe failures; and to my good friend Darlene Faye Adams, who not only was my sous-chef for numerous recipe tests but also accompanied me into the depths of the Library of Congress in Washington, D.C., in search of obscure Italian cookbooks.

Finally I wish to thank my two editors, Toula Polygalaktos and Gail Winston, whose creative talents made this a better book, and Claudia Hautaniemi, who suggested the title.

To all the people who helped me I am extremely grateful.

C.W.
Arlington, Massachusetts

Contents

I remembered Sicily while death triggered my soul to memories of being expelled from the paradise it was.

—AL-EDRISI

I loved Sicily in my youth; she seemed to me a garden of immortal felicity. But scarce had I come to mature years, when behold, the land became a burning gehenna.

—ABD AL-HALIM AS-SIKILLI

Oh that I could embark on the crescent moon,
fly to the shores of Sicily and there
crush myself against the breast of the sun!

—IBN HAMDIS

Part One

ONE

The Lost Paradise of Sicilian Cuisine

I fell in love with Sicily the moment our plane banked above the cerulean Golfo di Carini near the arid peninsula of Punta Ráisi airport west of Palermo.

This was the first day of a much-deserved vacation—my ex-wife and I were both changing jobs, and our first year with a newborn had left us exhausted. I had just spent three intellectually stimulating years at a research institute in Washington, D.C., where much of my work dealt with the Arab world.

The Sicily of my fertile imagination seemed the perfect Mediterranean destination for a carefree holiday. I couldn't wait to eat Sicilian food. I had learned to cook in Italian restaurants twenty years earlier and almost made a career of cooking, having once been offered a job as a sous-chef. In a sense I did make a career of it, since I have been cooking for family and friends ever since.

I longed to taste the exotic flavors of Sicilian cuisine—saffron, capers, golden raisins and currants, pine nuts, orange zest, fresh anchovy. I had no idea then that a vacation would turn into a fascinating quest for the lost paradise of medieval Arab flavors.

That quest later took me back to Sicily, and down into the depths of libraries, and into the kitchen over the course of several years.

My two loves, research and cooking, are woven together in this cookbook. I believe that enjoying food from foreign lands is heightened by knowing their history and culture. In writing this book, I've striven to place these wonderful Sicilian recipes in a historical context. I hope my efforts will reward both your palate and your sense of history.

Sicily is a sun-drenched island splashed by the azure waters of the Tyrrhenian, Ionian, and Mediterranean seas. Since antiquity Sicily has been known as the island in the sun. My enchantment with this island is amplified by its distinctive "eastern" air of dusty and languid towns built of brown tufa. The Sicilians themselves are a study in contrasts, dolorous and cheerful, friendly yet suspicious.

I found the sights, smells, and tastes of Sicily had an Arab feeling, an aura that was not a mirage, but a story waiting to be told. It became all the more intriguing when Tommaso d'Alba, a Sicilian gastronome and author of *La Cucina Siciliana di Derivazione Araba,* told me a Sicilian proverb: Scratch the skin of a Sicilian and you will find an Arab.

Later, d'Alba, a warm and engaging man, began to speak of *cucina arabo-sicula,* with an excitement that was infectious. What was it? As best I could make out at the time, *cucina arabo-sicula* was or is the cuisine of the poor, with lingering traces of sumptuous Arab fantasies of fragrance and taste. "Make no mistake," d'Alba said, "the Arabs produced a true and proper revolution in the food habits of Sicily."

This matter of Arab influence in Sicilian food had also popped up in Waverley Root's *The Food of Italy.* Root's enthusiasm about the Arab influence led him to claim, "Almost everything that strikes us today as typically Sicilian is typically Saracen."

My quest had begun. I had to find out what *cucina arabo-sicula* was. Did it exist? Were there recipes? Could I learn something about it and, more important, could I cook, taste, and communicate it? The answers were yes, yes, and, I hope, yes.

When I returned to Sicily later on a research trip, I arranged to meet Pino Correnti, the doyen of Sicilian gastronomes, and Enzo Siena of the Accademia Italiana della Cucina. I asked Correnti, "Is there an Arab-Sicilian cuisine?" "Yes," he said, "but although you can identify Arab-derived dishes you must look at Sicilian cuisine in its entirety to understand the diversity of influences, let alone one of them. Sicily is a rich civilization derived from all its conquerors. No one cuisine dominates; they are all woven together to produce the rich Sicilian cuisine of today."

Sicilian culture is inlaid with a thousand-year-old Arabian inheritance, embodied in the food of the island.

Correnti and Siena encouraged me to write this book. They provided me with recipe ideas and advice. Siena was the only Sicilian to ask me "How does someone named Wright come from three thousand miles away to write about the Arabs in Sicily?" I laughed, because it does seem strange, and explained that my grandfather was born near Benevento in Campania. My interest in the Arabs came about from my research work and from having an Arab wife.

As we talked at his summer home, spectacularly perched above the Ionian Sea in Torre Archirafi, Correnti mentioned two exemplary preparations that are Arab in inspiration. One was *Zuppa di Pesce alla Saracena*, fish stew made with grouper, red mullet, sole, shrimp, and squid simmered in a broth with saffron, parsley, hot red pepper, and sweet yellow pepper. He jumped up to get the second one, a pitcher full of an iced orange drink. "Now this is Arab-Sicilian," he announced with pride. It was heavenly and thirst-quenching, but must remain a secret—he didn't give me the recipe!

Sicilian cuisine is full of secrets. This cookbook is not the last word on Sicilian cuisine but merely a sampling of the food Sicilians call *cucina arabo-sicula*. The trendy food of northern Italy has eclipsed Sicilian cuisine, but I think you will find these recipes both exotic and familiar. Why? Because the foods of the Italian cuisine you may be acquainted with have some roots in the Sicilian cuisine of centuries long past.

The Arabs invaded Sicily in 827, and their culture remained there intact for four hundred years. The heart of Arab culinary influence is in western Sicily, where the Arabs maintained a presence for two hundred years after the Christian reconquest. This was my destination. I planned to meander through this mountainous area of the island, searching for lost dishes and meeting the people who could tell me about them. In small trattorias and private homes, I hoped to taste such inventions as *Sasizzeddi Agrassati*—beef rolls stuffed with pecorino cheese, parsley, golden raisins, and pine nuts, and sautéed in fine Marsala wine—a dish that melts in your mouth; or *Stigghiole*—the rustic charcoal-grilled caul fat stuffed with parsley, fresh sage, and lamb heart. Along the coast I would find *Gamberetti al Pomodoro*, a savory dish of shrimp, tomatoes, capers, raisins, celery, and pine nuts.

Eastern Sicily, which is often called the "Greek side" of the island, supposedly with no Arab influence, did have significant Arab influence at one time—it just ended sooner than on the west side. In the eleventh century, Catania was entirely Arabpopulated, and today there are several dishes from eastern Sicily that can claim Arab roots including *Pasticcio di Mohammed ibn ath-Thumna* (the chicken pie of the Emir of Catania Mohammed ibn ath-Thumna), a hollowed-out round bread stuffed with boned chicken, almonds, and pistachios, and bound with eggs; or *Crispelle di Riso alla Benedettina*, crisp deep-fried rice fritters flavored with lemon and served with orange-blossom honey.

When I asked Sicilians what the foundation was for *cucina arabo-sicula*, they nearly all gave the same answer—folklore and intuition. One has to look at what the Arabs brought to Sicily in the way of new crops and recognize what the Arabs themselves ate. It is also important to see how their traditions meshed with the ancient Greek, Roman, and Byzantine heritage they found in Sicily, and how those traditions were affected by the subsequent Norman, Swabian, French, and Spanish occupiers.

The last Arab Sicilians disappeared seven hundred years ago, so seeking the Arab roots can be frustrating. Untangling the culinary story is further complicated because Spain, which controlled Sicily for several centuries, had itself been ruled by the Arabs for six hundred years. Its own cuisine has many Arab-derived dishes, such as *paella*. In fact, an Arab-Spanish cuisine is also identifiable.

Although there is no agreement among Sicilians as to what Arab-Sicilian cuisine is, there are some common characteristics most agree on:

- The absence of *antipasti*. What the Sicilians call *grape 'u pitittu* are snacks or tidbits rather than appetizers. They are foods consumed *fuori tavola* (literally, away from the table), like *Arancine* and *Panelle*, which are basically what we would call street food.
- The *piatto unico* or one-pot meal. Some Sicilians believe the one-pot meal, combining many different elements, is an Arab vestige.
- Confectionery. Sicilians learned the art of making confections from the Arabs. The combination of pistachios, almonds, figs, and other fruit with sugar and honey is an Arab legacy. Ice cream and sherbet originated with the Arab Sicilians.
- Blends of nuts or breadcrumbs with raisins or currants and saffron. The Arabs used these to create exotic stuffings and seasonings.
- Stuffed and skewered foods. The Arab fondness for stuffed foods is shared by the Sicilians.
- Rice dishes. The Arabs introduced rice to Sicily, and although its cultivation died out, there are still many Arab-inspired Sicilian

rice dishes. Some food writers even argue that the famous *Risotto alla Milanese* is an Arab-Sicilian invention transplanted north.
• Sweet-and-sour dishes. Sour and sweet sauces are served with just about everything—chicken, rabbit, fish, meat, and vegetables.
• Citrus fruit married to meat and fish. Citrus fruits, especially oranges and lemons, are cooked with fish, meat, and vegetables.

A good clue to determining which dishes are Arab in origin is the linguistic connection. For example, Cuscusù, the Sicilian fish couscous, found exclusively in western Sicily; Cassata, a rich ricotta cake, that takes its name from the Arabic *qas'at*, the pan in which it is baked; *Cubbaita di Giuggiulena*, another dessert made with sesame seeds, honey, and almonds, comes from the Arabic *qubbayta*.

Why is the Arab influence so clearly identifiable and not, say, the Roman? How did Arab culinary inspiration and even recipes survive? One reason is that when Arab rule ended, Arab cooks found their way into the royal kitchens of the Norman kings. Another is that many recipes were kept safe in convents and monasteries. This is particularly true of confectionery, including such pastries as *Mecucka*, but also pizza (*Sfincione di San Vito*) and pasta dishes (*Pasta alla Paolina*).

The great Sicilian gastronome and Arabist Alberto Denti di Pirajno has a theory to explain how the convents became home for so many Arab-influenced dishes. During Arab rule, the inland town of Caltanissetta was called Qal'at al-Nissa, the castle of women, after the famous harem of the emir of that city. The harem women whiled away their time making sweets and cakes. After the Normans conquered Caltanissetta in the 1080s, the harems disappeared but not the Muslim Arab Sicilians. They even fled into the mountains, some converted, and, I believe, the women found refuge as crypto-Muslim nuns in the convents. They brought with them their secret recipes, which were handed down over the centuries within the confines of the convent walls.

My quest for the roots of Arab-Sicilian cuisine began in Palermo. As I stood before the stunning Cappella Palatina in the Palazzi dei Normanni in Palermo, I stared in wonderment at an inscription chiseled in Arabic script. An old man, a self-appointed curator standing just inside the Cappella, told me the chapel was founded in 1132 by the Norman King of Sicily Roger II, but the workmanship was definitely Arab.

The foundation of Sicily's rich medieval heritage was the symbiotic relationship between Normans and Arabs in the twelfth century. In the Cappella Palatina, Byzantine mosaics, scenes from the Old Testament with Latin inscriptions, and a purely Islamic wooden ceiling honeycombed with intricate painted panels coexist in perfect harmony. The ceiling panels, the earliest datable group of Arab paintings in existence, are sanctified in Arabic script to the glory of the king. The paintings depict delightful scenes of the so-called oriental life enjoyed by the Arabized Norman kings: people picnicking, enjoying their harems, and eating and drinking.

Two other Arab-inspired palaces survive in Palermo, La Cuba and La Zisa. In the twelfth century the Arab traveler Ibn Jubayr described these Norman palaces surrounding Palermo as "beads around the neck of a beautiful woman."

The Cappella is always a peaceful refuge from the dusty bustle of perpetually hectic Palermo. When I revisited Palermo several years later on a research trip with my friend Boyd Grove, nothing had changed—the city was still in a state of construction, destruction, and deterioration. Escaping the urban intensity and the heat, we found a small trattoria tucked away on a side street. Their specialty was *Pesce Spada alla Sfincione*, layered swordfish fillets baked with an aromatic blend of oregano, anchovies, and breadcrumbs.

Over some beer we caught up with some background history read from a collection of books bought from Flaccovio's, the best bookstore in Palermo. In the beginning three tribes inhabited Sicily, the Sicani, the Elmyi, and the Siculi, who gave their name to the island. Greek colonization began in about 735 B.C., and the Greeks made Sicily their greatest colony. Many famous Greeks, including Archimedes and Gorgias, were born there.

Under the Romans, the island became known as "the granary of Rome." Seventeen centuries ago Sicily was the summer playground of rich Romans whose palatial villas, such as the *Villa Romana del Casale* in Piazza Armenia, can be seen today.

As important as the Greeks and Romans were, they did not have a lasting influence on the cuisine of Sicily. In classical times, the diet of the masses consisted of little but bread and porridge with some vegetables, fish, and spices. Sicily may have been the granary of Rome but the wheat was not thoroughly cleaned before grinding and the result was flour of poor quality. And although many plants were known to the Romans, they were not extensively cultivated for the kitchen.

Early in the ninth century, two hundred years after the Arabs swept out of their desert home in the Arabian peninsula, they reached Sicily, bringing with them their religion, agriculture, science, and food. They brought in new crops, expanded the cultivation of old crops, and radically changed the foodways of Europe. Advances in European agriculture have long been attributed to the Crusaders, but scholars now credit the Arabs with these changes.

The Arab invasion force that landed on that fateful day in June 827 at Granitola, a few miles outside the town of Mazara del Vallo, changed the course of Sicilian history. Sicily was then ruled by Byzantium. The story goes that a romantic encounter between a Sicilian nun, Omoniza, and the Byzantine naval leader, Euphemius, was viewed as a rape by the nun's brothers, and they appealed to the Byzantine emperor Michael II to punish Euphemius. But Euphemius executed the emissary sent to arrest him and declared himself emperor of Sicily. Not long after, he sought refuge with the Arab dynasty of the Aghlabids, then ruling Tunisia, ninety miles across the Sicilian Channel. Euphemius offered the Arabs suzerainty over Sicily in return for their help against Michael II.

Reluctantly, because of a peace treaty with Byzantium, the Arabs agreed to invade Sicily. In a torpid but bloody campaign of pillage, it took fifty years to conquer Syracuse, the capital. It was the greatest triumph of all the triumphs in Islam in terms of wealth. Four hundred thousand pounds of sterling silver were hauled away. The Arabs moved the capital to Palermo, where it remains to this day, and created three governates (or *vilayet* in Arabic), to consolidate their rule. They exist today as the Val di Mazara, Val de Noto, and Val Demone; the word *val* coming not from "valley" but from the Arabic *wali*, the governor of the *vilayet*.

I drove out of Mazara early one morning to find Granitola, now marked by a lighthouse, and parked near an old Norman-Arab *giarre* (water tower). Surveying the windswept escarpment, I found it easy to imagine myself one of those medieval conquerors. Lunch that day clearly reflected their presence—*Riso alla Marinara*, rice, the cultivation of which was introduced by the Arabs, with seafood perfumed with saffron, the prototypical Arab flavoring. Such food has its roots in the golden age of medieval Sicily.

After a quarter century of peaceful rule, a revolt fueled by a devastating and horrible famine racked Sicily. The anonymous *Tarih Gazirat Siqilliah*, known as the Cambridge Chronicle, describes parents eating their children in desperation. Sicily's Arab rulers in North Africa sent the Arab general Al-Hassan ibn Ali al-Kalbi to quash the rebellion.

Al-Kalbi created his own independent dynasty, which opened

a new and brilliant chapter in Sicily's history. The Kalbite court was famous for its learning, generosity, magnanimity, and justice.

Nothing remains from the Kalbite dynasty of Sicily except perhaps the concept of kitchen gardens, which were expanded under the Normans. Such vegetables as eggplant and artichoke were introduced to Sicilian tables. One dish that supposedly has its origins in this era is *Cugghiune dell'Ortolano*, in which small eggplants are filled and fried, then served with a sweet-and-sour sauce.

From the Norman era of the twelfth century much more remains, primarily because the Normans were awed by Arab culture.

How did the Normans come to Sicily, of all places? At first restless Norman knights started spilling out of northwestern France because of overpopulation and a shortage of land in the early eleventh century. Mostly landless younger sons, they embarked on pilgrimages to Palestine in search of adventure and often returned by way of Sicily.

Not until later, in 1061, did the Normans set out to conquer Sicily under Count Roger, the "Great Count." Five years later, when William the Conqueror invaded England, he utilized the lessons Count Roger had learned during amphibious operations in Sicily.

It took thirty years for the Normans to conquer Sicily and bring an end to 264 years of Muslim rule. Arab culture did not die, however, since half the population was still Muslim Arab.

Roger II, son of the Great Count, became the most illustrious ruler of Norman Sicily. He admired Arab culture and lived as a caliph, with a court of Arab officials and attendants and a harem. His royal bodyguards and cooks, in the most trusted positions at court, were Arabs. The royal cook, known by his Arabic title *an-nazhir*, created magnificent dishes.

When Roger II died, the tolerant equilibrium of his kingdom diminished under his son, William the Bad, who was unable to control the marauding Norman barons who were attacking Arabs in the countryside. William was called "Bad" by the Norman barons, not by the Arab Sicilians. The barons were violent and ambitious men full of racial hatred of the Arabs. They captured William and sacked the treasury, also destroying priceless documents of Norman Sicily.

The Pope also wanted the Muslim Arabs of Sicily removed or destroyed, so Lombard settlers were brought in to settle around Qurlijum, an old ninth-century Arab fortress. (This later became Corleone, the home of Don Corleone in *The Godfather*.) The Lombards attacked the rural Arab villages, and the Arabs fled to the western part of Sicily and the cities of Palermo, Agrigento, and Trapani.

William the Good, grandson of Roger II, allowed a bit more tolerance of Arabs. He too liked to live like an Arab caliph. He was known as "good" because the barons approved of him—a bad omen for the Arabs.

The end was nearing for the Arab Sicilians. Daughters were encouraged to marry Muslims from other countries, and many left for exile never to return to their homes. Others, mostly farmers, hid in the mountains *ob metum Christianorum* (from fear of the Christians).

Although the Arab population was disappearing, Arab legacies were not. Government offices, such as fiscal administration and the navy, created by the Arabs, continued under the Normans. The chief of the navy office was *al-emir*. From this Arab-Sicilian innovation we derive our English word "admiral."

On Christmas Day 1194, the Swabians began their presence in Sicily with the coronation of Henry VI of the Swabian house of Hohenstaufen. A day later, Henry's wife Constance, the aunt of William the Good, gave birth to the future King Frederick II, who became known as Stupor Mundi (amazement of the world), the greatest of medieval kings.

Frederick's interest in Arabic learning gave rise to a new golden age and a legendary intellectual vibrancy in his court. He founded the University of Naples, one of the first in Europe, and required doctors to have degrees. He lived like a caliph, and his luxurious court was crowded with Arab philosophers, dancers, harem women, and astrologers. His understanding of Arabic led to the promotion of Arabic medical and scientific tracts and translations. Frederick was a famous epicure. *Turuna 'Ntianati* was probably an invention of Frederick's Arab chefs.

Frederick's court, as energized as it was by Arabic learning, did not translate into better times for the Arab Sicilians; they were further reduced to slavery and serfdom. The desolate mountainous lairs of western Sicily provided the remnant of Arab Sicilians a refuge from Christian attack. Some scholars believe that the secret guerrilla bands the Arabs formed in these mountains are the origin of the Mafia.

A previously unknown Arab Sicilian heroine of that period recently came to light. Known only as the Daughter of Ibn Abbad, she led a revolt against Frederick in 1222. She tricked Frederick into committing three hundred of his elite cavalry to accept her surrender, whereupon she massacred them.

In the end, Frederick's solution to the guerrilla groups was to round them up and deport them to Lucera in Apulia in 1246. This Arab-Sicilian community in Lucera remained loyal to Frederick, because he protected them against the Pope, who was even more ruthless.

With the death of Frederick, the days of the Arabs of Sicily were nearly over. When he died, a Muslim *qadi* in Palermo gave orders for a lament in Arabic to be carved into his tombstone: "Where is my land . . . Alas!"

One of the greatest contributions of the Arabs in Sicily was the medieval Arab Agricultural Revolution. One feature of this revolution was the development of kitchen gardens, which changed Sicilian diet and cuisine.

The *latifundia*, large unproductive Roman and Byzantine estates, were broken up by the Arabs into small farms, encouraged through taxes that promoted cultivated land. I noticed remnants of the *latifundia* one day as I drove out of Caltanissetta past the famous vineyards of Regaleali (from the Arabic *rahal 'ali*, hamlet of Ali), the home of Count Tasca d'Almerita. There one can still find small plots of land divided by stone walls.

The Arabs brought many plants to Sicily. There is little documentation, but we can get an idea by comparing cultivation before and after the Arab invasion. Rice, hard wheat, cotton, and sugar cane; orange and mulberry trees; odoriferous flowers, like asphodel and jasmine; spinach and artichokes; apricots, bananas, and watermelon; sesame seed and pistachio were all introduced by the Arabs.

They brought their knowledge of hydrology and irrigation. The control of water flow allowed the Sicilian farmer to regulate the harvest and grow more food. A new invention from the windy and arid regions of the Arab world, the windmill, arrived in the early tenth century. Now more flour could be milled and more bread eaten. Pizzas such as the tasty *Carbuciu,* a double pizza stuffed with tomatoes, oregano, and anchovy, became popular.

Bread, the basis of the Sicilian diet, was so ubiquitous that in the vernacular, people called all foods *companaticum* (accompaniment of bread). Fresh fruit played an important role in Sicily, as did fish. Eggs, as seen in such medieval dishes as *Taganu d' Aragona*, were common. This festive baked dish of rigatoni is a fusion of a dozen or more fresh eggs and pecorino and mozzarella cheeses, flavored with an aromatic mixture of saffron, parsley, and cinnamon.

Medieval peasant food was very simple. Farm workers ate semolina bread with onions and lemon with salt. In summer they ate olives. They ate vegetables like cabbage, cardoons, fennel, and onions and, rarely, some olive oil. On special occasions they might have a chicken or sausages with their pasta.

More people were needed to work the small Arab farms that began to change the Sicilian landscape. The result was earlier marriages, larger families, and more food needed to feed the growing population. The Arabs encouraged the establishment of these small farms through a new institution called *iqta*, originally a land grant for army troops. The *iqta* enabled the government to pass on income from land taxes, thus avoiding currency fluctuations. The *iqta* was important in Sicily because it put agriculture under the control of farmers who were free sharecroppers, not serfs, and therefore more productive.

The Arab–Sicilian farmer was encouraged to adopt new crops such as hard wheat, the most important Arab contribution, because of new demand for durable wheat. The high gluten content of hard wheat led to three culinary inventions: pasta, couscous, and hardtack. Hard-wheat products, unlike the summer wheat of the classical era, don't spoil and in medieval Sicily became a reserve food against famine.

A plentiful supply of hardtack made longer sea voyages possible. Pasta and couscous allowed speculators and governments to warehouse surpluses for use during years of low production or even famine and to offset inflation caused by high prices and demand.

Around 1100 Sicily was dotted with Arab market hamlets of about a hundred families. Sadly, under the weight of the oppressive Norman barons, the farms began to disappear and the Arabs clustered in larger villages for protection. Their small farms, orchards, and gardens were consolidated into large ranches and estates, which were owned by Norman barons and the church. The achievements of Arab agriculture were undone.

But the kitchen garden survived. The Arab–Sicilian kitchen garden evolved from the Islamic conception of the Garden of Paradise. The Koran describes gardens adorned with silken cushions arranged on rich carpets for lounging in the shade of broad-leafed trees, cooled further by the soothing tinkle of fountains. In paradise the *houris*, black-eyed beauties "with swelling breasts," and lovely boys, the *ghilman*, will attend every need in a purely sensual world of sight, sound, and taste.

The Arab emirs of Sicily fashioned royal gardens of verdant foliage and abundant springs. These gardens, *urtu* in Sicilian, were identical to the *huertas* of Spain that have their roots in the Arab era. The inspiration for these gardens came from the Arab *bustan*, the orchard-garden they longed for and remembered from their homelands, such as the luxuriant and abundant Ghurta of Damascus. In Palermo the gardens were planted with exotic fruits, such as oranges, herbs, and flowers. The gardens of paradise also evolved into kitchen gardens that provided Arab chefs with the raw material for their culinary inventions.

Islamic water-use laws encouraged irrigation, which brought new crops into the kitchen. Tax exemptions for such crops as olives, bananas, oranges, lemons, mangoes, and date palms assured the importance of olives and citrus in Sicilian cuisine. I discovered that the Sicilian dialect dealing with hydrology and irrigation is nearly all vestigial Arabisms, which indicates that Arabs were the original innovators and users.

The variety of crops in the kitchen gardens was enormous. Apples, pears, peaches, quinces, grapes, citron, *lumie* (a small, soft citron), bitter oranges, and pomegranates were cultivated.

Mangoes and bananas were introduced by the Arabs. The Arabic word for banana, *mawz* or *musa*, has survived in only one European language, Sicilian, as *musa*. The banana was prominent in the Arab gardens of Palermo because in the Koran the tree of the Garden of Eden is the banana tree, not the apple tree. Arab skill in artificial pollination boosted cultivation of pistachio nuts and palm trees.

Twelfth-century Sicily was a wondrous paradise, according to al-Edrisi, Count Roger II's court geographer. Arab chroniclers such as al-Istahri, Ibn Jubayr, and al-Andalusi describe markets selling fruit, hazelnuts, almonds, walnuts, dried figs, and rabbits.

Fourteenth-century contracts between the owners of these gardens and their farmers show the Arab heritage of these gardens. The contracts, now in the archives of Palermo, show that the kitchen gardens were identical to the ones described by the Arab agronomist Ibn al-Awwam when he visited Sicily in the twelfth century.

Sicilian food is different from Italian food, even when the ingredients are similar or the same. Alberto Denti di Pirajno attributes the difference to the fact that Sicily made no contribution to European mysticism and that skepticism was born on the island. What he means is that Sicilian cuisine is an earthly cuisine that "draws from the produce of its fertile soil a sunny delight for tastes educated by a twenty-five-century-long cooking tradition."

Culinary skepticism keeps the Sicilian cook close to the kitchen and garden. The ingredients of Sicilian cuisine are simple and fresh. Sicilian cooking is home cooking. It has never been influenced by professional cooking, as French cuisine has. Although some dishes can become complex and time-consuming, for the most part nothing is difficult to make.

The recipes in this book are Sicilian, in content and spirit. These dishes, and the customs, stories, and flavors they represent, offer us a chance to gaze back through history and to savor a lost paradise.

TWO
The Sicilian Pantry

Almonds

The almond was first cultivated by the Greeks in Sicily; it was revitalized later by the Arabs. For ease in preparation, buy blanched almonds. Store in the refrigerator or freezer.

Amaretti

These crisp, almond-flavored cookies are used, crushed, in some meatball preparations. They can be found in Italian groceries and gourmet food shops.

Aniseed

Aniseed was known to the Egyptians, Greeks, and Romans, but its cultivation in Sicily was introduced by the Arabs. In medieval times, Arab doctors used aniseed for its supposed medicinal properties. Today aniseed is used in some desserts and to make *Zammú*. Aniseed should be kept in a cool, dark place.

Apricots

The Arabs introduced the apricot to Sicily. The word "apricot" derives from the Arabic *al-berquq*. Though both the Greeks and Romans knew of this fruit, combining it with meat or rice is an Arab and Persian tradition.

Artichokes

The artichoke was developed by the Arabs, or perhaps the Berbers, from the cardoon, a wild edible thistle that looks like celery and tastes like artichoke. The artichoke first appeared in Italy in Naples and then in Tuscany in 1466, but it was being grown in Sicily as early as 1290 in the kitchen gardens of Palermo and possibly earlier.

Artichokes in the United States are tougher than those grown in Sicily, so look for young artichokes with tightly closed bracts or baby artichokes that have not yet developed a choke.

Frozen artichoke hearts and those imported and canned in water are satisfactory for many recipes, but the fresh are preferable.

Basil

Fresh basil is available year-round and preferable to dried.

Bay leaf

Bay leaves grow all over Sicily and are often used when grilling. If you are unable to find fresh bay leaves, soak dried bay leaves in water for an hour to make them less brittle.

Bread

Bread is a very important staple in the Sicilian diet as it is in Italian cuisine in general. See pages 64–74.

Breadcrumbs

Sicilians use breadcrumbs to thicken sauces, to sprinkle over pasta, and to add texture to many dishes. Make your own breadcrumbs from stale dry Italian or French bread in a food processor. Buy only unseasoned plain breadcrumbs in the supermarket or bags of plain breadcrumbs in an Italian grocery or in a bakery.

Broccoli

Broccoli is called *sparaceddi* in Sicilian. *Sparaceddi* also refers to broccoli rape or rapini. In Sicilian, green cauliflower is called broccoli, while white cauliflower is called *vrucculu*. If you can find green cauliflower, use it to replace white cauliflower.

Caciocavallo

Caciocavallo is a cow's-milk cheese that can be eaten as a table cheese when young. Aging up to a year produces a sharper, harder cheese good for grating. Use the mild version in all recipes. If you are unable to find caciocavallo, substitute imported provolone.

Traditionally, the cheese is shaped in balls that are tied together, two by two, with raffia. The most popular story of how this cheese got its name is that when it is hung to cure it resembles saddlebags thrown over the haunches of a horse—hence, *cacio*, meaning "cheese," and *cavallo*, meaning "horse." Another theory is that it was originally made from mare's milk and stamped with a horse, the seal of Naples. Or perhaps it is related to *Qashqawan*, an Arab-Turkish cheese.

Candied fruit

The art of candying fruit was taught to the Sicilians by the Arabs. The most common fruit used for candying are citrus fruits, specifically the peel. I have provided a recipe on page 240, but you might also check Middle Eastern markets, which often have wonderful candied peel. The tasteless supermarket variety should be avoided.

Capers

The use of capers in Sicilian food goes back to the Greeks. Being a desert plant, the caper bush needs very little water or nutrients. The best Sicilian capers come from Pantelleria.

Good Italian groceries will sell capers by the pound preserved in vinegar, brine, or salt. They will be much cheaper than the very expensive tiny jars of capers in vinegar. Keep them in a tight jar and rinse them as you need them.

Cauliflower

See Broccoli.

Cheese

Sicily was an important center for cheese production in the medieval Mediterranean. During the twelfth century cheese was exported in a trade involving Jews who provided kosher products for the Egyptian Jewish community. Only later did this trade develop with northern Italy. See individual cheeses.

Chicken

When buying chickens try to get the free-range kind. They have less fat and are more flavorful.

Chick-peas

Dried chick-peas need to be soaked overnight and cooked at length, but canned chick-peas are satisfactory. Chick-pea flour, used for *Panelle*, is available in Italian groceries, gourmet shops, and some health-food stores.

Chili peppers

Chili peppers are sometimes associated with the Arab influence by Sicilians, even though they came later from the New World, probably by way of Spain or Tunisia. Buy whole dried chili peppers and store them in a jar away from sunlight. Use rubber gloves when crumbling or cutting the peppers, or wash your hands with soap and water immediately.

Cinnamon

Cinnamon is the inner layer of the bark of the cinnamon tree. An ancient spice, it was popularized by Arab traders in Sicily, although it had been known as an exotic spice before then. Keep both ground and stick cinnamon on hand.

Cooking equipment

The absence of chimneys in thirteenth-century Sicilian homes has led historians to conclude that most cooking was done outdoors. Outdoor grilling is still a popular method of cooking in Sicily. In medieval Sicily, cooks used either a cooking tripod, called a *tripos*, or a slow braiser, called a *fucularu*, over a wood fire outside. Some outdoor ovens still exist in Sicily, in the baking sheds attached to some Sicilian homes, just as in North Africa. In aristocratic Sicilian households, cooking was done in a *tannura*, an in-ground baking oven, which the Arabs introduced and called a *tannur*. Indoor ovens are said to be a Norman introduction.

Several items will make cooking Sicilian dishes a lot easier. A *couscoussière* is necessary for making couscous. Earthenware or terra-cotta casseroles are authentic but can be replaced with heavy enameled pots and pans. An electric deep-fat fryer makes deep frying much simpler.

Currants

Called *ribes,* from the Arabic word for rhubarb, or *uvette zante*, currants are little black raisins. They may have been introduced to Sicily by Palestinian Arabs. California currants, called zante raisins, are quite satisfactory. Soak them if they seem dry.

Eggplants

The eggplant was introduced to Sicily by the Arabs around the late tenth century. It did not become popular in the rest of Italy for another five hundred years. The Italians once called the eggplant *radice araba*, Arab root.

The best eggplants, according to Sicilians, are a variety known as the Tunisian eggplant—large, egg-shaped, and pale purple, which is very sweet and does not have to be salted before cooking. Our oblong, deep-purple variety of eggplant absorbs too much oil when fried. I have tried to take this into account in the recipes by keeping the deep-frying temperature higher than usual and by calling for deep frying rather than shallow frying in less oil. More oil seems to work better than less oil.

Eggplant must be salted and left on paper towels to drain of its bitter water content before cooking. Pat the eggplant dry and then continue the preparation.

Fava beans

The fava bean is an important food in Mediterranean societies. In Sicily the fava goes back to before the Greeks. Sicilians eat fava raw and in *Frittedda*.

Fennel

Wild Sicilian fennel cannot be found in the United States, although Californians have access to a wild fennel of their own. For the rest of us I recommend a suggestion made by Paula Wolfert and Giuliano Bugialli to combine a bit of dill and fennel (see page 84).

Bulb or Florence fennel, called *finocchio* in Italian, is available almost year-round, with peak season in fall and winter.

Figs

Fresh figs are popular and abundant in Sicily. The only recipe in this book requiring figs uses dried figs.

Fish

See page 154.

Flour

Use unbleached all-purpose flour or bread flour if available.

Garlic

Garlic is one of the four cornerstones of Sicilian flavor, along with onions, parsley, and oregano.

Lard

In Sicilian folk medicine, raw pork fat was spread behind the ears to help recover from the mumps. The Koran prohibits the use of pork; the Arabs used sheep's tail fat instead of pork lard.

In Sicilian cooking, lard is usually used for browning meats for stews. You can use olive oil in its place.

Lemons

The first mention of the lemon tree in any language dates from the beginning of the tenth century and is from an Arabic source: Qustus al-Rumi, who wrote a book on farming, notes that the *laimun* tree is very sensitive to cold.

Sicilians are very fond of lemons, eating them raw with salt, in salads, in sherbet, and with meat and fish.

Lentils

Use green lentils, which you can find in an Indian market; otherwise, use the common brown lentils.

Mint

Mint is used extensively in Middle Eastern cooking and in Sicily and southern Italy. Some Sicilians consider the use of mint to be an indication of Arab influence, even though mint was known by the Greeks.

Mortadella

A large, smooth pork sausage from Bologna, it is marbled with pork fat and studded with peppercorns and sometimes pistachios.

Mozzarella

Mozzarella is a *pasta filata* (spun-curd) cheese; it was originally made with water-buffalo milk but now is made mostly with cow's milk, though water-buffalo mozzarella is still made in Italy for export and domestic consumption. The curds are bathed in hot whey and spun and kneaded into threads until they become soft and malleable. The pieces are cut off and formed into balls. The name "mozzarella" comes from *mozza*, the past participle of the verb *mozzare*, to cut.

Fresh mozzarella is always preferable. It will keep for a few days if covered with water that is changed once a day. Look for firm balls. If you must use the packaged commercial mozzarella, buy the whole-milk kind; it has more taste than the low-fat variety.

Nutmeg

Nutmeg is the kernel of the fruit of a tropical tree native to southeast Asia. Sicilians use nutmeg to flavor pasta, fish sauces, and some vegetable preparations. Buy a whole nutmeg and grate it as needed.

Olives and olive oil

Olive production did not suffer a setback under the Arabs, as some people claim. Since the olive is sacred in the Koran, it might be expected that the Arabs would greatly increase the number of olive trees in Sicily. But for some unknown reason the production of oil dipped in medieval Arab Sicily.

Although no Arab author of the period wrote about olive trees, we can assume their growth was encouraged, because in Sicilian dialect farmers call the strongest and most beautiful of the olive trees *saracinesco* (Saracen or Arab). In the area around Carini, the very old olive trees with their knurled trunks are believed by local farmers to be a thousand years old, planted by the Arabs. The olives from these trees are called *ulive saracini* (Saracen or Arab olives). Oil production, too, must have existed, because in Sicilian dialect *mazzaredda* is the bad layer or scum of oil that must be removed after a pressing. The word derives from the Arabic *ma'sa-ra* (the oil press).

Buy only imported black and green olives. The best imported olives come from Morocco, Spain, Sicily, Calabria, Apulia, Basilicata, and Greece. The large green Sicilian olives come from Paternò.

Olive oil—the most basic ingredient of Sicilian cuisine—is really a matter of taste, even though connoisseurs argue about where the finest olive oils can be found. All agree that the finest olive oil is cold-pressed extra-virgin olive oil. No heat-extraction process or chemicals are used in cold pressing, and in this first pressing the olive releases the purest oil with all its nutrients. A cold-pressed oil has not been further refined.

Olive oil is called extra-virgin when it is the first oil to come out of the olive, released with the least pressure being applied. The other grades are based on oleic acidity. Keep two or three grades of olive oil on hand. For deep frying, use a lower-grade oil, such as "pure" or "pure virgin." For direct use on food, on the other hand, use only the very best first cold-pressed extra-virgin oil. Sunlight spoils olive oil, so you should buy it in cans.

Onions

Onions were grown in abundance in Palermo, according to the tenth-century Arab traveler Ibn Hawqal, and are still popular. Medieval Arab chroniclers attributed the so-called stupidity and laziness of the Arab Sicilians to their excessive onion eating.

The Arabs considered onions to be an aphrodisiac. A typical Arab-influenced preparation is *Cipolline in Agrodolce*.

Yellow onions are fine for all recipes calling for small amounts of onions. For dishes where the onion is the star, such as *Insalata di Cipolle*, use a sweet onion, such as a Georgia Vidalia, or a red onion; we call it a Bermuda, and in Italy it is known as a Calabrian onion.

Oranges

The orange was first introduced to Europe by the Arabs via Sicily. This was the bitter orange. The Arab emirs of Palermo created orangeries and used the bitter orange, lime, and shaddock for candying, preserves, and essences. One thousand years ago the bitter orange was precious because very few citrus fruits were known, and the ones that were usually had almost no juice. The Arabs sprinkled sugar on the bitter orange and sucked the juice out. The meager juices of these fruits were used for drinks and to season meats, fish, poultry, and sweets.

The earliest recorded appearance of the orange in Italy is in 1002. Leo Ostiensis reports that a prince of Salerno gave a present of *poma citron* (bitter orange) to a Norman prince for delivering the Salernitans from the Arabs.

In Arab Sicily, the roads must have been lined with orange trees. A deed from 1094 records a *Via de Arangeris* (street of orange trees) near the village of Patti.

In Sicily the sweet orange is known as the Portugal orange. It is commonly thought to have been introduced to Europe by Portuguese traders returning from China in the seventeenth century. But there is evidence of it in the orangerie of Francesco Abatellis, the royal magistrate and harbor master in fifteenth-century Palermo. One scholar says that it was introduced a century earlier.

Another orange grown in Sicily is the blood orange, called *tarocco*, ideal for orange salads. The mandarin is also popular, as is the tangerine.

Orange flower water

This fragrant water is made by a distillation using orange blossoms. The bottles of orange water sold in gourmet stores are very expensive. Look for them instead in a Middle Eastern market.

Oregano

Oregano is a powerful flavoring in Sicilian cooking. Both fresh and dried oregano are used, often with garlic, onion, and parsley.

Pancetta

Pancetta is Italian bacon. It is sold in Italian groceries. Substitute blanched bacon if pancetta is unavailable.

Parmesan

Parmesan is probably the most famous Italian cheese. It is usually grated. Though not originally a Sicilian cheese, it is commonly used everywhere now. Buy only imported Parmigiano-Reggiano.

Parsley

Parsley is used extensively in Sicilian cooking, both as a flavoring and as a garnish. I use the flat-leaf variety, but curly parsley will do.

Pasta

Pasta should be cooked in furiously boiling, abundantly salted water until al dente. I use both fresh and dry pasta, depending on the sauce and my mood. I find the Italian dried pasta to be the best. I am including only one recipe for homemade pasta, a dessert (see page 229).

Pecorino

Pecorino is a hard sheep's-milk cheese. In the early stages, after the milk curdles but while it is fresh and no salt has been added, the cheese is known as *tuma*; this will keep only for a few days. Once the cheese receives its first salting, it is called *primu sale*. After several months and another salting, it becomes pecorino. In Sicily, *tuma* and *primu sale* are very popular.

Aged pecorino is also called *canestrato* or *pecorino siciliano*. It is usually dry, sharp, and salty. When peppercorns have been added to *pecorino siciliano* curd, it is called *pecorno, maiorchino,* or *pepato.* (You can add crushed peppercorns to grated pecorino to get the same effect.) Another kind, this one with pepper and saffron, is called *piacintinu ennisi* in Sicilian. *Pecorino romano,* which is made in northern Italy, is similar to *pecorino siciliano.* It can be used as a substitute.

You can sometimes find a young pecorino, less than sixty days old, sold under the name "eating pecorino" or *pecorino crotonese* in Italian markets. This is close to *primu sale.*

Pepper

Where pepper is called for, use freshly ground black (or white) peppercorns.

Pine nuts

Pine nuts are an essential ingredient in *cucina arabo-sicula*. In Sicilian markets they are found mixed with currants. Called *pignoli* in Italian, they are from the cone of the stone pine and are native to the Mediterranean. They are used in many sweet-and-sour dishes and fillings.

Buy pine nuts in bulk at a Middle Eastern market; you will find they cost far less than elsewhere. Store them in the refrigerator.

Pistachios

Pistachios are another essential ingredient in *cucina arabo-sicula*. The Arabs introduced the pistachio in Sicily. The Sicilian word for nut is *fastuca*, which comes from the Arabic word for pistachio, *fustuq*. Sicilians will tell you that the best variety is the *pistacchio di Sicilia*, which comes from Bronte in the province of Catania. Pistachios are also used extensively in sweets.

You can buy imported pistachios in bulk at Middle Eastern markets. Never use the red-dyed nuts, which are not meant for cooking. Pistachios should be a bright light-green color when crushed. Store them in the refrigerator.

Pomegranates

The Prophet Muhammad recommended the Koran's sacred fruit: "Eat the pomegranate, for it purges the system of envy and hatred." The pomegranate was first brought to Spain and Sicily by the Arabs to grace their pleasure gardens. It is an Asian bush that can attain a height of twenty feet.

Magnificent dishes of chicken or meat with raisins and pomegranate seeds were served to the caliphs. These dishes were reinvented five hundred years later by cooks of the Italian Renaissance.

Primu sale

See Pecorino.

Prosciutto

Several of my recipes call for prosciutto. Prosciutto di Parma, the best prosciutto, is very expensive, but you only need a little.

Provola

Normally a cow's-milk cheese, in Sicily it is sometimes made from a mixture of cow's and sheep's or goat's milk. It is shaped in the form of a demijohn.

Provolone

For a more authentic taste, use imported provolone. Aged provolone can be used interchangeably with caciocavallo.

Raisins

Several kinds of raisins are used in Sicilian cooking. One is the *uvetta sultanina*, the small golden raisin, quite rare in Sicily; it is called sultana in England. Another raisin, the *uva passa*, comes from the Zibibbo grape. *Zibib* means "raisin" in Arabic. *Uvette passoline* are little black raisins. See also Currants.

Rice

The rice used in Sicilian cooking is Arborio or Vialone rice. These are both short-grained rices, with Vialone being smaller. They take a little longer to cook than the long-grained rice most Americans are familiar with. Italians like their rice creamy; Sicilians like theirs al dente, with the grains more separate.

Ricotta

Ricotta is not a cheese but a creamy curd that has been cooked twice. Hence the name ricotta—literally, "recooked." The leftover hot whey of milk used to make cheese is reheated and the solid milk parts are skimmed off to drain. The foam of the whey when it is being recooked is called *zabbina* in Sicilian, which comes from the Arabic word *zarb,* thought also to be the root of the word for the custard dessert *zabaione* (see page 236). The best ricotta is made with sheep's milk.

Buy part-skim-milk ricotta. Freshly made ricotta is available in markets in cities with Italian communities.

Rosemary

Rosemary, a strongly scented herb, is often used in lamb dishes. A bunch of rosemary twigs can be tied together and used as a brush for basting grilled foods with their marinade.

Saffron

Medieval Sicily, with its subtropical climate and loamy soil, was found to be ideal for growing saffron. The Arabs introduced it around the year 920. The medieval Arab writers who visited Sicily—Al-Baghdadi, Qazwini, and Yaqut—all confirm that saffron was cultivated near Erice. Any dish with saffron is certainly Arab in origin.

Nowadays, most saffron comes from Spain, although Iran is also an exporter. The best saffron is orange-red, not bright red, and sometimes labeled "very select." It is a powerful, almost magical, spice, both in taste and coloration.

Saffron is expensive, but you will be using very small amounts, usually just a pinch. The saffron threads have to be steeped first in tepid water.

One Arab contribution to European cuisine transmitted through Sicily was endoring, the coating or coloring of food with saffron or egg yolks for a yellowing effect. The Arab introduction of endoring spread to France by the fourteenth century. For red coloring they used alkanet (from the Arabic *al-hinna*), a plant of the borage family whose root gives a red dye. Pistachios, coriander, and spinach were used for green.

When the tomato was first introduced to Sicily people were not sure how to use it. They added small amounts of tomato to saffron for a less expensive coloring effect. Coloring food was a kind of alchemy, and Arab pharmacologists and alchemists were always looking for an elixir.

Sage

Sage, when dried, is an herb with a strong, musty aroma; it is slightly bitter. It is not used often in Sicily but does appear in several of the recipes in this book. Always use fresh sage leaves.

Salt

Some culinary historians believe that the Arabs taught the Sicilians how to salt fish. Salt industries are today based around Trapani. Use whatever salt you normally use and sea salt where called for, especially when preparing *Bottarga*.

Sesame seeds

Sesame seeds were introduced by the Arabs. They are often used on bread, in sauces, and for sweets.

Soppressata

This famous salami is made in Basilicata, in Calabria, and in Sicily. The pork meat is coarsely chopped and mixed with salt, pepper, chili peppers, and red wine. It is fairly widely available, but you can substitute another salami.

Squash

Marrow or summer squash was cultivated in medieval Sicily in fields called *nuara,* a dialect word from the Arabic *nowar.* Today these squash are called *zucca.*

When the hard or winter squashes of the New World were introduced to Italy, they also were called *zucca.*

In the fall you will see *zucca gialla,* a hard yellow squash unique to Sicily, sold whole or by the piece in the market. Pumpkin, Hubbard, or butternut squash are excellent substitutions for *zucca gialla.*

Stock or broth

Nothing rivals homemade broth, but in dishes calling for small amounts of stock I often take the easy way out and use a bouillon cube. Very fine Italian cooks I know do this all the time.

Sugar

The Arabs introduced sugar cane and sugar-milling techniques to Sicily. Cultivation was well established by the year 950. Although the Romans imported granulated sugar and sugar cane, they apparently never had seen the plant.

The sugar industry of Arab Sicily was centered at Palermo. Sugar was exported to North Africa, often in the form of confections. Confectionery became a rich trade as Arab-Sicilian expertise and originality grew to meet the demand of the North African Arab caliphs and emirs. Sicilian confections were so famous that they appeared on the Pope's table and were used to bribe the Arab customs officials in Tunisia.

Sunflower-seed oil

The sunflower was introduced to Sicily by the Spaniards after its discovery in the New World, and now there are fields of sunflowers in Sicily. The seeds are pressed to produce a delicate and light oil that is often used for deep frying.

Tarragon

Tarragon was introduced to Sicily by the Arabs, but it is not in common use there today.

Thyme

Both dried and fresh thyme are used in Sicilian cooking.

Tomatoes

Tomatoes are a New World fruit, but that does not preclude their use in *cucina arabo-sicula*. One theory holds that the color of the tomato was as important as its taste: Once it became rooted in Sicilian culture, it was used as a less expensive substitute for saffron.

Any kind of firm ripe tomato will do for the recipes in this book, but plum tomatoes are preferable. Of the canned products, the best are imported whole peeled Italian plum tomatoes from San Marzano. The label on the can will say "San Marzano."

Tomato extract

A highly concentrated tomato extract is sold in tubes in gourmet and specialty stores. You can substitute tomato paste.

Tuma

See Pecorino.

Vinegar

Use only the highest-quality imported white and red wine vinegars. Because *agrodolce* sauces, a foundation of *cucina arabo-sicula*, are based on vinegar, it is imperative you use the best. Malt vinegar and balsamic vinegar are never used in Sicilian cooking.

Watermelon

The Arabs introduced the watermelon to Sicily, probably in the mid-tenth century. The seeds were roasted, then pounded into a paste or crushed into cakes.

There are two kinds of watermelon in Sicily. One is round with a light green skin; the other is larger with a dark green skin.

Wine

In the eleventh century, the greatest of Arab-Sicilian poets, Ibn Hamdis, wrote about the excellence of local wine and expressed nostalgia for the "paradise of delights." "Sicilian wine resembles flower petals," he said, "and is drunk in cups which seem like entrance halls of palaces."

Very little wine is used in Sicilian cooking in general and even less is used in *cucina arabo-sicula*. When a recipe calls for wine, try to use a Sicilian wine, such as Corvo. Marsala, the famous dessert wine, is also used in some recipes.

Part Two

A Note About the Recipes

With the Arabs we finally come to a delicious sector of our Sicilian culinary zodiac.

—PINO CORRENTI

All the recipes I have chosen for this book are traditional dishes from Sicily that belong to *cucina arabo-sicula*—that is, they are in some way Arab-inspired or -derived. Although I never found unanimity among Sicilians about the precise Arab heritage of these recipes, one thing is true for all of them: They are delicious and well suited for the American home cook.

Many of the recipes have fallen out of fashion or are unfamiliar to contemporary Sicilian cooks. The joy of rediscovering these flavors of a lost tradition was always exciting and surprising. I collected the ideas for the recipes in Sicily, mostly through conversations and correspondence with ordinary Sicilians, food writers, researchers, and some chefs. While I was developing a recipe, I consulted many cookbooks and food writers to make sure that I was capturing the right flavor. In the end I have changed and adapted the recipes to reflect my personal cooking style, but without losing authenticity.

Each recipe is given with its English translation and original Italian or Sicilian name. In some cases I've used the Sicilian name if I thought it interesting or unique in some way.

Often the recipes are for six to eight portions or more, partly because Sicilian food lends itself to leftovers in a way that few other cuisines do. Many dishes are served at room temperature and are excellent, if not better, the next day.

Recipes are not chemical formulas. While these recipes are wonderful when followed to the letter, there is always room for a certain amount of improvisation. If you are unfamiliar with Italian or especially Sicilian cuisine, though, I recommend you stay close to the recipe the first time. Be sure to read each recipe through once or twice before starting so you have a clear picture of what happens when.

I know you will have fun, and *buon appetito!*

THREE
Appetizers
GRAPE 'U PITITTU

The absence of appetizers in Sicilian cuisine is thought to be an Arab legacy. The antipasto course has been integrated into Sicilian restaurant menus, but at home what Sicilians eat as appetizers are more accurately called *grape 'u pitittu* (literally, mouth openers). These tidbits are often served on large, colorful ceramic platters called *lemmi* (an Arabic word). Many of the recipes in this chapter can be served as appetizers, side dishes, or main courses, whichever you prefer.

Deep-Fried Rice Balls

ARANCINE

Pinch of saffron
2 cups Arborio rice, washed
2 cups chicken stock
(Ingredients continued)

Arancine are balls of saffron rice filled with a tomato ragoût and deep-fried until they are golden. They look like

Salt
2 tablespoons butter
1½ cups grated caciocavallo
 or pecorino
2 eggs, separated
1 small onion, chopped
2 tablespoons olive oil
¼ pound ground beef, cooked
 and drained of fat
1 small tomato, peeled,
 seeded, and chopped very
 fine
1 tablespoon fresh rosemary
 leaves
Pinch of pepper
½ cup cooked peas
¼ cup white wine
Flour, for coating
Breadcrumbs, for coating
Olive oil, for deep frying

little oranges, hence their name. The famous Sicilian gourmand Alberto Denti di Pirajno argues that *arancine* were created by Arab cooks experimenting with pilaf. In a thirteenth-century Baghdad cookery book there is a recipe for an *arancine*-like preparation called *naranjiya*.

Arancine reflect the complexity and richness of Sicilian history. The rice and saffron are an Arab influence; the stuffing is probably French; the tomatoes were brought from America by the Spaniards; and the cheese is an ancient Greek contribution. Saffron was popular because yellow was thought by the Arabs to be a source of gaiety.

There are many kinds of *arancine*, including a sweet one; others are filled with sweetbreads, some with fresh cheese or egg yolks, chicken, chicken livers, and tomatoes, and even béchamel sauce. In the eastern part of Sicily, *arancine* have an oval or pyramid shape; in the western part they are round, similar to blood oranges in size. *Arancine* freeze well; they need only to be reheated in the oven.

1. Steep the saffron in ½ cup of warm water for 30 minutes.

2. Place the rice in a pot with the chicken stock. Add the saffron solution, ½ teaspoon of salt, and the butter. Stir and bring to a boil. Once the stock is boiling, lower the heat and cook the rice, tightly covered, until it has absorbed all the water, about 20 minutes. Spoon the rice onto a platter and mix in the cheese and egg yolks. Spread the rice out to cool.

3. Sauté the onion over medium heat in the 2 tablespoons of olive oil for about 7 minutes, or until translucent. Add the cooked ground beef, tomato, rosemary, ¼ teaspoon of salt, and the pepper and cook, covered, for about 8 minutes. Add the peas and the white wine. Cook until the wine has evaporated. The mixture will look like a thick ragoût.

4. Spread some flour for coating on a piece of wax paper.

Lightly beat the egg whites in a shallow bowl. Spread bread-crumbs for coating on a piece of wax paper.

5. To form the rice balls, spread some rice flat in the palm of your hand, then cup your hand slightly, using the thumb of your other hand to make an indentation. To keep the rice from becom-ing sticky, keep a plate of cold water nearby to dip your hand into each time you form a rice ball. Place about 1 tablespoon of the meat mixture into the indentation and fold the edges over. Cover with some more rice and shape it with both hands into a ball the size of a lemon, about 2¼ inches in diameter. Squeeze just tightly enough to make a firm ball, but not so hard that it falls apart.

6. Roll each ball in the flour, dip it in the beaten egg white, and roll it in the breadcrumbs, coating it evenly. Refrigerate the rice balls for 30 minutes before frying.

7. Heat the oil for deep frying to 360°F.

8. Deep-fry the rice balls for 4 minutes or until golden. Do not fry too many at once. As the *arancine* finish cooking, drain on paper towels. *Arancine* are usually served warm or at room tem-perature.

Makes 12.

Butter Rice Balls

ARANCINE CON BURRO

Pinch of saffron
2 cups milk
2 cups Arborio rice, washed
8 tablespoons (1 stick) butter
1½ teaspoons salt
4 eggs, lightly beaten
½ teaspoon black pepper
½ pound fresh mozzarella,
   finely diced
⅓ cup small fresh or frozen
   peas
Olive oil, for deep frying
Breadcrumbs, for coating

I like this recipe even better than the more traditional one—it's simpler and more elegant.

1. Dissolve the saffron in 1 tablespoon of tepid water. Let stand while cooking the rice.

2. In a heavy pot with a heavy lid, bring the milk and 2 cups

of water to a boil. Add the rice, 2 tablespoons of the butter, and the salt. Stir. Cover and reduce the heat to low and cook for 15 minutes. Check the rice; if it is soft but there is liquid left, strain it. If it is still al dente, continue cooking for another 5 minutes or until the liquid is absorbed, being careful that the rice is not too mushy.

3.   When the rice is ready, stir in the saffron and half the eggs. Stir gently until all the rice turns yellow. Spread the rice out on a platter or marble surface. Let it cool completely.

4.   In a bowl mix together the remaining 6 tablespoons of butter and the pepper, mozzarella, and uncooked peas. Place rice in the palm of your hand, shape it, and fill it as described in Step 5. Cover with some more rice and shape it with both hands into a ball the size of a lemon, about 2¼ inches in diameter.

5.   To form the rice balls, spread some rice flat in the palm of your hand, then cup your hand slightly, using the thumb of your other hand to make an indentation. To keep the rice from becoming sticky, have a plate of cold water nearby to dip your hand into each time you form a rice ball. Place about 1 tablespoon of the meat mixture into the indentation and fold the edges over. Cover with some more rice and shape it with both hands into a ball the size of a lemon, about 2¼ inches in diameter. Squeeze just tightly enough to make a firm ball, but not so hard that it falls apart.

6.   Heat the oil for deep frying to 360°F. Preheat the oven to 450°F.

7.   Pour the remaining lightly beaten eggs into a shallow bowl. Spread the breadcrumbs on a piece of wax paper.

8.   Dip each ball into the eggs, then roll it in breadcrumbs. Deep-fry, 3 or 4 at a time, for about 4 minutes, or until they are an orange-brown. When all the balls are fried, place them in a baking pan and put them into the oven for 10 minutes. Serve hot.

Makes 14 to 20.

Fresh Tuma with Anchovies

TUMA CON LE ACCIUGHE

6-ounce ball of tuma or fresh mozzarella
24 anchovy fillets
Olive oil
White pepper

This preparation is from the Syracusan chef Pasqualino Giudice. To create a nice cocktail appetizer, cut the cheese into bite-size chunks and skewer them with the anchovies. Fresh mozzarella can be substituted for *tuma,* a very young fresh pecorino from Sicily.

1. Cut the cheese into sticks 4 inches long and ½ inch thick or into 1-inch cubes. Rinse the anchovies under cold water, add enough olive oil to cover, sprinkle with white pepper to taste, and let marinate for 30 minutes.

2. When ready to serve, arrange the anchovies over the cheese in a dish.

Serves 4.

Chick-pea Flour Fritters

PANELLE

1⅓ cups chick-pea flour
  (about ½ pound)
1½ teaspoons salt
2 tablespoons finely chopped
  parsley
Sunflower-seed oil, for deep
  frying

Panelle will always be well received by family and guests. They are a light and delicious snack requiring no adornments or condiments except a sprinkling of salt. Try making them into a sandwich, as they do in Palermo, between two slices of Italian bread with a squirt of lemon.

1. In a pot, dissolve the chick-pea flour in 4 cups of cold water. Add the salt and parsley and cook over medium heat, stirring continuously, until the mush becomes fairly thick, about 20 minutes. It will resemble yellowish farina. You may not think it is done, but it is. Remove immediately from the heat.

2. Spread the mush over a large baking sheet to cool slightly, spreading evenly until it is about ⅛ inch thick. After it has cooled and dried a bit but is still warm, cut the dough into small rectangular pieces about 2 x 3 inches.

3. Heat the oil for deep frying to 360°F.

4. Deep-fry the pieces in the oil until golden, about 1 minute. Drain on paper towels and serve warm or reheat later.

Serves 4 to 6.

Eggplant "Buttocks" Sandwiches

SCIATRE E MATRE

3 medium eggplants (about 3
  pounds)
Salt
2 tablespoons butter
2 tablespoons flour
1 cup hot milk
Pepper
Freshly grated nutmeg
Olive oil, for deep frying
6 or 7 eggs, lightly beaten
Dry breadcrumbs, for coating
Mint leaves and chopped
  mint, for garnish

Today Sicilians use the expression *scia-tre e matre* as an exclamation of wonder. The expression comes from the Arabic *sciateru ya ma tara*, which the Arabs say sarcastically when someone from whom you expect very little actually accomplishes something. The Sicilians use this expression to describe the taste of the eggplant, from which we expect so little. But what about the "buttocks" part? Michele Pasqualino in his eighteenth-century dictionary suggests that *sciatre e matre* is a Sicilian euphemism for buttocks, which this dish resembles . . . at least to the imaginative cook who originally named this preparation.

1. Slice the unpeeled eggplants crosswise ⅝ inch thick, keeping the slices together in the order in which you cut them so that you will be able to make even-sized sandwiches later. Lay the eggplant pieces on paper towels and sprinkle with salt. Leave them to drain of their bitter juices for 1 hour or longer. Pat dry with paper towels.

2. Prepare a béchamel sauce. Melt the butter in a small saucepan, add the flour, and stir until smooth. Add the hot milk a little at a time, whisking constantly until the sauce is thick, like a pancake batter, about 5 minutes. Add salt and pepper to taste. Remove from the heat.

3. Spread a very thin layer of béchamel on each side of eggplant, as if you were buttering bread. Don't be tempted to slather it on or the taste will be overpowering and unpleasant. Grate a small amount of nutmeg over the béchamel and lay the matching slice of eggplant on top to make a sandwich.

4. Heat the oil for deep frying to 360°F.

5. Pour the eggs in a bowl and spread the breadcrumbs on a piece of wax paper. Dip each eggplant sandwich in the egg and

then in breadcrumbs, making sure all sides are breaded, including the edges.

6. Deep-fry the sandwiches until golden brown on one side, then carefully turn over with tongs to the other side, about 90 seconds a side. Drain the sandwiches on paper towels. Salt them while they are still hot and let them cool. Decorate the border of the serving platter with mint leaves and sprinkle some chopped mint over all. Serve at room temperature.

Makes 14 to 20 sandwiches.

Green Vegetable Medley

FRITTEDDA

1 pound fresh peas, shelled (from about 2½ pounds of pods)
2 pounds fresh fava beans, shelled (from about 5 pounds of beans)
6 young artichokes (if you use older artichokes, with fully developed bracts, cook them longer)
Juice of 1 lemon
½ cup olive oil
8 ounces scallions, white part only, finely chopped
Salt and pepper
Freshly grated nutmeg
4 mint leaves, chopped (optional)
1 teaspoon red wine vinegar (optional)
4 teaspoons sugar (optional)

In western Sicily, where *frittedda* was born, it is served as a *grape 'u pitittu*. None of the Sicilian food authorities I know believe this dish has Arab roots, but I feel there is some evidence. The Arabs introduced the artichoke and the scallion; in fact, the word "scallion" comes from the Palestinian Arabic for the name of the town most famous for scallions, Ascalon. It has the sweet-and-sour trademark of Arab cuisine, and finally, it comes from western Sicily where so many Arab-influenced dishes originated.

The young artichokes needed for this dish can be hard to find. They should be very tender, without chokes. Since the dish is affected by the age and size of the vegetable, you will have to judge for yourself the right cooking time and how much salt, pepper, and nutmeg you want to use—so keep tasting.

1. Rinse the peas and fava beans and set aside. Trim the artichokes, quarter, and leave them in cold lemon water until they are all prepared. Heat the olive oil in a large pan and sauté the scallions over low to medium heat until soft, about 3 minutes.

2. Add the artichokes and cook an additional 5 minutes (long-

er if they are larger), then add ⅔ cup of hot water. Bring to a boil and simmer for 5 minutes. Add the peas and fava beans. Season to taste with salt, pepper, and nutmeg. Cover and simmer for 20 minutes.

3. Moisten the vegetables with more hot water if they look dry. Cook up to 40 minutes, or until tender; keep checking. If you serve this as a cold summer dish, stir in the mint, vinegar, and sugar while the vegetables are still hot.

Serves 8.

Preserved Tuna

SURRA

2 pounds tuna, cut from the
   lower belly
1 tablespoon sea salt
Olive oil, for deep frying
Extra-virgin olive oil, for
   preserving

The lower part of the tuna belly toward the tail fin, called *ventresca* in Italian, is the most delicious part of the fish. In Sicilian it is called *surra*, a word derived from the Arabic. It is the same prized part of the tuna which the Japanese use for making sashimi. At the fish market, ask for a slice in one piece from the belly of the tuna and then cut it up yourself.

1. Using a very sharp knife, cut the tuna belly into 2 x ½ -inch pieces. Salt the tuna and let rest for 15 minutes.

2. Heat the oil for deep frying to 360°F.

3. Deep-fry the tuna pieces until they are golden, about 90 seconds. Drain and arrange on a tray in the refrigerator, lightly covered with wax paper, for 24 hours.

4. Remove tuna pieces from the refrigerator and place tightly and neatly, as if you were packing sardines, in a large, wide-mouthed jar with a lid. Cover with extra-virgin olive oil. Store in the refrigerator but serve at room temperature.

Makes 2 pounds.

Mixed Fried Little Fish

SCIABBACHEDDU

Olive oil, for deep frying
2 pounds mixed tiny fish
1½ cups flour
Sea salt
Lemon wedges, for garnish
1 pound spaghetti, cooked
   (optional)

Sciabbacheddu is a Sicilian word that refers to the little fish caught in trawl nets. It comes from a kind of net the Arabs introduced called a *scia'beka*. Neighborhood fishmongers, especially ethnic ones, might carry very small fish such as *papalina* or even baby sand eels—both of which would work well in this recipe. My fishmonger carries these small fish a couple of times a year, and I buy several pounds at a time and freeze them.

Deep-fried little fish can be served plain or used as a topping for spaghetti. You should eat the fish whole, heads and all. As the Italians would say, you will be nourished by all those good enzymes.

1. Heat the oil for deep frying to 360°F.
2. Wash the fish under cold water and drain. Roll it in the flour, shaking off any excess, and deep-fry in batches for 30 seconds, breaking apart with a fork any fish that have clumped together.
3. Drain on paper towels, sprinkle with sea salt, and serve immediately with a wedge of lemon or as a topping for spaghetti.
   Serves 6.

Grilled Baby Squid and Baby Cuttlefish

SPITINI GRAPE 'U PITITTU

2 cups dry breadcrumbs
¾ cup olive oil
½ cup finely chopped parsley
2 garlic cloves, very finely
  chopped
1½ teaspoons salt
½ teaspoon pepper
3 tablespoons dry white wine
4 pounds baby squid and
  cuttlefish, cleaned and cut
  into small pieces
3 lemons, sliced
1 tablespoon dried oregano

Along the coastline of rural Sicily it is popular to eat barbecued morsels while awaiting the pasta. Traditionally this particular *grape 'u pitittu* was made with the small squid and cuttlefish dragged in by the fishermen with their *sciabbica* (trawl net). While the women prepared dinner, the fishermen would grill these morsels to satisfy their hunger. But first all the squid and cuttlefish had to be cleaned, their cartilage and ink sacs removed.

This is a delightful way to spend a summer's night, outdoors with friends, eating *spitini* as they come off the grill. As Pino Correnti, the noted Sicilian food writer, says, "*È un buon cominciare una lunga notte di mezza estate al mare*" (It's a beautiful way to start a long mid-summer night by the sea).

As it is unlikely that you will find baby squid or cuttlefish, substitute four pounds of the smallest squid available.

1. Preheat the grill so the charcoal has died down a bit but is still glowing or preheat a gas grill to medium.
2. Toast the breadcrumbs in a frying pan with 2 tablespoons of the olive oil over medium heat for 4 minutes. Transfer to a bowl and add the parsley, garlic, 1 teaspoon of the salt, and ¼ teaspoon of the pepper, 1 tablespoon of the olive oil, and a sprinkling of the wine. Add the squid and cuttlefish in and toss well.
3. Thread the squid and cuttlefish onto 8 long skewers, making sure the pieces are well covered with breadcrumbs. After every few squid or cuttlefish pieces thread a slice of lemon on the skewer.
4. Place the skewers on the grill. Mix together the remaining olive oil, the oregano, the remaining ½ teaspoon salt, and the

remaining ¼ teaspoon pepper, and baste the skewers. Turn occasionally, basting each time. When they look crisp, about 30 to 40 minutes, they are ready to eat.

Serves 8 to 10.

FOUR
Pizza and Breads

SFINCIONE E PANE

> The major influence on Sicilian cuisine
> was exerted by the Arabs.
>
> —FELICE CÙNSOLO

In his magnificent work *Pani e Dolci di Sicilia* (*The Breads and Sweets
of Sicily*), Antonio Uccello describes bread as sacred and versatile in
Sicily. The many different kinds of Sicilian breads, often sculpted
into various shapes, are often associated with festivals or served as
devotional foods. They have delightful names; here are some ex-
amples: *pucciddatu, vastidduni, ciumi-tortu, jadduzzu. Pupidda, ciuri,
scuzzaria* are breads made for children. *Panuzzi di Morti* are ritual
breads made for the dead, while *sacra famiglia* is a sculptured bread
in the shape of a family.

    In Sicily, bread is often a meal in itself. Sometimes it is dressed
with olive oil, salt, pepper, and oregano, or served as a sandwich
with olives, caciocavallo cheese, and fresh tomatoes ripe off the
vine, or simply grilled. Stale bread is used for breadcrumbs or
zuppa di pancotto (bread soup). Stale bread is also mixed with
olives, artichoke hearts, green peppers, raisins, and pine nuts and
seasoned with vinegar for a kind of bread salad.

    Not all these breads are Arab-derived but one Arab contri-
bution is *u 'nciminatu,* cumin-seed bread. Two others are *pane e
birra* with sesame seeds, and *muffolette,* a soft roll made with flour,

boiled potatoes, lard, yeast, saffron, salt, and cumin or sesame seed. *Muffolette* can also be stuffed with pork and aniseed or with onions, pine nuts, and golden raisins.

The typical bread of Sicily is called *pane rimacinato* because it is made from fine semolina flour that has been milled twice. It is an earthy bread, crusty, porous, chewy, and yellow. Sometimes it is sprinkled with sesame seeds and baked in ten-inch rounds about three inches high. *Pane rimacinato* is the best bread I have ever had.

The way the Sicilians break bread is very much part of the Arab heritage. It is similar to what one finds in North Africa. In Sicily, bread is still often broken by hand into chunks rather than cut with a knife; in most of the rest of Italy, bread is cut by holding the loaf against the chest and slicing it with a knife drawn toward the body.

Bread has long had a symbolic value in the Mediterranean, playing an important part in religious rituals. In Sicily, too, this tradition exists.

David Abulafia and Henri Bresc, scholars of medieval Sicily, citing Christian documents in the archives of Palermo, report that in 1329, long after the Muslim Sicilian community was vanquished, some Arab merchants in Palermo took oaths *tacto pane ad legem Mukumet* (touching bread according to Islamic law).

Pizza seems to have been developed in Sicily and North Africa. Michele Amari, the preeminent authority on Arab Sicily, proposed that *sfincione*, a Sicilian word for pizza, derives from the Arabic *sfang* (or *isfang*), a fried dough or pastry that was perhaps fermented.

The typically Sicilian stuffed pizza called *carbuciu* is very similar to the griddle pizzas of the Kabylie region of North Africa. In Sicily it is seasoned with breadcrumbs, olive oil, and oregano while the North African version uses onions and herbs. In Malta, too, one finds a pizza stuffed with tomatoes, olives, and anchovies. The Arabs also traditionally stuffed half-moon-shaped breads. These evolved into *focaccia, calzone,* and *impanatas* and other pastries.

Pizza or Bread Dough

PASTA DI PANE O PIZZA

1⅓ cups warm water
3 teaspoons yeast, fresh or dry
1½ teaspoons salt
(Ingredients continued)

This basic pizza and bread dough can be used for all the *sfincione*, pizza, bread, and *impanata* recipes in the book.

4 cups bread flour, sifted
4 tablespoons olive oil (only
*   if making pizza)*

In recipes calling for bread dough, omit the olive oil. This recipe is based on the one found in Carlo Middione's *The Food of Southern Italy*.

1. Pour the warm water into a large mixing bowl previously warmed under hot running water and dissolve the yeast. Stir with a fork. Let it rest for 5 minutes, then add the salt and shake gently.

2. Add the flour (and olive oil, *only if you are making pizza*) and mix until you can knead the dough with your hands without its sticking. Once it has formed into a smooth ball, place it on a lightly floured surface and knead for 12 minutes. If you are making pizza you may need to add flour. Add only a light sprinkling at a time. If making bread do not add flour until at least the eighth minute of kneading.

3. Once the ball of dough is smooth, place it in a lightly greased bowl, cover with a kitchen towel, and let it rise in a warm (80°F.) place for 2 hours, or until double in bulk. At this point, it is ready to make into a pizza. If you are making braided sesame seed bread, go to Step 4. If you are making rolls, go to Step 5. If you are making a round loaf, go to Step 6.

4. For braided sesame seed bread, punch down the dough and divide in two. Cover the dough with a kitchen towel and let it rise for 1 hour, until double in bulk. Roll each ball back and forth into a 24-inch-long strip. Braid the 2 strips and place on a baking stone or pan. Cover with a kitchen towel and let rise 1 hour, or until almost double in bulk. Lightly drizzle the top of the braided bread with a little water. Sprinkle sesame seeds to cover. This slow proofing process is necessary for good-tasting bread. Go to Step 7.

5. For rolls, punch down the dough and divide into 6 balls. Cover with a kitchen towel and let them rise for 1 hour. Punch down and let them rise for 1 hour. Lightly drizzle the top of the rolls with water. Sprinkle sesame seeds to cover. Place the rolls on a baking stone or pan. Go to Step 7.

6. For a large round loaf, place on a baking stone or pan, cover with a kitchen towel and let it rise for 1 hour. Punch down and let it rise again for 1 hour. Go to Step 7.

7. Preheat the oven to 475°F. With a razor blade score the bread or rolls several times in diagonal slashes. Place a pan of boiling water in the oven to create enough steam for crusty bread. Place the bread or rolls in the oven. Reduce the heat to 425°F. and bake for 40 minutes. Cool on a rack.

Makes four 9-inch pizzas, one round or braided loaf, or six rolls.

Palermo Pizza

SFINCIONE ALLA PALERMITANA

1 recipe Pizza Dough (page
65)
¾ pound fresh sardines (or
anchovies), cleaned and
gutted, with heads, tails,
and backbones removed
Sea salt
1 pound plum tomatoes,
peeled and seeded
1 medium onion, chopped
½ cup olive oil
½ pound caciocavallo or
provolone, diced or sliced

In New York City nearly every street corner pizza joint sells "Sicilian" by the slice. These thick pizzas have their roots in the *sfincione* of Palermo.

Canned sardines will not work for this recipe. You simply must find fresh sardines or anchovies (see pages 158 and 155). Fresh anchovies can be found in Italian and Greek neighborhoods. If that proves to be impossible, make something else!

1. Prepare the pizza dough as described on page 65.
2. Wash the sardines and roll them in the sea salt. Cut up the tomatoes and let them drain for about 1 hour.
3. Sauté the onion in the olive oil over medium heat for about 6 to 7 minutes, or until translucent. Lower the heat, add the tomatoes, and cook for 30 minutes. Add half the sardines to the tomatoes and cook for 10 minutes. Turn off the heat and set aside.
4. Preheat the oven to 375°F.
5. Divide the pizza dough into quarters if you are making 4 pizzas. Roll out the dough and lay it in a lightly oiled pizza pan, flattening the dough with your hands to cover the whole area. The dough should be about ⅛ inch thick. Make sure that the sides are not too thin or they will brown too fast. Using half the tomato sauce and all the cheese, cover each pizza and bake for 20 minutes.
6. Add the rest of the sauce and place the remaining sardines on top in a spoke-like fashion. Bake for 10 minutes. Serve immediately.

Makes one to two large pizzas or four 9-inch pizzas.

San Vito's Pizza

SFINCIONE DI SAN VITO

1 recipe Pizza Dough (page 65)
Juice of 1 lemon, strained
¼ cup chopped onion
3 tablespoons chopped parsley
½ pound pork shoulder, fat removed and cut into very small pieces (save ¼ cup for later use)
¾ cup (6-ounce can) tomato paste
4 tablespoons olive oil
2 links fennel sausage, removed from casing and crumbled
¼ cup cut-up soppressata
½ cup red wine
1 cinnamon stick
1 cup diced primu sale or fresh mozzarella
Salt and pepper
1 tablespoon fennel seeds
¼ cup dry breadcrumbs
1 teaspoon fresh oregano leaves

This *sfincione* is called "San Vito" because it has been made for centuries by the sisters of the San Vito Convent in Palermo. Some recipes do not call for a second sheet of dough over the topping, but this recipe is probably closer to the original.

1. Prepare the pizza dough as described on page 65, incorporating the lemon juice into the pizza dough. Let the dough rise to double in bulk.

2. Meanwhile, sauté the onion, parsley, pork shoulder, and tomato paste in 2 tablespoons of the olive oil over medium heat. Stir several times, scraping any stuck bits from the bottom of the pan. After 5 minutes, add the sausage and soppressata. After another 5 minutes, add the wine and the cinnamon stick. Lower the heat and simmer for 15 minutes.

3. Preheat the oven to 400°F. When the dough has risen, divide it in two and roll out 2 circles 16 inches in diameter and

about ⅜ inch thick. Don't flatten the edges. Lay the first pizza down on an oiled baking stone or pizza pan. Remove the cinnamon stick and cover with the sauce, setting aside 4 tablespoons. Sprinkle the cheese over the sauce along with salt and pepper to taste, the pork fat, and the fennel seeds. Cover with the other circle of dough and pinch the edges together. Puncture the top of the pizza all over with a fork.

4. Put the pizza in the oven. Sauté the breadcrumbs in a small pan, stirring with a wooden spoon. As they begin to turn golden, moisten with the remaining olive oil and remove from the heat. When the pizza just begins to turn color, about 15 minutes, remove it from the oven for a moment and spread it with the remaining sauce, breadcrumbs, and oregano. Continue baking for 15 minutes.

Serves 6.

San Giovanni's Pizza

SFINCIONE DI SAN GIOVANNI

1 recipe Pizza Dough (page 65)
½ cup olive oil
½ medium onion, finely chopped
½ cup peeled, seeded, and chopped ripe tomatoes
Salt and pepper
30 anchovy fillets
⅔ cup diced caciocavallo
⅔ cup dry breadcrumbs

For a unique taste try grilling this earthy *sfincione*, using a baking stone on your grill.

1. Prepare the pizza dough as described on page 65. Divide in half.

2. Preheat the oven to 375°F.

3. Heat 2 tablespoons of the olive oil in a skillet and sauté the onion over medium heat for 7 minutes, or until translucent. Add the tomatoes and salt and pepper to taste. Cook for another 7 minutes.

4. Rinse the anchovy fillets. Dice them together with the cheese. Add the mixture to the sauce and cook for another 2 minutes. Set aside.

5. Heat 3 tablespoons of the olive oil in a small saucepan and fry the breadcrumbs, stirring a little. Set aside.

6. Flatten 1 ball of dough in a lightly oiled 12-inch pizza pan. Pinch the sides to make a raised edge. Pour in half the sauce, spreading it around. Sprinkle half the breadcrumbs on top, then drizzle half the remaining olive oil over all. Bake for 30 minutes or until the bottom is light brown. Serve immediately. Repeat the process for the other pizza.

Makes two 12-inch pizzas.

Double Pizza

CARBUCIU

1 recipe Pizza Dough (page 65)
¾ cup dry breadcrumbs
½ cup olive oil
Salt and pepper
2 tablespoons fresh oregano leaves
36 anchovy fillets
6 plum tomatoes, sliced

Carbuciu is a unique Sicilian type of filled pizza. The word carbuciu derives from the Arabic word for bread bakery.

Try grilling the carbuciu. Place a baking stone on a grill with a cover, making sure the fire is very hot. Place the carbuciu on the baking stone and put the cover down. It will be done in fifteen minutes.

1. Preheat the oven (or grill) to 500°F., using a baking stone.

2. Prepare the pizza dough as described on page 65, divide it into 6 balls, and roll each one out into a 5-inch circle, ½ inch thick. Bake until golden on top. If using the grill, bake until there are black spots on the bottom, about 15 to 25 minutes. Remove from the heat.

3. Slice each pizza in half horizontally, using a serrated knife. Mix the breadcrumbs with the olive oil, salt and pepper to taste, and the oregano. Season one of each pizza half with the breadcrumb mixture.

4. Carefully place 6 anchovy fillets and enough slices of ripe tomato to cover the breadcrumbs and anchovies. Cover this half with the other half and serve.

Makes six 5-inch pizzas.

Fried Pizza with Anchovies

TARONGIA

1 recipe Pizza Dough (page 65)
Olive oil, for deep frying
24 anchovy fillets
Freshly ground black pepper

Tarongia is a Sicilian name for a large fried pizza, or *frittelle*. The word comes from the Arabic *turung*, which means citron or orange, reflecting the golden color after it is cooked. It can be made with a variety of different ingredients, but anchovies are the most common. Another version uses wild fennel.

1. Prepare the dough as described on page 65, divide in four, and roll out into 9-inch circles, ⅜ inch thick.
2. Heat the oil for deep frying to 370°F.
3. Deep-fry the pizzas until golden. Set aside to drain on paper towels.
4. Layer the anchovies on the top, add pepper to taste, and eat. Makes four 9-inch pizzas.

VARIATION

For a fennel topping, trim 1 fennel bulb and cook whole in salted water until tender but still firm. Drain well and chop fine. Sauté in 2 tablespoons olive oil together with 1 thinly sliced medium onion for 10 minutes. Spread this mixture on top of each *tarongia* and sprinkle generously with grated provolone, if desired. Place under the broiler to brown.

Stuffed Pizza

CRISPEDDI

1 recipe Pizza Dough (page 65)
1 cup crumbled ricotta salata
24 anchovy fillets, rinsed
Olive oil, for deep frying

Crispeddi is a kind of pizza that is stuffed with ricotta salata cheese and anchovies, then deep-fried until golden. The dough needs to rise for a long time before it is shaped into half-moons.

1. Prepare the pizza dough as described on page 65, letting it rise for 2 hours. Punch down and let rise 2 more hours. Divide into 8 balls and roll each out into an 8-inch circle.

2. Place 2 tablespoons of cheese and 3 anchovy fillets on half of each circle. Fold the other half over to form a half-moon and press the edges together with a fork so they are closed tight.

3. Heat the oil for deep frying to 370°F.

4. Deep-fry the half-moons until golden, about 2 minutes per side. Drain well on paper towels and serve.

Makes 8 pizzas.

Spinach Pie

IMPANATA DI SPINACI

1 recipe Bread Dough (page
  65)
2 pounds fresh spinach,
  trimmed
Salt
3 tablespoons olive oil
3 garlic cloves, lightly crushed
6 tablespoons golden raisins
24 black olives, pitted and
  chopped
½ dry red chili pepper,
  crumbled

The Arabs introduced spinach to Sicily and Spain, but for some reason, it never became popular in Sicilian cuisine. I have come across only four spinach recipes in all of my Sicilian cookbooks, this being one of them.

There is circumstantial evidence that the Sicilian *impanata*, also known as a *calzone*, derives from the half-moon-shaped filled breads of the Islamic tradition. In Sicily they are typically filled with vegetables, cheese, meat, stockfish, or eel.

1. Prepare the bread dough as described on page 65.

2. Wash the spinach thoroughly and boil it in salted water in a large pot for 8 minutes. Drain very well in a colander, pushing the water out with the back of a wooden spoon. Chop the spinach.

3. In a large frying pan, sauté the spinach in the olive oil with the garlic for 4 minutes over medium heat, stirring often. Add the raisins, olives, and chili pepper. Taste for salt and add more if you like. Mix all the ingredients well and sauté for 2 more minutes, stirring. Set aside.

4. Preheat the oven to 375°F.

5. Divide the dough into two pieces and roll each out into a 12-inch circle. Oil a pizza pan and put down one circle of dough. Evenly layer half of the spinach mixture on top of half of the

dough. Fold the other half over it to form a half-moon. Crimp the edges together. Repeat for the second pizza. Poke a fork through the top layer in several places and bake in the oven for 35 minutes, or until the top is golden.

Serves 6.

Eel and Broccoli Pie

IMPANATA DI CALTANISSETTA

1 recipe Bread Dough (page 65)
1 medium onion, sliced
4 tablespoons olive oil
½ pound boned, skinned, and chopped eel (page 156)
½ pound plum tomatoes, peeled, seeded, and chopped
Salt
2 anchovy fillets
½ small onion, sliced thin
1 tablespoon caciocavallo, sliced into tiny strips
2 tablespoons pitted and chopped black olives
1 pound broccoli florets
¼ cup red wine

This is an earthy preparation from Caltanissetta, a medieval town in the interior of Sicily. This unusual combination of ingredients makes for very tasty fare.

1. Prepare the bread dough as described on page 65.

2. Brown the medium sliced onion in a large skillet with 2 tablespoons of the olive oil for 10 minutes over medium heat, stirring very often. Stir in the eel. Add the tomatoes and a pinch of salt. Simmer over low heat for 10 minutes.

3. In another skillet, combine the anchovy fillets, the ½ small sliced onion, the caciocavallo, and half the black olives. Layer the broccoli on top. Drizzle the remaining olive oil over the top, add the remaining black olives, and sprinkle with salt. Sprinkle the wine over the broccoli. Cover and simmer over low heat, shaking the pan from time to time. Do not stir. After 12 minutes, check the broccoli; it should be slightly resistant when pierced with a fork. Add the eel and tomato sauce and remove from the heat with one last shake.

4. Preheat the oven to 375°F.

5. Roll out the dough in a 16-inch circle. Place on a lightly oiled pizza pan or baking stone. Using a slotted spoon to make sure the filling is well drained, spread it over half the dough. Fold the other half over it to form a half-moon. Crimp the edges and puncture the top with a fork in several places. Bake in the oven for about 35 minutes or until the top is golden.

Serves 6 to 8.

Fried Pizza

MITILUGGHIA

Olive oil, for deep frying
1¼ cups flour
⅔ cup warm water
Salt

These small fried white pizzas have a curious name that may derive from the Arabic *mitilua,* which means risen or fermented, except that, curiously enough, these aren't leavened.

1. Heat the oil for deep frying to 360°F.

2. Mix the flour with the water in a bowl and knead until you can form a smooth ball. Roll out the dough on a lightly floured surface to about ¹⁄₁₆ inch thick. Make 10 circles about 4 inches in diameter.

3. Deep-fry for 10 seconds. After 1 side turns golden, turn over to the other side for 5 more seconds. Remove and drain on paper towels. Sprinkle with salt and eat hot immediately.

Makes ten 4-inch pizzas.

FIVE
Salads, Sauces, Soups, and Oils

SALATE, SALSE, MINESTRE, E OLIO

Some of the most delicious and stunningly beautiful salads in Sicily are made with vegetables, seafood, and citrus fruit. These salads—for example *Insalata di Arance*—are even more exquisite when made with the sweet blood oranges of Sicily.

The sauces I've included are versatile, and I suggest a variety of ways they can be used. Nearly any Sicilian soup that includes rice can be traced to the Arabs, because rice production died out in Sicily centuries ago. The soups I've included are meals in themselves and quite flavorful.

Orange Salad

INSALATA DI ARANCE

8 Florida juice oranges or 16 blood oranges, peeled and cut into ⅛-inch slices
(Ingredients continued)

This popular orange salad from Palermo is an excellent accompaniment to grilled meat. It can also be served

3 tablespoons extra-virgin
   olive oil
½ teaspoon salt
Pinch of black pepper
1 tablespoon finely chopped
   mint

between courses to refresh the palate. Some cooks top the salad with leek or onion; others add sliced red onion or even chopped herring and celery. This is a dish that requires the absolutely best extra-virgin olive oil. The oranges should not be swimming in oil, but don't be timid either.

Sicilians use Portugal oranges, which are similar to Valencias or Florida juice oranges. A stunningly beautiful—and sweeter—dish can be made by using blood oranges if they are available.

Orange salad may also be good for your health. In the twelfth century, al-Edrisi, the Arab geographer of the Norman King Roger II's court in Palermo, described orange salad as being beneficial for the intestines.

1. Arrange the orange slices on a platter in an attractive spiral and sprinkle with oil, salt, pepper, and mint.

2. Let marinate for 1 hour before serving and serve at room temperature.

Serves 8.

Fresh Lemon Salad

INSALATA DI LIMONI

6 lemons, peeled and sliced
   thin
4½ tablespoons extra-virgin
   olive oil
½ teaspoon black pepper
Coarse salt

I have seen Sicilians sink their teeth into a lemon, an act that would make most North Americans cringe. Let me provide some conditions you should satisfy to enjoy this salad. Make it in the summer as a between-course refresher. Choose very fresh hard lemons. Make believe you are Sicilian.

Arrange the lemons in a spiral on a platter. Pour the olive oil over, then sprinkle with pepper and a liberal amount of salt. Leave to marinate at room temperature for 1 hour, then serve.

Serves 10 Americans or 2 Sicilians.

Arab Olive Sauce

SALSA SARACENA DI OLIVE

1 potato
Pinch of saffron
1 cup pitted and finely
  chopped large green
  Sicilian olives
2 tablespoons extra-virgin
  olive oil
1 anchovy fillet, mashed
1 tablespoon dried oregano
1 tablespoon pine nuts
1 tablespoon golden raisins

The sauce is powerful and pungent and contrasts nicely with a white-fleshed fish, poached chicken or turkey breast, or veal roast.

   1. Grate the potato and leave in a bowl with cold water to cover for 1 hour. Remove 3 tablespoons of the water and dissolve the saffron in it. Drain and reserve ½ teaspoon of the sediment at the bottom of the bowl.
   2. Place the chopped olives in a bowl large enough to hold all the ingredients. Add the olive oil, anchovy, oregano, pine nuts, raisins, and saffron in water. Add the ½ teaspoon of potato sediment. Mix well and let stand, covered, for 1 hour.
   Makes 1 cup (enough for 6 servings).

Onion Salad

INSALATA DI CIPOLLE

6 tablespoons extra-virgin
  olive oil
2 tablespoons white wine
  vinegar
2 large sweet onions, such as
  red Bermudas or Vidalias,
  peeled and sliced
Chopped mint leaves, for
  garnish

As Ibn Hawqal noted in 974, the Arab Sicilians loved onions, in large quantities and eaten raw.

They eat it at home morning and evening among all their classes so it spoils their imagination and damaged their brains and confused their senses and changed their minds and lessened their understanding and discolored their faces.

This very simple onion salad may derive from those roots. The pride of Catania, it was served in November 1964 to Archbishop of Krakow Karol Wojtyla, the future Pope John Paul II. That he liked this modest but flavorful dish was reported in *La Sicilia*, the biggest daily newspaper of the island.

Mix the olive oil and vinegar together and pour over the onions. Garnish with the mint.

Serves 4.

Orange and Clam Rice Salad

RISO ALL'ARANCIA

12 littleneck clams
1 tablespoon cornstarch
1 cup Arborio rice, washed
1 tablespoon butter
½ teaspoon salt
1 garlic clove, peeled and
    crushed
2 tablespoons extra-virgin
    olive oil
Peel from 1 orange, very
    finely chopped
1 tablespoon very finely
    chopped parsley

I first tasted this exquisite rice salad sitting on the sun-parched terrazzo of the Villagio San Lorenzo in Marzamemi, a tiny port named from the Arabic *Marsa al-Hamman*, port of the baths. It is refreshingly light and cool, perfect for hot Sicilian-like summer days.

1. Place the clams in a bowl of cold water with the cornstarch for 30 minutes to cleanse them. Drain, wash, and shuck the clams, saving the juice. You should have ½ cup or more. Chop the clams very fine and set aside. Add ½ cup of cold water to the clam juice and set aside.

2. Combine the rice with the butter, clam juice and water, and salt in a heavy pot with a tight-fitting lid. Bring to a boil, then reduce and simmer for 15 to 20 minutes. If the rice is not done, add ½ cup boiling water.

3. Meanwhile, sauté the garlic in the olive oil until it begins to turn brown. Discard the garlic. Add the clams and cook on low

to medium heat for 5 minutes. Remove the clams from the heat and gently toss with the rice, orange peel, and parsley until thoroughly mixed. Spread on a serving platter and serve at room temperature.

Serves 4.

Almond Sauce

SARADUSU

½ cup blanched almonds
1 tablespoon sugar
2½ tablespoons red wine
   vinegar
2 tablespoons tomato paste
1 cup finely chopped onion
5 tablespoons olive oil
1½ tablespoons flour
¼ cup pitted and finely
   chopped large green
   Sicilian olives
1 tablespoon capers, washed
   and chopped
1 red chili pepper (optional)
2 anchovy fillets
Salt and pepper

Saradusu is a Sicilian dialect word from the Arabic indicating "sweet and sour." The thirteenth-century Baghdad cookery book Khall Wa-Kardal lists an almond-and-vinegar sauce for fish that may be the root of this spicy, sweet-and-sour Sicilian almond sauce.

Saradusu is best served thick with baked white fish steaks such as hake, cod, or halibut or over a whole grilled fish. It can also be poured over a whole steamed head of cauliflower.

1. Chop the almonds into small bits in a food processor and toast them under a broiler until they begin to turn brown, about 4 minutes. Set aside. Dissolve the sugar in the vinegar and set aside. Dilute the tomato paste in 1 cup hot water and set aside.

2. Sauté the onion in 4 tablespoons of the olive oil over medium heat until translucent, about 6 to 7 minutes. Stir in the flour and cook for 2 minutes. Lower the heat, add the diluted tomato paste, and stir. Add the olives and the capers, bring to a boil, then reduce the heat to very low. Add the chili pepper, if desired. Simmer for 15 minutes, uncovered.

3. Meanwhile, heat the remaining tablespoon of olive oil and stir the anchovies in it until disintegrated. Add the sugar-vinegar mixture and almonds. Simmer over low heat until the vinegar evaporates, about 5 minutes.

4. After the tomato sauce has cooked for 15 minutes, com-

bine both sauces and cook together for 5 minutes. Season to taste with salt and pepper.

Makes about 2 cups.

Orange Sauce

SALSA ALL'ARANCIA

2 tablespoons butter
3 egg yolks
Salt and pepper
2½ tablespoons white wine
   vinegar
2 tablespoons orange juice
Grated zest of ½ orange

This sauce is common in France, too, where it is known as *sauce maltaise*. It is wonderful over steamed vegetables such as asparagus, green beans, or fennel.

Melt the butter in the top of a double boiler. Remove from the heat and add all the other ingredients. Return to the double boiler and start whisking constantly over medium heat. The sauce should thicken in about 2 to 3 minutes. Remove from the heat immediately.

Makes about ½ cup.

Yellow Saffron Sauce

SALSA GIALLA ALL "ZAFRAN"

4 egg yolks
1 tablespoon olive oil
Juice of ½ lemon
1½ tablespoons flour
1 tablespoon butter
Pinch of saffron
Salt and pepper
Freshly grated nutmeg

This bright yellow saffron sauce is typically served with a Sicilian *frutti di mare*, a medley of sea creatures that might include date shells, warty venus, murex, *Venus gallina,* sea eggs, mussels, sea urchins, oysters, limpets, abalone, and cockles. In place of such an exotic array, you may use a selection of mussels, scallops, shrimp, oysters, limpets, periwinkles, littleneck clams, and sea urchins.

In the top of a double boiler whisk the egg yolks off the heat. While beating, slowly add the olive oil and lemon juice. Turn the heat on low and continue whisking as you add the flour, butter, and saffron. Add salt and pepper to taste and, while still whisking, add ½ cup of water. Cook, whisking, until the sauce is dense, like a loose mayonnaise. Remove from the heat, adjust the salt and pepper, and add a pinch of nutmeg.

Makes about 1 cup.

Mint and Parsley Pesto

ZOGGHIU

⅔ cup chopped parsley
  (loosely packed)
⅔ cup chopped fresh mint
  (loosely packed)
3 garlic cloves, peeled
½ cup olive oil
1 tablespoon white wine
  vinegar
Salt

This interesting pesto goes very nicely with grilled fish or turkey, poached chicken, or roast game. *Zogghiu* is a Sicilian dialect word that comes from the Arabic *zait*, which means to add oil to food, and it is prepared like a pesto. Perhaps *zogghiu* has roots among the Yemenis who settled in Palermo in the tenth century. The Yemeni *zhug* is a hot coriander sauce that sounds similar. On the other hand, the Sicilian anthropologist Giuseppe Pitrè attributes this sauce to mariners operating out of Palermo.

1. Pound the parsley, mint, and garlic in a mortar until you have a homogenous paste. If you use a food processor, chop them by pulsing with very short bursts.

2. Put the paste in a bowl and slowly whip in the olive oil and vinegar a tablespoon at a time. Add salt to taste.

Makes ½ cup.

Smooth Tomato Sauce

SALSA DI POMODORO PASSATA

2 pounds plum tomatoes
2 medium onions, finely
  chopped
Salt to taste
4 tablespoons olive oil
Pinch of sugar
10 basil leaves

This is Palermo's own tomato sauce; in Sicily, nearly every village has its own.

1. Chop the tomatoes and drain for 30 minutes. Put the tomatoes and onion in a large frying pan with the salt. Cook the tomatoes and onions for 1 hour over very low heat, stirring occasionally. Do not bring to a boil. If the sauce begins to thicken too quickly add a few tablespoons of water and stir.

2. Push the tomatoes through a sieve or food mill. Transfer the tomato sauce to another saucepan coated with olive oil, add the sugar and basil, and cook on low heat for 30 minutes.

Makes 2 cups.

Tomato Sauce

SALSA DI POMODORO

2 garlic cloves, peeled and
  slightly crushed
4 tablespoons olive oil
1 medium onion, finely
  chopped
2 pounds tomatoes, peeled,
  seeded, and finely chopped
6 basil leaves
Salt and pepper
1 tablespoon dried oregano
  (optional)

This sauce has bits of tomato in it and is also faster to make than Smooth Tomato Sauce (above). It is particularly good with pasta.

1. Sauté the garlic in the olive oil in a deep sauté pan until it turns brown. Remove and discard the garlic and add the onion.

Cook the onion until translucent. Add the tomatoes with their liquid, the basil, and salt and pepper to taste. Cook on high heat for 25 minutes, uncovered.

2. When the sauce is finished, turn the heat off, add the oregano, if using, and let it steep for 10 minutes before serving.

Makes 2 to 3 cups.

Meatball Soup-Soufflé

SCIUSCIEDDU

1¼ pounds ground beef
½ cup grated caciocavallo or pecorino
¼ cup dry breadcrumbs
Salt and pepper
5 eggs
2 tablespoons olive oil
1¾ cups ricotta
4 cups Beef Broth (page 86)
Ground cinnamon, for sprinkling

Everything about this spectacular meatball soup with its soufflé topping is open to question: its origin; the meaning of the name; whether to call it a soup or a stew; whether it should be made in a peasant or baronial style; how it is spelled; even where it is from. This version is from Messina. Fiammetta di Napoli Oliver, a food writer from Mondello, and Enzo Siena, a culinary historian from Syracuse, both think the roots might be Arab, perhaps related to the Arabic *shourbat al Qeema*, a meatball soup also flavored with cinnamon.

1. Mix together the beef, ¼ cup of the grated cheese, the breadcrumbs, and the salt and pepper. Lightly beat one of the eggs and add it. Knead the meat well and make little meatballs, no more than 1 inch in diameter. Sauté the meatballs in the olive oil for about 15 minutes on low heat, shaking the pan occasionally. Remove the meatballs with a slotted spoon and leave to drain on paper towels.

2. Separate the remaining eggs, putting the yolks in 1 bowl and the whites in another. Mix the yolks with the ricotta. Fold in the remaining grated cheese. Whip the egg whites until they form peaks.

3. Preheat the oven to 350°F.

4. Bring the broth to a boil in a deep ovenproof casserole or tureen. Using a large serving spoon, add the meatballs and egg-yolk mixture by the spoonful. When the broth returns to a boil,

turn the heat off, sprinkle the top with cinnamon, and pour in the egg whites. Place in the oven for 20 minutes. Serve immediately.
   Serves 6.

Vegetable and Bean Soup

MINESTRA DI VERDURA E FAGIOLI

½ cup dry fava beans
½ cup dry haricots or other
   white beans
Salt
2 medium onions, cut into
   eighths and separated
1 carrot, peeled and coarsely
   chopped
1 celery stalk, coarsely
   chopped
1 bay leaf
1 bulb fennel, coarsely
   chopped, and 1 bunch dill,
   chopped (about 2 pounds)
3 cabbage leaves
1 bunch beet leaves or Swiss
   chard leaves, or 1 pound
   spinach leaves
3 Belgian endive leaves
Pepper
1 cup Arborio rice, washed
Extra-virgin olive oil, for
   drizzling
Grated parmesan cheese, for
   serving (optional)

The Vucciria, the old street market of Palermo, reminds me of an Arab souk, with its close-quartered warrens and noisy hustle-bustle. Today you can find in the Vucciria every variety of vegetable, from giri (a kind of edible leafy Sicilian green) and sparacelli (broccoli) to dandelion and sweet Tunisian eggplant to swordfish and pine nuts.

   Since vegetables are plentiful in Sicily, soup dishes are very popular. I've included several that have an ancient but not necessarily Arab history.

   You can replace wild fennel with fennel and dill, as suggested to me by cookbook writer Paula Wolfert. Beet greens or Swiss chard can be used in place of giri.

   1. Soak the dry beans for 1 hour in cold water; drain. Bring a large pot of lightly salted water to a boil. Add the beans, onions, carrot, celery, and bay leaf.
   2. After the water returns to a boil, reduce the heat so that the soup slowly simmers. Check the beans after 45 minutes, and if they still feel hard, continue cooking until they are almost soft.
   3. Add the bulb fennel and dill, cabbage, beet leaves, and endive leaves. Taste for salt and pepper. Simmer for 25 minutes, uncovered.

4. Add the rice. Cover and cook for 15 minutes. Serve with a generous amount of extra-virgin olive oil drizzled on each serving. You can also sprinkle some parmesan cheese on top.
Serves 8.

Rice Balls in Broth

BADDUZZI DI RISU 'NTO BRODU

¼ teaspoon saffron
Enough beef marrow bones to
  yield 3 tablespoons beef
  marrow
4 tablespoons butter
1 small onion, finely chopped
⅓ cup white wine
2 cups Arborio rice, washed
10 cups Beef Broth (page
  86)
4 tablespoons freshly grated
  caciocavallo or pecorino
¼ pound caciocavallo or fresh
  mozzarella, cut into tiny
  cubes
Sunflower-seed oil, for deep
  frying
3 eggs
Flour, for dredging
Freshly grated parmesan
  (optional)

If these rice balls seem familiar it is because they are similar to *arancine* (pages 53–56). The basic preparation is like that of *Risotto alla Milanese*, which most Sicilian gastronomes consider to be of Arab-Sicilian origin. The rice balls are very delicate and will fall apart in the broth.

1. Soak the saffron in 1 tablespoon of tepid water. Extract the marrow from the bones with a small spoon. If the marrow does not come out easily, boil the bones for 10 minutes or microwave them for 1 minute on high.

2. Melt 2 tablespoons of the butter in a large heavy pan. Sauté the onion and bone marrow until the onion is translucent, stirring often. Add the wine and cook until it is reduced to a few tablespoons. Stir the rice into the pan and sauté over medium-low heat for 3 minutes.

3. Bring the broth to a boil and add 1 cup to the rice; the broth will sizzle. Stir once and let cook until the broth is absorbed,

shaking the pot once in a while. Continue in this manner, 1 cup at a time, until you have used 3½ cups of broth. Stir very gently and shake until the rice is al dente. This should take about 20 minutes.

4. Add the saffron by sprinkling over the rice and stir gently. Remove from the heat and gently stir in the remaining butter and the grated cheese. Cover and let stand for a few minutes. Uncover and spread the rice on a large platter to let it cool completely.

5. Shape the rice into small balls the size of a walnut, putting a cube of cheese into the center, in the same manner as for the rice balls on page 55.

6. Heat the oil for deep frying to 360°F.

7. Beat the eggs in a shallow bowl. Spread some flour for dredging on a piece of wax paper.

8. Roll the balls in egg and then in flour. Deep-fry them until they are golden. Serve them in the remaining hot broth, adding some grated parmesan, if desired. Serve very hot with 4 or 5 rice balls per serving. Any remaining rice balls can be frozen for later use.

Serves 8.

Beef Broth

BRODO DI CARNE

4 pounds cracked beef
    marrow, shin, and/or
    shank bones, with meat on
    them
1 large onion, peeled and cut
    into eighths
4 plum tomatoes, cut in half
2 celery stalks, cut up
10 peppercorns
Bouquet garni, tied together
    in cheesecloth (2 parsley
    sprigs, 1 fresh thyme sprig,
    2 fresh sage leaves, 1 bay
    leaf)
Salt and freshly ground black
    pepper, to taste

This is a flavorful broth that can be used as a base to various soups.

1. Put all the ingredients except the salt and ground pepper with 4 quarts of cold water into a stockpot and bring to a boil,

then reduce to a simmer. Skim the surface of the foam. Partially cover and simmer on very low heat for no less than 6 hours.

2. Pour the broth through a strainer and discard all the bones, meat, vegetables, and bouquet garni. Pour the broth through the strainer lined with cheesecloth. Season to taste with salt and pepper.

3. To degrease the broth, place in the refrigerator. The fat will congeal on top and can be lifted off. The broth can be frozen until needed.

Makes 2 to 3 quarts.

Holy Oil

OLIO SANTO

1 quart first cold-pressed
  extra-virgin olive oil
1 tablespoon black
  peppercorns, very coarsely
  ground
1 tablespoon white
  peppercorns, very coarsely
  ground
1 red chili pepper, chopped
2 bay leaves, broken in half
4 garlic cloves, finely chopped
4 cardamom seeds, shelled
½ teaspoon salt

I like to use this cardamom-flavored olive oil for dipping crusty bread or to dress plain foods. Cardamom, a member of the ginger family, was part of the spice trade known to the Greeks and Romans, but the Arabs popularized it in Sicily. The Arab practice of flavoring coffee with cardamom may be the inspiration for its use here.

Pour out ½ cup of the olive oil and reserve for another use. Mix together the pepper, chili pepper, bay leaves, garlic, cardamom, and salt. Add this mixture to the bottle of olive oil. Cork or cap the bottle and leave for 20 days.

Makes about 4 cups.

SIX

Pasta, Rice, and Couscous

PASTA, RISO, E CUSCUSÙ

PASTA

Marco Polo did not introduce macaroni to Europe. The word "macaroni" does not come from Macco, a character in Atellan farces; nor from *macco*, a word used in Sicily today for flour-and-water dough; nor from *makaria*, a food of the blessed described by the Greek lexicographer Hesychius.

As difficult as the history of macaroni is to trace, scholars now know that all suggestions that do not base this history on the Arab discovery of hard wheat (*Triticum durum*) can be dismissed. Mixing flour and water to make threads had been known for millennia, but mixing hard-wheat flour and water to make macaroni was unique and important. The Arabs introduced hard wheat to Sicily in the ninth or tenth century, where it replaced the soft Roman wheat known as *emmer* or *poulard*. Hard wheat was unknown to the Romans and played no role in the classical diet of Sicily. The hardness and high gluten content of the hard wheat meant it could be stored for long periods without spoilage. As a result, the world literally changed because pasta and couscous reduced the severity of the famines that periodically attacked the people of the Middle Ages.

The first mention of *maccherone* in Italian is in a document written in 1041 that comes from Calabria. The word is used in a metaphorical sense as a name for a "silly person." Only later does it come to mean pasta. The first clear use of the word to refer to pasta appears in a Genovese notarial document from 1279: an inventory that lists the possessions of a soldier named Ponzio Bastone as containing a chest of macaroni.

But 120 years before that, al-Edrisi, the Arab geographer of the Norman court in Palermo and author of the *Kitab al-Ruger* (Book of Roger), wrote that "to the west of the outskirts of habited Trabia, enchantingly situated, rich in perennial water and swathed in a beautiful plain and broad farms, is made a vermicelli (*itriya*) in such a large quantity."

A fourteenth-century Italian cookbook mentions different kinds of pasta made from hard wheat and refers to it as *tria*. *Tria* is a Sicilian word borrowed from the Arabic *itriya*. Ibn Butlan's eleventh-century medical treatise mentions it too. An astonishing picture depicting the making of *trij*, or pasta, is in the Vienna copy of his *Taqwim al-Sihha* or *Tacuinum Sanitatis*, an Arabic medical text translated into Latin under the auspices of the Sicilian King Manfred, son of Frederick II, who was known as the "lover of science." Al-Jawhari and Isho Bar Ali, lexicographers of the ninth century, also mention the word. The Syrian Bar Ali indicates that *itriya* is made from semolina, which is then dried and cooked. In the tenth century, the Arab agronomist Ibn Wahshiya described a wheat product that is "viscous," clearly a reference to hard wheat's high gluten content.

Pasta, in all its varieties, was known by the fourteenth century: vermicelli, macaroni, lasagne, and so on. Lasagne, suggests the French scholar Maxime Rodinson, may come from the Arabic *lawzinag*, a kind of pasta in layers, made in strips, quadrangles, or rhomboids.

In medieval Palermo pasta was made at home by hand; the aristocracy already had special machines for kneading the pasta dough. In the fifteenth century this privilege was carried on by the Jews, who may have inherited it from the Arabs in Norman Sicily. The notion that the Jews carried on Arab-Sicilian cuisine and brought it north is also evidenced in a baked pasta dish of Jewish origin. Popular in Ferrara, it is called *Hamin* and is made with *tagliolini*, goose fat, golden raisins, and pine nuts.

The Sicilian food researcher Felice Cùnsolo spoke the truth when he said, "The Sicilians are formidable eaters of pasta." Every Sicilian family eats pasta at least once a day and many eat it more often than that. Even in the fourteenth century, Sicily was the major exporter of pasta and rice to Genoa.

Pasta with Cauliflower and Saffron

PASTA CON BROCCOLI "ARRIMINATA"

½ cup golden raisins or
  currants
Pinch of saffron
1 medium cauliflower head
  (about 2 pounds)
Salt
⅓ cup olive oil
1 medium onion, thinly sliced
2 garlic cloves, finely chopped
6 anchovy fillets, rinsed and
  coarsely chopped
1½ cups peeled and chopped
  plum tomatoes
⅓ cup pine nuts
Pepper
1 pound perciatelli (bucatini)
  or spaghetti
2 tablespoons grated pecorino
2 tablespoons finely chopped
  basil leaves
Extra-virgin olive oil, for
  drizzling

This wonderfully aromatic dish from Palermo imbued with saffron is one of my favorite uses for cauliflower. *Arriminare* in Sicilian means "to shake," which is how you mix the ingredients together.

1. Soften the raisins in warm water for 20 minutes. Put the saffron in 3 tablespoons of tepid water to steep.
2. Cook the cauliflower whole in salted water until half done, 12 to 18 minutes at a vigorous boil. There should be a bit of resistance when it is pierced with a knife. Drain, saving the water. Chop the cauliflower into small florets.
3. Heat the olive oil in a deep pan and sauté the onion and garlic until translucent, about 6 minutes over medium heat. Stir often to keep the garlic from burning. Add the anchovies and tomatoes and cook for 20 minutes over low heat, stirring often. Drain the raisins. Add the cauliflower, pine nuts, raisins, and saffron, a few tablespoons of cauliflower water, and salt and pepper to taste. Cover and cook over very low heat for 30 to 40 minutes.

4. Cook the pasta in the remaining cauliflower water until al dente. Drain and transfer to the pan with the sauce. Shake the pan vigorously with the lid on to mix. Lift the lid, put a paper towel underneath to absorb water, replace lid, and let stand for 10 to 20 minutes. Before serving, sprinkle with pecorino and finely chopped basil leaves. Pass extra-virgin olive oil for drizzling.

Serves 4.

Ziti and Cauliflower Gratin

ZITI CON BROCCOLI IN CROSTATA

Salt
1 medium cauliflower head
  (about 2 pounds)
Pinch of saffron
1 garlic clove, lightly crushed
  and peeled
3 anchovy fillets, rinsed and
  patted dry
5 tablespoons olive oil
1½ tablespoons pine nuts
1¼ pounds ziti
½ cup freshly grated pecorino

This oven-baked ziti from the area around Caltanissetta and Ragusa is very pretty, with the vermilion flecks of saffron against the yellow pasta.

1. Bring a pot of salted water to a boil and place the whole cauliflower in it. Cook until the cauliflower is slightly resistant to a fork, about 12 minutes. Drain, saving the cooking water, and break up the cauliflower into small florets. Set aside. Remove ¼ cup of the cauliflower water and dissolve the saffron in it.

2. In a large frying pan, sauté the cauliflower, garlic, anchovies, and 4 tablespoons of the olive oil over high heat for 2 minutes. Add the pine nuts and sauté for 1 minute. Remove from the heat and set aside.

3. Bring the cauliflower water to a boil and add a bit more salt. Parboil the ziti until they are about half done. Drain well.

4. Preheat the oven to 375°F.

5. Pour the ziti into a large, deep, oiled ovenproof casserole. Stir in half the cauliflower and half the cheese. Sprinkle with the saffron water and mix gently. Spread the remaining cauliflower and cheese on top. Drizzle with the remaining tablespoon of olive oil and place in the oven for 15 minutes. Serve immediately.

Serves 8.

The Friars' Pasta

PASTA ALLA PAOLINA

1 medium cauliflower head
  (about 2 pounds)
½ cup olive oil
1 medium onion, finely
  chopped
1 tablespoon tomato paste
1 tablespoon pine nuts
1 tablespoon golden raisins or
  currants
Salt and freshly ground black
  pepper
Pinch of ground cloves
  (optional)
Pinch of ground cinnamon
  (optional)
6 anchovy fillets, rinsed and
  mashed
¾ pound spaghetti

The vegetable concoction used in this recipe can be served separately as a side dish. The original recipe was developed by the friars of San Francesco di Paola monastery in Palermo; they used cloves and cinnamon as flavoring.

1. Cut all the florets off the cauliflower and slice them ½ inch thick. Peel the tender portion of the stem and cut into thin slices.

2. Heat the olive oil in a heavy pot and sauté the onion over medium heat until translucent, about 6 minutes. Add the tomato paste, stirring it in the oil over medium-high heat until the onions are bright red.

3. Add the cauliflower, stirring over high heat until well coated. Reduce the heat. Add the pine nuts, the raisins, ½ teaspoon salt, and ½ teaspoon pepper; cover and cook over medium-low to low heat for about 20 minutes, or until almost tender, stirring every now and then. Turn off the heat. Add the cloves, cinnamon, if desired, and anchovies, and mix well. If you want a milder flavor, use fewer anchovies. Season to taste with salt and pepper.

4. Cook the pasta in a large pot of boiling salted water until al dente. Drain and pour into the pot with the cauliflower. Mix well. This dish can be served lukewarm.

Serves 4.

Pasta with Sardines

PASTA CON LE SARDE

Pinch of saffron
Salt
1 bulb fennel, trimmed (about
   2 pounds)
1 pound perciatelli (bucatini)
   or spaghetti
½ cup olive oil plus 2
   tablespoons
2 medium onions, thinly
   sliced
6 anchovy fillets, rinsed
2 pounds fresh sardines,
   gutted; head, tail, and
   dorsal fin removed; and
   boned
Pepper
2 tablespoons currants, soaked
2 tablespoons pine nuts
2 tablespoons tomato paste
   (optional)
¼ cup blanched almonds,
   toasted and chopped
   (optional)

Pasta con le Sarde is one of the most celebrated dishes of Sicilian cuisine. It is a specialty of Palermo, but there are variations throughout western Sicily. A version of this dish, called alla sciacchitana, from the town of Sciacca, which was founded by the Arabs, uses breadcrumbs and roasted almonds. Another, Pasta con le Sarde a Mare, is the poor man's version: The sardines are still in the sea! This recipe is the classic one.

One non–Sicilian food writer described this dish as an "eyesore," but he was rightly dismissed by the Sicilian writer Alberto Denti di Pirajno as clearly not a gourmand, a philosopher, or a historian. Here is Denti di Pirajno's rhapsodic recipe for Pasta con le Sarde:

Gather the fennels on the mountains where Pan's reed pipe and the Oreads' songs still echo. Fish the sardines in the seas where Athens' triremes were beaten, and prepare them in the Muslim fashion, with raisins and pine nuts. The sun will have ripened for you the tomatoes to cover the pasta with a purple-red mantle which will become golden in the oven received from Norman seamen.

An amusing legend about the birth of this dish is recounted by a number of writers. Byzantine chronicles claim that Admiral Euphemius, when he landed in Mazara del Vallo in 827 at the head of an Arab invasion force, ordered his Arab cooks to prepare a meal. They found sardines in the harbor, wild fennel, pine nuts, saffron, and currants in the hills and mixed them all together. I tried to trace this legend through the relevant chronicles of Theodosius Continuatus, Constantine Porphyrogenitus, and Simon Logothete and also the Arab chronicle by Ibn al-Athir but never found this story. Then again, that's what legends are for.

1. Dissolve the saffron in a small bowl with 2 tablespoons of tepid water. Bring a large pot of water to a boil and salt it abundantly. Boil the fennel whole in the water on medium heat for about 10 minutes. When it is slightly resistant to a fork, drain, reserving the fennel water. Press the remaining water out with the back of a wooden spoon. Chop into small pieces. Set aside.

2. Bring the fennel water back to a boil. Add a bit more salt and the pasta. Cook until half done. Drain, reserving ½ cup of the water. Sprinkle with 2 tablespoons of the olive oil and toss well.

3. In a frying pan, sauté the onions in the remaining olive oil until translucent, about 6 minutes. Add the anchovies and cook until they disintegrate. Add half the sardines and sauté for 2 minutes over medium heat. Add the fennel and salt and pepper to taste. Cook for 5 minutes.

4. Drain the currants and add along with the pine nuts and saffron. Continue cooking for 5 minutes. Add the pasta and mix well.

5. Butterfly the remaining sardines. Dissolve the tomato paste, if using, in the fennel water reserved in Step 2.

6. Preheat the oven to 425°F.

7. Put the pasta into a large baking pan and cover with any remaining sauce. Lay the butterflied sardines on top of the pasta and sprinkle with almonds, if desired. Top with the diluted tomato paste, if desired. Bake for 10 minutes. Remove and serve immediately.

Serves 6.

Spaghetti with Moorish Sauce

SPAGHETTI ALLA SALSA MURISCA TARATATA

1½ tablespoons sugar
1 tablespoon white wine
 vinegar
Pinch of ground cinnamon
1 teaspoon orange water
⅓ cup dry breadcrumbs, toasted
4 tablespoons pine nuts
1 garlic clove, peeled
3 tablespoons bottarga (page
 185), rinsed
2 anchovy fillets, rinsed
1 red chili pepper
3 tablespoons coarsely
 chopped parsley
1 teaspoon strained fresh
 orange juice
1 teaspoon strained fresh
 lemon juice
7 tablespoons extra-virgin
 olive oil
1½ pounds spaghetti
Salt
Freshly grated parmesan, for
 sprinkling

I heard about this unusual dish from Pino Correnti, the Sicilian culinary historian. It supposedly commemorates the eleventh-century battle between the Arab-Sicilian Emir Ibn al-Hawwas and the Norman Count Roger I. In the dialect of the county of Mòdica, *taratata* means "clash," as between two armies, but it also refers to a wild dance that is said to drive out the poison from a tarantula bite. *Taratata* may also be a reference to the Arab and Ottoman *tarator* sauce made with nuts and bread beaten into a cream with a mortar and pestle.

1. Dissolve the sugar in the vinegar and set aside. Dissolve the cinnamon in orange water and set aside.

2. Make a pesto of the breadcrumbs, pine nuts, garlic, *bottarga*, anchovy fillets, chili pepper, and parsley in a food processor using short bursts, until the mixture is uniform. Scrape into a bowl.

3. Moisten the pesto with the vinegar-and-sugar mixture and stir until blended. Add the orange juice and lemon juice and the cinnamon-orange water, stirring well to combine. Add 1 tablespoon of the olive oil at a time, whisking as you go. You can make the pesto several hours ahead of time and refrigerate it at this point.

4. Cook the spaghetti in a large amount of boiling salted water until al dente. Drain and toss with the sauce, mixing very well. Pass the remaining olive oil for drizzling. Pass some parmesan, if desired.

Serves 6 to 8.

Spaghetti with Fried Breadcrumbs and Raisins

SPAGHETTI CON LA MOLLICA FRITTA E CON L'UVA PASSA

1 clove garlic, crushed and
  peeled
¼ cup olive oil
4 to 5 tablespoons
  breadcrumbs
½ cup golden raisins or
  currants
Salt
1 pound spaghetti
1 teaspoon finely chopped
  parsley
Pepper

This unusual rustic dish combines raisins, breadcrumbs, and garlic, making an interesting change from cheese. It's a particular favorite with my children.

1. Lightly brown the garlic in the olive oil, then discard the garlic. Sauté the breadcrumbs in the oil, stirring constantly, over medium heat for about 2 minutes. Soak the raisins in a bowl of tepid water.

2. Bring a large pot of abundantly salted water to a boil. Add the pasta and cook until al dente. Drain well. Drain the raisins and toss with the pasta, parsley, and breadcrumbs, and salt and pepper to taste. Toss well, making sure all the pasta is thoroughly covered with breadcrumbs. Serve immediately.

Serves 4 to 6.

Spaghetti with Broccoli and Lentil Pesto

TRIA BASTARDA ALLE LENTICCHIE

Salt
¾ pound lentils (1½ cups)
¾ cup broccoli florets
⅓ cup lard, cut into pieces
2 small onions, finely chopped
2 carrots, peeled and diced

This lusty peasant dish from the area around Palermo is similar to a Persian one described by Claudia Roden in *A Book of Middle Eastern Food. Tria* comes from the Arabic word *itriya*, a kind of pasta made in twelfth-century Sicily.

½ cup white wine
¼ cup extra-virgin olive oil
Pepper
1 pound spaghetti
Holy Oil (page 87) or
    extra-virgin olive oil, for
    drizzling

1. Bring salted water to cover to a boil and cook the lentils and broccoli together for 12 to 20 minutes, or until tender. Purée the mixture in a food processor or in a food mill.

2. Melt the lard and sauté the onions and carrots for 12 minutes over medium heat. Add the purée and mix well. Add the wine and cook until it evaporates, 2 to 3 minutes. Taste and add olive oil as needed and salt and pepper to taste.

3. Bring a large pot of abundantly salted water to a boil. Add the spaghetti and cook until al dente. Drain. Place the spaghetti in a serving bowl, cover with sauce, and toss until all the spaghetti is coated. Serve immediately. Pass Holy Oil or olive oil at the table.
Serves 4.

Yellow Vermicelli

VERMICELLI GIALLI

Pinch of saffron
Salt
¾ pound vermicelli
1 cup heavy cream
3 ounces (¾ cup) prosciutto,
    cut into little bits
½ cup freshly grated
    parmesan
2 egg yolks, beaten
1 hard-boiled egg yolk, riced
2 tablespoons finely chopped
    parsley

It is sometimes forgotten that the Arabs use milk or cream with pasta. Even in the Maghreb, where dairy products are scarce and expensive, there is a vermicelli dish, called *Shahriyet el-Hamrak,* that is made with milk and cinnamon. In Lebanon, vermicelli is mixed with milk, eggs, parsley, and cheese. This Sicilian version uses saffron, the little "Arab fantasy," as Tommaso d'Alba calls it.

This preparation goes quickly, so have your ingredients ready at the start.

1. Dissolve the saffron in 3 tablespoons of tepid water. Bring a large pot of salted water to a boil. Add the vermicelli and cook it until al dente. Drain.

2. While the vermicelli is cooking, put the cream in a sauté pan over medium heat. As it begins to reach a boil, but before it bubbles, add the prosciutto and parmesan. Stir a little. When little bubbles begin to form around the edges, add the saffron water.

3. Just as the cream reaches a boil, remove from the heat and incorporate the egg yolks. Season with the hard-boiled egg yolk and parsley. Toss with vermicelli and serve very hot.

Serves 4.

Spaghetti with Almonds

SPAGHETTI ALLE MANDORLE

½ cup olive oil
1 medium onion, finely chopped
1 garlic clove, peeled and finely chopped
1 cup whole blanched almonds, finely chopped
⅔ cup dry breadcrumbs
1 teaspoon black pepper
Salt
1 pound spaghetti
Holy Oil (page 87) or extra-virgin olive oil, for drizzling (optional)

This recipe is a variation of a dish common to western Sicily called *Pasta che' Nuci* (Pasta with Walnuts). The Arabs probably introduced the notion of mixing pasta with nuts. In fact, the Sicilian word for nut (*fastuca*) comes from the Arabic word for pistachio (*fustuq*).

1. Heat the oil in a frying pan and sauté the onion and garlic over medium heat, stirring often, for 6 minutes, or until the onion is translucent. Add the almonds and continue cooking over medium heat for 4 minutes. Add the breadcrumbs and cook for another 3 minutes, mixing and stirring often. Add the pepper and salt to taste.

2. Bring a pot of abundantly salted water to a boil and cook the spaghetti until al dente. Drain and toss with the sauce until the spaghetti is completely coated with breadcrumbs and almonds. Pass some oil for drizzling, if desired.

Serves 4 to 6.

Spaghetti with Lobster and Pantelleria Pesto

SPAGHETTI ALL'ARAGOSTA "CULL'AMMOGHIU"

1 medium live lobster (2½ pounds) or ½ pound lobster meat
Sea salt
Juice of 1 lemon
2 tablespoons capers, rinsed
2 tablespoons white wine vinegar
8 basil leaves
3 garlic cloves, peeled
4 large ripe tomatoes, peeled, seeded, and well drained
½ cup parsley leaves
1 teaspoon black pepper
½ cup extra-virgin olive oil
¾ pound spaghetti

Ammoghiu is another raw sauce, this one from the island of Pantelleria, famous for capers.

1. Steam the lobster for 20–30 minutes. Drain. When it is cool, remove all the meat and the tomalley, if any. Cut the lobster meat into pieces and season with a little sea salt and lemon juice. Set aside in the refrigerator.

2. Combine the capers, vinegar, basil, garlic, tomatoes (make sure they are well drained, otherwise the sauce will be too watery), parsley, and pepper in a food processor and process in short bursts. Slowly pour in the olive oil, with the processor turned on.

3. Remove the lobster from the refrigerator. When the pesto is all mixed, pour it over the lobster pieces and set aside to allow the lobster to come back to room temperature.

4. Bring a large pot of abundantly salted water to a boil and cook the spaghetti until al dente. Drain well and place in a serving platter. Pour the lobster sauce over the spaghetti, toss gently, and serve.

Serves 4.

Silly Spaghetti

SPAGHETTI AL MATAROCCU

2 pounds plum tomatoes,
   peeled, seeded, and cut up
12 cloves garlic, peeled
½ cup olive oil
8 basil leaves, finely chopped
1 cup freshly grated pecorino
½ cup blanched almonds,
   crushed
Salt
1 pound spaghetti

Mataroccu is a Sicilian word meaning "silly." I don't know what the context is here, but this raw sauce, familiar to the Marsala region, is delicious when added directly to steaming-hot spaghetti.

1. Put the tomatoes in a bowl and leave to drain. Crush the garlic in a mortar with a pestle. Transfer to a deep bowl.
2. Drain the tomatoes of all their juice and add to the garlic. Mix and pound the tomatoes into the garlic with the pestle. This is the *mataroccu.*
3. When the *mataroccu* is uniformly blended, add the olive oil, basil, ½ cup of the cheese, and the almonds and mix a little. Leave aside to let the flavors mingle for up to 1 hour.
4. Bring a large pot of abundantly salted water to a boil and cook the spaghetti until al dente. Drain and toss with the sauce and serve immediately. Pass the remaining cheese at the table.
    Serves 4 to 6.

Spaghetti with Lobster, Basil, and Saffron

SPAGHETTI CON ARAGOSTA ALLA TRAPANESE

Pinch of saffron
¾ cup dry white wine
2 medium live lobsters (2
   pounds each) or 1 pound
   lobster meat

This blend of basil, saffron, and lobster has a flavor you will never forget. I was inspired to create this recipe after tasting a similar dish prepared in Trapani and the Egadi Islands.

½ cup plus 2 tablespoons
  extra-virgin olive oil
Sea salt
3 garlic cloves, peeled and
  very finely chopped
2 garlic cloves, crushed and
  peeled
½ small onion, finely
  chopped
1 pound plum tomatoes,
  peeled, seeded, chopped,
  and drained
2 dried red chili peppers
10 basil leaves
¾ pound spaghetti

1. Dissolve the saffron in 3 tablespoons of the wine.

2. Steam the lobsters together until they are done, about 20 to 30 minutes. When they are cool, remove all the meat and tomalley, if any.

3. Cut up the lobster meat and place it in a bowl. Cover with the dissolved saffron and remaining wine. Drizzle ¼ cup of the olive oil over the lobster so that it is well covered, leaving a small pool at the bottom of the bowl. Toss the lobster with a little sea salt and the chopped garlic. Cover and place in the refrigerator to marinate.

4. Pour ¼ cup of the olive oil into a saucepan and sauté the crushed garlic until it just begins to turn brown. Discard the garlic, add the onion, and sauté over high heat, stirring constantly, until translucent, about 5 minutes. Add the tomatoes.

5. Lower the heat to medium–high and cook the sauce for 10 minutes, uncovered. Add the chili peppers and continue cooking for 10 minutes. Add the marinated lobster along with the basil leaves and cook for 2 minutes.

6. Meanwhile bring a large pot of abundantly salted water to a rolling boil and add the spaghetti. When it is al dente, drain it and put it in a serving bowl. Toss with the remaining olive oil. Pour the sauce over the spaghetti, toss, and serve.

Serves 4 to 6.

Pasta with Anchovies

PASTA CON LE ACCIUGHE

1 tablespoon golden raisins or
   currants
10 anchovy fillets, rinsed and
   mashed
1 tablespoon pine nuts
1 small garlic clove, peeled
   and finely chopped
3 tablespoons finely chopped
   parsley
½ teaspoon salt
1 teaspoon black pepper
2 cups Smooth Tomato Sauce
   (page 82)
¾ pound bulb fennel mixed
   with 6 to 7 dill sprigs
   (optional)
½ pound spaghetti or trenette
½ cup dry breadcrumbs,
   toasted
½ teaspoon red pepper flakes
   (optional)

This recipe and the next are glorious and hearty dishes I enjoy serving to people who love—or hate—anchovies. Here the anchovies blend together with the raisins and pine nuts to help create a delicately seasoned tomato sauce.

In Enna, in the interior of Sicily, this dish is called *milanisa,* which the Sicilian food authority Pino Correnti thinks might be a reference to the Lombards from Milan who immigrated in the twelfth century to work for the Norman sericulture industry established with Arab expertise.

1. Soak the raisins in a cup of warm water for 15 minutes. Drain well and mix together with the anchovies, pine nuts, garlic, parsley, salt, and pepper. Set aside.

2. Heat the tomato sauce. When it just begins to boil, add the anchovy mixture and turn off the heat. Let stand for at least 30 minutes before mixing it with the pasta.

3. Bring salted water to a boil in a large pot and add the fennel, if using, and the pasta. Cook until al dente. Drain and toss well with the tomato sauce. Sprinkle 2 tablespoons of the breadcrumbs and the pepper flakes, if using, on top and serve immediately. Pass the rest of the breadcrumbs at the table.

Serves 4.

Arab-Style Penne

PENNE ALLA SARACENA

1 pound plum tomatoes,
  peeled, seeded, finely
  chopped, and drained
2 garlic cloves, peeled and
  finely chopped
3 tablespoons finely chopped
  parsley
3 tablespoons finely chopped
  mint
¼ cup olive oil
Salt
1 pound penne
3 tablespoons freshly grated
  pecorino
3 tablespoons ricotta

What identifies this dish as Arab is the earthenware vessel used to combine the penne and the sauce. In Sicilian it is called a *coccio*. A similar terra-cotta baking casserole is used with *Taganu d'Aragona*.

I was always delighted to see ricotta appearing on pasta dishes in Sicily; it's a delicious addition. The distinguished Sicilian historian Santi Correnti told me of the medieval roots of ricotta in Sicily. Frederick II and his hunting party came across the hut of a farmer who was making ricotta. Frederick, who was ravenous, asked for some ricotta. He pulled out his loaf of bread and poured the hot ricotta and whey on top and ordered his retinue, "*Cu' non mancia ccu' so' cucchiaru lassa tutto 'o zammataru* (Those who don't eat with a spoon will leave all their ricotta behind).

1. Mix together the tomatoes, garlic, parsley, mint, olive oil, and salt to taste. Cook the penne in abundantly salted boiling water until al dente. Drain.

2. Put the cooked penne in an earthenware pot, add the sauce, and cook over slow heat for a minute or two. Add the pecorino. Mix well and serve on a terra-cotta platter with the ricotta sprinkled on top.

Serves 6.

Pasta with Anchovies and Toasted Breadcrumbs

PASTA ALLE SFINCIONE

2 garlic cloves, peeled and
  chopped
2 tablespoons chopped parsley
3 tablespoons extra-virgin
  olive oil
1 cup anchovy fillets (about
  30 fillets), rinsed, half
  mashed in a mortar with a
  pestle, half left whole
4 cups Smooth Tomato Sauce
  (page 82)
1 teaspoon black pepper
Salt
1 pound tagliatelle or
  fettuccine
⅓ cup dry breadcrumbs,
  toasted

The sauce for this pasta dish was probably a pizza topping at one time, since sfincione is the Sicilian word for pizza. Don't let the amount of anchovies deter you from making this delicious dish. To ensure success, you may want to read about anchovies on page 155.

1. Combine the garlic and parsley and sauté in the olive oil over medium heat for 2 minutes. Remove the pan from the fire, add the mashed anchovies, and stir. Add the tomato sauce and pepper. Simmer, covered, for 20 minutes.

2. Preheat the oven to 450°F.

3. Bring a pot of salted water to a rolling boil and add the pasta. Cook until al dente. Drain and transfer to a baking dish. Pour the hot sauce over the pasta. Scatter the whole anchovies on top and sprinkle evenly with breadcrumbs. Bake for 10 minutes, or until the breadcrumbs begin to look a bit crusty.

Serves 6.

Pasta with Tuna

PASTA COL TONNO

1/4 pound fresh or canned tuna
   (poached in water, if fresh)
1 1/2 tablespoons pine nuts
1 1/2 tablespoons golden raisins
1 garlic clove, peeled and
   finely chopped
1/2 teaspoon black pepper
2 cups Smooth Tomato Sauce
   (page 82)
3/4 pound penne or spaghetti
Salt
2 tablespoons very finely
   chopped parsley

Fresh tuna mixed with pine nuts and golden raisins makes for an appetizing sauce in this recipe from the Palermo area.

1. Mix together the tuna, pine nuts, raisins, garlic, and black pepper. Heat the tomato sauce. When the sauce is hot, mix in the tuna mixture and let stand for 30 minutes.

2. Cook the pasta in plenty of boiling salted water until al dente. Drain well and mix with the sauce. Sprinkle with the parsley. Serve hot or at room temperature.

Serves 6.

Pasta with Eggplant

PASTA CON LE MELANZANE

2 large eggplants, peeled and
   cut into 1 1/2-inch cubes
   (about 3 pounds)
Salt
Olive oil, for deep frying
3 dried red chili peppers
1 garlic clove, peeled and
   lightly crushed

(Ingredients continued)

As the Italian gourmand Alberto Consiglio once said of this Arab-inspired dish, "Pasta con Melanzane is so heavenly that it would make even a Christian say, 'La ila'ha il Allah, abu Mohammad rasoui Allah!' (There is no God but God, and Mohammed is his messenger!) under his breath."

Pepper
¾ pound vermicelli
*1 tablespoon extra-virgin
   olive oil*
1 teaspoon chopped parsley

1. Spread the eggplant pieces on paper towels and sprinkle with salt. Leave them to drain for 1 hour or longer, then pat dry with paper towels.
2. Preheat the oil for deep frying to 370°F.
3. Put the chili peppers and garlic in the oil. When the garlic turns light brown, remove it and discard. Leave the red peppers in the oil. Deep-fry the eggplant in batches until brown. Drain the eggplant on paper towels and salt and lightly pepper them.
4. Meanwhile, bring a large pot of salted water to a boil. Once the pot of water is at a rolling boil, drop in the vermicelli and cook it until al dente. Drain and transfer to a bowl. Toss carefully with the extra-virgin olive oil and parsley. Add the eggplant pieces and toss again. Serve very hot.
   Serves 4.

Penne Rigate with Tuna Roe and Herring Roe

MACCARRUNEDDA A SARAUSANA
CULL'OVA RI TUNNU E L'OVA D'ARINGA

1 pound kippered herring
*2 tablespoons herring or
   salmon roe*
*¼ cup bottarga, rinsed and
   sliced thin (page 185)*
*2 tablespoons extra-virgin
   olive oil*
*1 garlic clove, peeled and
   lightly crushed*
Pinch of cayenne
Salt
1 pound penne rigate
*3 tablespoons finely chopped
   parsley*

Pasqualino Giudice, a magnificent chef and engaging raconteur, generously shared his reinterpretation of an old Sicilian dish with me. Kippered herring was probably introduced to Sicily by the Greeks or Normans; *bottarga* is an Arab invention.

1. Remove the head, tail, skin, and bones from the herring, and the roe if there is any, and set aside. Dice the herring into small pieces. Add the herring roe (or salmon roe if there was no herring roe) to the *bottarga*. Heat the oil in a sauté pan and sauté the garlic with the herring head, skin, and bones, adding the cayenne. Sauté for 10 minutes. Bring a large pot of salted water to a boil for the pasta.

2. Strain the juices from the sauté pan into a large pan, discarding the herring bones. Add the herring pieces. Cook for 3 minutes. When the water for the pasta reaches a rolling boil, cook the pasta until al dente.

3. Combine the herring and *bottarga* and mix gently. As soon as the pasta is cooked, drain and add to the pan. Return to the heat and add the parsley. Toss in the pan. Transfer to a hot dish, cover, and let stand for 5 minutes. Serve.

Serves 4 to 6.

Pasta with Dried Tuna Roe Sauce

PASTA CON SALSA DI BOTTARGA

1 cup sliced bottarga, *rinsed and finely chopped (page 185)*
¼ cup extra-virgin olive oil
2 garlic cloves, peeled and chopped
2 tablespoons finely chopped parsley
2 dried red chili peppers, crumbled
Salt
¾ pound macaroni
1 teaspoon black peppercorns, crushed

Before making this pasta dish, you will need to make the *bottarga* (dried tuna roe). This recipe shows off its powerful and wonderful flavor.

1. Mix together the first 5 ingredients in the top of a double boiler, heating for 7 minutes over medium-low heat.

2. Bring a large pot of salted water to a boil and cook the macaroni until al dente. Drain and toss with the sauce and pepper.

Serves 4.

Tagliatelle with Dried Tuna Roe

LINGUE DI PASSERO ALLA BOTTARGA

1 pound tagliatelle
Salt
½ cup olive oil
1 tablespoon green
  peppercorns
2 tablespoons finely chopped
  parsley
3 tablespoons bottarga,
  rinsed and chopped (page
  185)

This recipe was given to me by Michele Papa, president of the Associazione Siculo-Araba in Catania. Papa, a knowledgeable and enthusiastic student of the Arabs in Sicily, is a lawyer who defends the rights of Sicily's newest Arabs, immigrants from Libya and Tunisia.

Use fresh Italian bread to soak up the very flavorful sauce. *Lingue di Passero* (literally, sparrow's tongues) is a large linguine. You can use linguine, fettuccine, or tagliatelle in this recipe.

Cook the pasta in salted water until al dente. Drain. Heat the olive oil in a clay pan or heavy enameled iron skillet. Add the pasta and toss with the green peppercorns and parsley. Add the *bottarga*, toss again, and serve hot.

Serves 4 to 6.

Pasta with Chick-peas

CICIRI CON PASTA

Salt
1 cup canned chick-peas,
  drained and rinsed
1 onion, cut into eighths and
  separated
¾ pound spaghetti
¼ cup olive oil
1 tablespoon freshly ground
  black pepper

I love simple peasant dishes with big flavors such as this pasta with chick-peas. Chick-peas were part of Sicilian cuisine long before the Greeks and Arabs arrived, but most probably it was the Arabs who first combined them with pasta.

If you want to spice up this pasta dish, add some parsley, red pepper flakes, or grated caciocavallo.

1. Bring a large pot of abundantly salted water to a rolling boil. Add the chick-peas and onion. When the chick-peas are still hard but reaching an al dente stage, in about 15 minutes, add the spaghetti and cook until al dente.

2. Drain the spaghetti and chick peas. Mix with the oil and pepper and serve.

Serves 4.

Taglierini with Squash Blossoms

TAGLIERINI COI FIORI DI ZUCCA

½ pound squash blossoms (about 10 to 12)
Pinch of saffron
⅓ cup chicken broth
Salt
1 small onion, peeled and finely chopped
3 tablespoons olive oil
Pepper
2 egg yolks
4 tablespoons grated pecorino
½ pound fresh taglierini or fettuccine

If you grow your own zucchini and find their yellow flowers stunning, remember, you can eat them too. This recipe, a specialty of Enna, is as beautiful as it is flavorful.

1. Pick the flowers, including any tiny zucchini that have formed. Put the saffron into the chicken broth to steep. Boil the flowers for 1 to 2 minutes in lightly salted water. Drain and chop fine.

2. Sauté the onion in the olive oil along with the flowers over medium heat for 10 minutes, stirring often. Add salt and pepper to taste and the chicken broth and saffron. Cook on low heat until the sauce becomes creamy, about 10 to 12 minutes, stirring occasionally. Remove from the heat and let stand until tepid. Bind the sauce by gently stirring in the egg yolks and pecorino.

3. Cook the taglierini in a large pot of abundantly salted water until al dente. Drain and toss with the sauce until well seasoned.

Serves 2.

Baked Pasta with Eggs and Cheese

TAGANU D'ARAGONA

Pinch of saffron
1⅓ cups chicken broth
Salt
2½ pounds rigatoni
3 tablespoons olive oil
Vegetable oil
8 slices stale Italian
  rustic-style bread
2¼ pounds fresh mozzarella
  or tuma, sliced
16 eggs
1 cup finely chopped parsley
⅔ cup freshly grated pecorino
¼ teaspoon ground cinnamon
Pepper

Cinnamon and saffron give this dish the exotic flavor so typical of *cucina arabo-sicula*. The name of this dish refers to the kind of pan used by the Aragonese chefs. This magnificent preparation is an Eastern dish inherited from the influence of the Spanish viceroy in Sicily at the beginning of the seventeenth century. I believe that *Taganu d'Aragona* is the Sicilian version of the North African stews called *tagines*. Further proof of its Arab origins is that the word *taganu* derives from the Arabic *tajin*, which refers to a shallow earthenware pan. If you don't have an earthenware or terracotta baking dish, use a cast-iron enameled baking pan.

1. Dissolve the saffron in ⅓ cup of warm chicken broth. Fill a very large stockpot (one that can hold 3 to 4 gallons of water) with water and bring it to a rolling boil. Add salt. Add the rigatoni and partially cook it. Drain the rigatoni and top it with olive oil so it doesn't stick together. Arrange a third of the rigatoni on the bottom of a well-oiled casserole large enough to hold all the ingredients.

2. Lay 4 slices of the bread on top of the rigatoni. Layer a third of the mozzarella on top of the bread. Spread half of the remaining rigatoni on top of the mozzarella.

3. Preheat the oven to 350°F.

4. Layer half of the remaining mozzarella on top of the rigatoni. Beat the eggs with the parsley, pecorino, cinnamon, and saffron with chicken broth, and add pepper and salt to taste. Pour evenly over the contents of the casserole.

5. Spread the remaining rigatoni on top and cover with the remaining mozzarella. Place the remaining 4 slices of bread on top. Add the remaining chicken broth, drizzling it over all. Place in the oven, uncovered, and bake for 35 to 45 minutes, or until the eggs and liquid have been absorbed but the dish does not look dried-out. Remove from the oven and let stand for 10 minutes.

6. Run a knife around the sides of the pasta. Place a large platter over the top of the casserole, invert it, and unmold the pasta so that it can be sliced on the platter.

Serves 12 to 15.

VARIATION

The *Taganu* can be made with meatballs as well. For the meatballs, knead together ¾ pound ground beef, 1 beaten egg, 2 tablespoons finely chopped onion, ½ cup dry breadcrumbs, and 2 tablespoons chopped parsley. Form into small marble-size balls and sauté in 1 tablespoon of olive oil until brown. Pour in 2 cups of Smooth Tomato Sauce (page 82) and continue cooking for 20 minutes over medium heat. Add to the *Taganu* at the end of Step 2.

RICE

The Arabs introduced rice to Egypt in the seventh century and to Sicily shortly after their conquest, growing it in irrigated paddies. There is evidence that it was exported from Sicily in 867. It was grown in the area of Sambuca di Sicilia, Ribera, and Sciacca. A number of famous rice dishes are believed to have originated in Sicily, especially those where rice is married to saffron—*Risotto alla Milanese* and Spanish dishes such as paella. Riziculture died out in Sicily for unknown reasons and is commonly thought to have moved north to Lombardy with the Spanish Aragons.

Petrus de Crescentiis, a thirteenth-century commentator, describes rice only medicinally and not as a food crop. In medieval Arab cooking, and we can presume in Arab Sicily, rice was prepared in countless ways, alone or with other ingredients. A number of soups were made with rice and are found in forms today that derive from the original Arab soups such as Badduzzi di Risu 'nto Brodu (page 85). Dessert recipes that use rice are purely Arab in origin, especially when they are cooked with milk and sugar or honey (pages 231 and 232).

Rice with Seafood

RISO ALLA MARINARA

Pinch of saffron
20 mussels, scrubbed and
  debearded

When I hear that romantic word *marinara*, I dream of this extraordinary dish that is so common in coastal Sicily.

20 *littleneck clams, scrubbed*
1 *small (1 pound) live lobster
or ¼ pound lobster meat*
4 *tablespoons finely chopped
parsley*
4 *garlic cloves, peeled and
finely chopped*
½ *cup olive oil*
¼ *pound squid, cleaned and
cut into small pieces or
rings*
2 *cups Arborio rice, washed*
Salt
Pepper

Rice tossed with seafood is delicious alone, but seasoned with saffron and garlic it reaches new heights.

1. Put the saffron in a small cup with 3 tablespoons of tepid water to steep. Steam the mussels and clams until they open. Discard any mussels or clams that do not open. Remove the clams and mussels from their shells. Reserve ¾ cup of the clam and mussel juice for this recipe and save the rest for another use. Set aside. Steam the live lobster for 12 to 15 minutes. Drain. When it is cool, remove the meat, chop, and set aside.

2. In a large pan, sauté the parsley and garlic in ⅓ cup olive oil for 2 minutes over medium heat. Add the squid and reduce the heat to low. Continue cooking, uncovered, for 12 minutes.

3. In a heavy pot with a tight-fitting lid, sauté the washed rice in the remaining olive oil for 1 minute. Add the reserved clam and mussel juice and 1⅓ cups water. Check the clam and mussel juice to see how salty it is, then add salt to taste. Stir and bring to a boil. Reduce to a low simmer and cook until al dente, about 12 minutes, but check before that time. Add a few tablespoons of boiling water if the rice is too hard.

4. Add the lobster meat, clams, and mussels to the pan with the squid. Stir and add pepper to taste. Pour the saffron water over the seafood. Stir again and cook over low heat for 10 minutes.

5. Pour the rice into a mixing bowl and mix with half the seafood. Spread the mixture on a serving platter and cover with the remaining seafood. Serve hot or at room temperature.

Serves 4.

Rice with Angels

RISO CON GLI ANGELI

½ cup olive oil
2 garlic cloves, peeled and
  chopped
3 tablespoons chopped parsley
6 ounces squid, cleaned and
  cut into ¼-inch rings
6 ounces medium shrimp,
  peeled and cut in half
1 pound mussels, scrubbed
  and debearded
Salt and pepper
1½ cups Arborio rice, washed
1 teaspoon salt
1 tablespoon butter
3 tablespoons freshly grated
  parmesan

What are the "angels" of this dish? Could it be that the spreading mussel shells are the angel wings and the squid rings the halos? Heavenly in any case.

1. Heat the oil in a frying pan or casserole and sauté the garlic and parsley for 2 minutes. Add the squid, shrimp, and mussels. Add salt and pepper to taste. Simmer, covered, until the mussels open, in about 6 to 8 minutes. Discard any mussels that don't open.

2. Combine the rice, 1 cup water, the teaspoon of salt, and the butter in a large saucepan and bring to a boil. Reduce to very low heat and cover. Check the rice after 10 minutes and add ½ cup boiling water if you have to. The rice should be cooked in 20 to 25 minutes. Spoon the rice onto a serving platter and pour the seafood over it. Mix well and sprinkle with parmesan. Let the rice stand, loosely covered with aluminum foil, for 5 minutes.

Serves 4.

Festive Baked Rice

TUMMÀLA

1 chicken, about 3 pounds
2 medium onions, cut into
  eighths
2 celery stalks, cut into
  chunks
4 tomatoes, peeled, seeded,
  and quartered
5 parsley sprigs
10 black peppercorns
1½ cups breadcrumbs
3 tablespoons milk
¾ pound chopped veal
¾ pound pecorino pepato,
  grated (page 41)
1 garlic clove, finely chopped
4 tablespoons finely chopped
  parsley
Salt
¼ teaspoon pepper
5 eggs
1 medium onion, finely
  chopped
2 tablespoons lard
½ pound Italian sweet
  sausage, sliced ½ inch thick
¼ pound pork rind, cut into
  thin strips
2 tablespoons tomato paste
2½ cups Vialone or Arborio
  rice, washed
Butter
2 hard-boiled eggs, sliced
½ pound tuma or
  mozzarella, sliced
¼ pound caciocavallo, thinly
  sliced
¼ pound pecorino, grated
2 cups Smooth Tomato Sauce
  (page 82) (optional)

Tummàla is a magnificent feast dish, which should be shared with many friends. A Christmas specialty in Sicily, it is also prepared for all sorts of festive occasions when a grand culinary gesture is warranted.

The Italian translation of the Sicilian tummàla is timballo, leading one to believe that this dish is derived from the French timbale. In fact, the name comes either from Mohammed ibn ath-Thumna, the eleventh-century Emir of Catania, or from tummala, the Arabic name for a certain kind of plate.

Don't let the list of ingredients intimidate you. Great length, in this case, does not mean great difficulty.

1. Place the chicken with the gizzard and the heart but not the liver in a large stockpot. Add the onions, celery, tomatoes, parsley sprigs, and peppercorns. Cover with cold water and bring to a boil. Reduce to a simmer and cook the chicken for 2 hours, or until the meat falls off the bone when pushed with a fork.

2. While the chicken is cooking, prepare the veal croquettes. Soak ½ cup of the breadcrumbs in the milk. If mixture looks soggy, squeeze the milk out. Add the veal, half of the *pecorino pepato*, the garlic, 2 tablespoons of the chopped parsley, ½ teaspoon salt and the pepper. Lightly beat 1 egg and add it to the mixture. Mix well with a fork or your hands. Form croquettes the size and shape of your thumb. Cover and put aside in the refrigerator.

3. Drain the chicken, saving all the broth in a smaller pot. Remove all the skin and bones from the chicken and cut up the meat into small pieces.

4. In a large frying pan, sauté the chopped onion in 1 tablespoon of the lard over medium heat until golden, about 8 minutes. Remove from the pan and set aside. Add the remaining lard to the pan and sauté the veal croquettes until they are browned. Add the sausage and pork rind and sauté for 10 minutes. Add the sautéed onion, the remaining parsley, and the tomato paste diluted in 1 cup hot water. Cook over low heat for 10 minutes. Set aside.

5. Bring the chicken broth to a boil and reduce it by one-third. Pour 2½ cups into a heavy saucepan and add the rice and about 1½ teaspoons salt. Cook, covered, until al dente, about 15 minutes. Pour about ¾ cup broth into the veal-sausage mixture.

6. Drain the rice, if necessary, and mix it with the remaining *pecorino pepato*.

7. Preheat the oven to 350°F. Butter a deep baking dish and spread the remaining breadcrumbs over the bottom.

8. Spread the rice on top of the breadcrumbs, about ¾ inch high. Spread three-quarters of the chicken and half of the veal croquettes and sausage mixture on top of the rice. Make a layer of hard-boiled egg. Layer the *tuma* on top of the eggs. Cover with the remaining veal and sauce. Spread on a layer of caciocavallo. Mix the remaining chicken with the remaining rice and spread it on top.

9. Beat the remaining 4 eggs lightly and combine with the pecorino. Add salt and pepper to taste. Pour the sauce evenly over the top.

10. Bake until the top has a nice golden crust, about 1 hour. Check from time to time to be sure it doesn't dry out. The *tummàla* can be served directly from the baking dish with pan sauces or with tomato sauce.

Serves 8 to 10.

Baked Rice

RISO AL FORNO

1 pound veal shoulder, cut
    into ½-inch dice
⅔ cup olive oil
2 cloves garlic, peeled and
    crushed
¾ cup (6-ounce can) tomato
    paste
Salt and pepper
1 teaspoon sugar
3 tablespoons pine nuts
3 tablespoons golden raisins
3 cups Arborio rice, washed
5 tablespoons lard or butter
2 teaspoons salt
3 hard-boiled eggs, minced
⅔ cup breadcrumbs
⅓ cup grated pecorino
¼ pound prosciutto, sliced ¹⁄₁₆
    inch thick and diced
¾ pound tuma or
    mozzarella, diced

This opulent rice dish laced with finely minced veal, pine nuts, golden raisins, and sugar is perfect for a large gathering. This dish probably began as a simple peasant dish in the Arab era and later evolved into this richly baroque preparation.

1. Brown the veal in the oil with the garlic over medium-high heat. Remove the garlic cloves after about 10 minutes. Dissolve the tomato paste in ⅔ cup warm water and add it to the meat. Add salt and pepper to taste and simmer over low heat for 30 minutes.

2. When the meat is done, mince it in a food processor, making sure all pieces are cut very small but not mushed. Mix the veal with 1 cup of the sauce in which it was cooking, the sugar, pine nuts, raisins, and salt and pepper to taste. Let sauce stand for 20 minutes.

3. Place rice in a heavy pot with 3 cups water, 2 tablespoons of the lard, and the salt. Bring to a boil, then reduce to a simmer, cover, and cook until done, about 15 to 20 minutes. Add a small amount of boiling water if it is not done and continue cooking. Mix with the remaining sauce, eggs, ⅓ cup of the breadcrumbs, and the pecorino. Mix gently and spread on a platter to cool.

4. Preheat the oven to 425°F.

5. Grease a baking casserole with 2 tablespoons of the lard and coat it with 3 tablespoons of the breadcrumbs. Place half the rice in the casserole and cover evenly with the meat mixture, the prosciutto, and the *tuma*. Cover with the remaining rice. Sprinkle with the remaining breadcrumbs and remaining lard. Bake for 20 minutes, or until golden.

Serves 8 to 10.

Sicilian Paella

RISO IN PADELLA

2 pounds mussels, washed and
  debearded
1 pound squid, cleaned and
  cut into rings
¾ pound medium shrimp,
  saving shells and head, if
  available
8 peppercorns
1 celery stalk, cut into pieces
1 small onion, quartered
Bouquet garni, tied together
  in cheesecloth (4 parsley
  sprigs, 2 fresh thyme
  sprigs, 2 fresh sage sprigs,
  1 bay leaf)
1 green pepper, seeded and
  sliced into thin strips
1½ cups peas, fresh or frozen
2 cups tomato purée
¾ cup finely chopped parsley
½ cup white wine
2 pinches of saffron
6 tablespoons olive oil
1 small chicken (fryer), cut
  into eighths, fat and skin
  removed
¾ pound hot Italian sausage,
  sliced
1 dried red chili pepper,
  crumbled

(Ingredients continued)

There is no doubt that a rice dish with saffron is an Arab-influenced dish. In this case we don't know which came first, Spain or Sicily—*padella* and *paella* both mean frying pan.

1 medium onion, chopped
3 garlic cloves, peeled and
  crushed
Pepper
2½ cups Arborio rice, washed

1. Keep the mussels, squid, and shrimp in the refrigerator while you work. Place the shrimp shells and heads, if any, in a 2-quart saucepan, along with the peppercorns, celery, onion, and bouquet garni; add 1 quart of cold water. Bring to a boil, then lower to a simmer, partially covered, for 1 to 2 hours. Strain the shrimp broth, reserving 1 cup. Save the rest for another use.

2. Combine the green pepper with the peas, if using fresh; do not combine if using frozen. Pour the tomato purée in with the peas and peppers. Set aside.

3. Set aside 4 tablespoons of the parsley and place the mussels in a large pan or a paella pan, if you have one. Sprinkle the wine and remaining parsley over the mussels. Cook the mussels, covered, over high heat until they begin to open, about 5 minutes. Discard any that do not open. Drain the mussels, reserving the broth. Add the saffron to the broth and set aside to steep.

4. Heat 3 tablespoons of the olive oil in the paella pan over medium heat. Add the chicken and brown for 5 minutes. Add the sausage and chili pepper. Sauté, stirring occasionally, until uniformly browned, about 10 minutes. Remove with a slotted spoon and set aside. Remove the excess oil and fat from the pan.

5. Put the shrimp and squid in the paella pan, without mixing the two, on medium heat, stirring frequently, for about 5 minutes. Remove from the pan and set aside separately.

6. Heat the remaining olive oil in the paella pan over medium heat. Add the chopped onion, the garlic, and 4 tablespoons of the parsley and fry, being careful not to burn, for 3 to 4 minutes. Add the tomato purée, green pepper, and fresh peas (not the frozen). Cook, uncovered, for 10 minutes, stirring occasionally.

7. Put the chicken and sausage pieces into the paella pan and cook for 2 minutes. Add the squid and cook for 1 minute. Add the mussels. Add half the mussel broth with saffron and salt and pepper to taste. Bring the broth to a boil over high heat.

8. When it reaches a boil, add the rice, remaining mussel broth, and strained shrimp broth and reduce the heat to low. Stir a little with a wooden spoon to distribute the ingredients evenly and submerge the rice. Cover tightly and simmer for 20 minutes.

9. After 15 minutes, add frozen peas (if using) and reserved shrimp. After another 5 minutes, check the rice, pushing it around so that it is completely submerged. Add more broth if needed.

The rice tends to get stuck in the mussel shells, so make sure you push the shells down. Cook the rice another 10 minutes, if necessary. Bring the paella pan to the table and serve directly.

Serves 8 to 10.

Baked Rice with Eggplant

RISO CON LA MELANZANE ALLA PALERMITANA

3 medium eggplants (about 3 pounds), sliced into ½-inch rounds
Salt
Pinch of saffron
Olive oil, for deep frying
1 large onion, chopped
3 tablespoons olive oil
¼ cup finely chopped parsley
¼ cup finely chopped basil
1½ cups peeled, seeded, and chopped tomatoes
Pepper
2 cups Arborio rice, washed
2 tablespoons olive oil
½ cup freshly grated pecorino pepato (page 41)

This substantial dish is rich with the typical ingredients of *cucina arabo-sicula*: eggplant, saffron, and rice. *Pecorino pepato* is an earthy Sicilian cheese with cracked peppercorns thrown into the curd.

1. Spread the eggplant slices out on paper towels and sprinkle with salt. Let stand for 1 hour or longer, then pat dry with paper towels. Put the saffron in 2 cups salted water to steep while you work.

2. Preheat the oil for the deep frying to 370°F.

3. Deep-fry the eggplant in batches until golden. Drain and set aside on paper towels.

4. Sauté the onion in the 3 tablespoons of olive oil, stirring in half the parsley and half the basil. Cook over low to medium heat for 8 to 10 minutes. Add the tomatoes and salt and pepper to taste. Continue cooking for 10 minutes, stirring occasionally.

5. Bring the water with the saffron to a boil. Pour in the rice in a slow stream and cook until al dente, about 8 to 10 minutes.

6. Preheat the oven to 450°F.

7. Oil a baking dish with the remaining olive oil. Spread a third of the rice on the bottom. Cover the rice with tomato sauce, then a layer of eggplant. Continue in this manner until all the ingredients are used up, ending with eggplant. Sprinkle the *pecorino pepato* on top.

8. Put the casserole in the oven, uncovered, and bake for 15 minutes. Sprinkle the remaining parsley and basil over the top and continue baking for 5 to 10 minutes. Serve immediately.

Serves 6 to 8.

COUSCOUS

Couscous was one of the most important inventions, along with pasta, emanating from the Arab discovery and dispersal of hard wheat, *Triticum durum*. No one knows for sure when couscous was invented or when it arrived in Sicily, but an educated guess would place it around the mid-twelfth century. In Sicily one of the first written appearances of couscous is in municipal tariff records from Palermo showing its regulation in the sixteenth century. The kneading trough and fixed roller used to pulverize the hard-wheat semolina can be placed in the fourteenth century. The writer–pastry chef Nick Maglieri notes that the Santo Spirito Monastery in Agrigento makes a dessert couscous specialty that they attribute to an Arab servant about the time of the founding of the monastery in the late thirteenth century.

The starting point for all couscous recipes is the same. In Sicily the semolina grains are slowly poured into a large, round terra-cotta dish with sloping sides called a *mafaradda* (from the Arabic *mat'arad*, meaning a large drinking bowl, or from *marfada*, a big clay dish) and formed into small pellets by hand. The process of raking, rolling, aerating, and forming the pellets is called *incocciata* by the Sicilians.

Cuscusù is the apex of Arab-Sicilian cuisine; its successful preparation is considered the height of culinary art. In Sicily, the home of *cuscusù* is on the western shores. Trapani, Marsala, Mazara, Erice, and even the tiny village of San Vito lo Capo, where it is called *tha'am* (a purely Algerian-Arabic expression), all claim to have the best.

Preparing *cuscusù* is a long, involved process, so I suggest you read carefully through the recipe, imagining everything before you start. The whole process should take about four and a half hours from start to finish.

You will need some specialized equipment, including a *mafaradda*, or some other large terra-cotta platter with angular shallow sides, for raking and forming the pellets. Another essential piece of equipment is a *cous-*

coussière, for steaming the couscous over the fish broth. A large pot with a colander sitting on top is a satisfactory alternative. You will also need a large-holed flat sieve and cheesecloth or a white kitchen towel, and for those who want to be authentic, a woolen blanket. Be sure to use raw couscous. It can usually be found in health-food stores. Do not use the packaged or precooked variety.

The fish used in the broth, called *la ghiotta* in Sicily, is critical, so try to have a good mix of as many fish as possible. There should be a three-to-one ratio of white fish to oily fish. (See pages 154–160 for more information on types of fish.) When asked what fish to use for the broth, Sicilians typically would answer *"pesci del giorno"* (catch of the day), and I would advise you to do the same.

Choose at least four of the following white fish: scabbard fish, cod, hake, scorpion fish, bogue, amberjack, bream, monkfish, porgies, red-fish, red snapper, blue-mouth, gray mullet, red mullet. Choose at least two of the following oily fish: moray eel, conger eel, shark, mackerel, bluefish, sardines. Try very hard to get an eel.

The fish for the broth will not be eaten. If you want to serve some fish on top of the couscous, set aside a few small fish and shrimp, grill them, and serve with the finished couscous. In fancy versions mussels, shrimp, or lobster is used. This is often done in restaurants, but it is not necessary, in my opinion.

Traditionally *cuscusù* is served as a first course.

Sicilian Fish Couscous

Cuscusù

2 pinches of saffron
1 tablespoon sea salt
1 cup white wine
3 pounds mixed white fish,
   cleaned and gutted, with
   heads and tails
2 pounds oily fish, cleaned
   and gutted, with heads and
   tails
2 pounds raw couscous
1½ cups olive oil
Pinch of cinnamon
3 medium onions
½ celery stalk
(Ingredients continued)

3 garlic cloves
2 pounds plum tomatoes,
  peeled, seeded, and chopped
1½ tablespoons chopped
  parsley
1 bay leaf
13 large basil leaves
Red pepper flakes
Salt and pepper
Pinch of nutmeg
1 clove
2½ cups boiling water
Extra-virgin olive oil, for
  sprinkling on couscous
1 cup flour

1. Dissolve 1 pinch of the saffron in 2 cups of water with the sea salt. Dissolve the other pinch of saffron in the white wine. Clean the fish under cold running water. Chop the larger fish into chunks and keep the smaller fish whole. Set aside in the refrigerator.

2. Put half the couscous in a large earthenware dish with shallow sides and sprinkle with some of the salted saffron water. Work the grains with your fingers to separate them and moisten them evenly. Work in a circular rotating motion, constantly raking and forming small "marbles" of soft dough. Rake them with one hand and rub with the other, to form pellets the size of a half grain of rice. If the mixture becomes too wet, add a little dry couscous and start again. Continue in this manner, adding more couscous and more water, until all the grains are moistened. The couscous should be evenly wet, not soggy, and uniform in size. If necessary, shake the couscous through a large-holed sieve, breaking apart any large pellets with your hand. You may want to sieve 2 or 3 times to make sure that each pellet is separate.

3. Arrange the couscous on white kitchen towels and leave to dry for 1 to 2 hours, depending on the humidity in the air. Using ½ cup olive oil in all, brush each one of the little pellets with oil, using your fingers, and sprinkle cinnamon over all.

4. Chop one of the onions, the celery, and 2 garlic cloves very fine. In a large stockpot that will hold all the fish, fry the onion, celery, and garlic in 1 cup of the olive oil until golden.

5. Add the white wine with saffron, the tomatoes, parsley, bay leaf, 1 basil leaf, and 2 generous pinches of red pepper flakes. Season with salt and pepper to taste. Add a pinch of nutmeg and

the clove. Simmer, uncovered, for 3 minutes. If you like spicy food, add 2 more pinches of red pepper.

6. Add 1½ cups hot water. Simmer, covered, for 25 minutes. Add the fish and simmer, covered, for another 25 minutes. Add the boiling water. Bring to a boil again. The broth should have the consistency of a light cream soup. If it looks too thick, add some water. If it looks too thin, boil for 5 to 10 minutes.

7. Remove from the heat and put half the broth into the bottom part of the *couscoussière* along with 1 cup of hot water. Make sure that there is not too much broth in the bottom. It should never touch the couscous.

8. Chop the remaining onion and garlic very fine.

9. Bring the broth to a boil, and as you see steam rising, cover the holes of the top part of the *couscoussière* with the remaining 12 basil leaves.

10. Place the cloth with the couscous pellets on top of the basil leaves. Sprinkle the couscous with olive oil if needed, and mix in the small chopped onion and garlic and a little salt and pepper. Mix very gently. Fold the edges of the cloth or dish towel in and cover the pot.

11. Seal the 2 parts of the *couscoussière* together with a long rope of flour and water, so that no steam escapes. Cook over low heat for 1 hour. Keep the remaining broth warm.

12. Spoon out the couscous onto a large platter and rub the grains with salted water to separate any pellets that may have stuck together. Let the couscous cool for 10 minutes, then put it back into the *couscoussière* for 30 minutes.

13. Strain the remaining broth, throwing away all the fish, and reheat. Transfer the couscous into a large deep pan with a cover and pour in half of the broth. Cover tightly, then wrap in a wool blanket and let rest for 30 minutes in a warm place. This step is probably no longer necessary in our modern centrally heated homes, but go ahead anyway . . . it can't hurt. The grains will absorb the broth and swell up. Serve in individual bowls with extra broth passed around.

Serves 6 as a main course or 12 as a first course.

SEVEN
Meat, Poultry, and Game

CARNI, POLLAME, E SELVAGGINA

Sicily remains separate by virtue of her Islamic heritage even while this heritage penetrates the very pores of her culture.

—HENRI BRESC

MEAT

Until recently, meat was rare and very expensive in Sicily. In medieval times it was almost nonexistent. For this reason one finds many preparations using aromatic stuffings of dry breadcrumbs and other ingredients—fruit, spices, eggs, and vegetables. An elaborate meat dish could then be made to feed the typically large Sicilian family on a special occasion or holiday. Because Sicily was plentifully supplied with bread, dry breadcrumbs were natural for stuffing in meat.

Today meat is more commonly found. Although I found the quality quite poor in Sicily, there is no reason that we cannot avail ourselves of our excellent meats and use flank steak or top round, for instance, in the various *spitini* preparations that follow.

Grilled Beef Rolls with Prosciutto and Mozzarella

INVOLTINI ALLA PAESANA

*12 beef slices, cut from the
top round or flank, 3 x 5
inches, 1/8 to 1/4 inch thick
(about 1¾ pounds)*
*18 large bay leaves,
preferably fresh*
2 tablespoons golden raisins
1 small onion, finely chopped
1 cup breadcrumbs
*½ cup finely diced fresh
mozzarella*
2 tablespoons pine nuts
*1 slice prosciutto, 1/16 inch
thick, finely chopped*
Salt
1 egg, beaten
Breadcrumbs, for coating
Olive oil

Throughout Sicily you find all kinds of stuffed meat and fish rolls that are often grilled. Many are double-skewered in a manner reminiscent of Arab kebabs. Spit grilling probably goes back to Greek Sicily, or perhaps even Neolithic Sicily, but the practice of mixing pieces of meat with vegetables on a skewer is very common in the Arab Mediterranean and all of the Middle East.

Use wooden or bamboo skewers six to eight inches long for these and other brochettes. Soak the skewers in water first or wrap the ends in foil to prevent burning.

1. Prepare a very hot charcoal fire or preheat a gas grill.

2. Place the beef slices between 2 pieces of wax paper and flatten with a mallet or the side of a cleaver until they are about 1/16 inch thick.

3. If using dry bay leaves, soak them in water. Soak the raisins in water.

4. Mix together the onion, breadcrumbs, mozzarella, pine nuts, and prosciutto. Drain the raisins and stir in. Place a heaping tablespoon of stuffing on each beef slice. Freeze leftover stuffing. Carefully roll up the slices and secure with toothpicks. Dip the beef rolls into the salted beaten egg and then the breadcrumbs, making sure all surfaces are breaded.

5. Using 2 skewers, side by side, skewer a bay leaf then a beef roll, another bay leaf, another beef roll, and a bay leaf.

6. Drizzle olive oil over the rolls and place on the grill for 7 minutes. Brush more olive oil over the rolls and turn for another 7 minutes.

Serves 4 to 6.

Grilled Beef Rolls with Pecorino, Currants, and Pine Nuts

Involtini alla Siciliana

12 beef slices, cut from the
   top round or flank, 3 x 5
   inches, ⅛ to ¼ inch thick
   (about 1¾ pounds)
1 tablespoon currants
12 large bay leaves,
   preferably fresh
6 tablespoons breadcrumbs
2 tablespoons olive oil
2 tablespoons grated pecorino
1 tablespoon pine nuts
6 tablespoons finely chopped
   onion
Salt and pepper
Olive oil, for basting
1 large onion, peeled,
   quartered, and separated

These *involtini* are very common in Bagheria, near Palermo. Called *Braciolettine Arrostite* in Sicily, they are referred to as *Involtini alla Siciliana* in the rest of Italy.

1. Prepare a very hot charcoal fire or preheat a gas grill.

2. Place the beef slices between 2 pieces of wax paper and flatten with a mallet or the side of a cleaver until they are about ¹⁄₁₆ inch thick.

3. Soak the currants in water to cover for at least 15 minutes. Soak dried bay leaves in water.

4. Sauté the breadcrumbs in the olive oil for about 5 minutes. Remove from the heat. Drain the currants and add to the breadcrumbs with the pecorino, pine nuts, and chopped onion, and salt and pepper to taste. Mix thoroughly and set aside.

5. Brush each slice of beef with oil and layer with the stuffing, rolling up tight. Freeze leftover stuffing. Using 2 skewers side by side, slide on a bay leaf, an onion slice, and a beef roll. Grill close to the fire, basting with olive oil, for about 5 to 7 minutes a side.

Serves 4 to 6.

Beef Rolls in Marsala

SASIZZEDDI AGGRASSATI

8 beef slices, cut from the top
  round or flank, 3 x 5
  inches, ⅛ to ¼ inch thick
  (about 1¼ pounds)
½ cup breadcrumbs
½ cup grated pecorino
1 tablespoon finely chopped
  parsley
2 tablespoons golden raisins,
  soaked and drained
2 tablespoons pine nuts
¼ teaspoon salt
½ teaspoon pepper
Olive oil
1 large onion, thinly sliced
½ cup Marsala

Involtini are sometimes fried or braised, as in this French-inspired recipe with its Arab ingredients. The wine used in this dish is Stravecchio, a very special wine from Vittoria. It is unobtainable in this country, as only five hundred bottles are produced every year. You can use Marsala instead. Look for the designation S.O.M. (Superior Old Marsala).

Sometimes a large stuffed beef roll is prepared using a whole butterflied flank steak, which is stuffed with hard-boiled eggs and cheese and braised in red wine. This is called a *farsumagru* in Sicilian.

1. Place the beef slices between 2 pieces of wax paper and flatten with a mallet or the side of a cleaver until they are 1/16 inch thick.

2. Mix together the breadcrumbs, cheese, parsley, raisins, pine nuts, salt and pepper. Divide the stuffing among the beef slices and roll them up like little sausages. Secure with toothpicks, if necessary.

3. Heat the olive oil in a large frying pan and add the onion. Cook over medium-low heat until translucent, about 6 minutes. Add the beef rolls and brown them over low heat for 12 minutes, turning once. Add the Marsala and continue cooking, covered, for 20 minutes. Serve immediately, spooning the sauce over the meat rolls.

Serves 4.

Grilled Veal Rolls with Pine Nuts and Raisins

INVOLTINI DI VITELLO

12 pieces of veal scaloppine,
  3 x 5 inches, ⅛ to ¼ inch
  thick (about 2 pounds)
18 large bay leaves
1 small onion, finely chopped
5 tablespoons olive oil
2 cups breadcrumbs
½ cup grated caciocavallo or
  pecorino
½ cup golden raisins, soaked
  and drained
⅓ cup pine nuts
8 very thin slices soppressata,
  cut into small bits
1 plum tomato, peeled,
  seeded, and finely chopped
Salt and pepper
2 eggs, beaten
1 medium onion, peeled,
  quartered, and separated
Olive oil, for basting

These veal rolls are particularly savory grilled over bay twigs, thyme twigs, or applewood chips.

1. Prepare a very hot charcoal fire or preheat your gas grill.
2. Place the pieces of veal scaloppine between 2 pieces of wax paper and flatten with a mallet or the side of a cleaver until they are about 1/16 inch thick.
3. Soak the bay leaves in water.
4. Sauté the chopped onion in 2 tablespoons of the olive oil over medium heat until translucent, about 7 to 8 minutes. Add 1 cup of the breadcrumbs and 2 more tablespoons of the oil and cook for 1 to 2 minutes, mixing thoroughly. Remove from the heat. Add the cheese, raisins, pine nuts, soppressata, and tomato, and salt and pepper to taste, and mix again.
4. Place a heaping tablespoon of stuffing on each veal slice and carefully roll up. Secure with toothpicks. Dip the veal rolls

into the beaten eggs and then the remaining breadcrumbs, making sure all surfaces are breaded.

5. Using two skewers, side by side, skewer a bay leaf, a piece of onion, and a veal roll. Repeat, ending with a bay leaf.

6. Drizzle olive oil over the rolls and place on the grill for 8 minutes. Brush with more olive oil, turn, and grill for 8 minutes on the other side.

Serves 6.

Grilled Veal Rolls with Mortadella and Pecorino

BRACIOLETTINE ARROSTITE ALLA MESSINESE

8 pieces of veal scaloppine, 3 x 5 inches, ⅛ to ¼ inch thick (about 1¼ pounds)
8 thin slices butter (about 3 tablespoons)
8 slices mortadella
½ cup breadcrumbs
2 tablespoons finely chopped parsley
2 garlic cloves, very finely chopped
⅓ cup freshly grated pecorino
Pepper
Olive oil
Salt
Melted lard or butter, for basting

There are a number of variations on this classic grilled dish from Messina. The noted Sicilian food writer Anna Pomar says that there is so much of a cult around its preparation that butcher shops in Messina employ special assistants to cut the veal.

1. Prepare a very hot charcoal fire or preheat a gas grill.

2. Place the pieces of veal between 2 pieces of wax paper and flatten with a mallet or the side of a cleaver until they are about ¹⁄₁₆ inch thick.

3. Place a thin slice of butter on every rectangle of meat, then cover with slices of mortadella, trimming to the same size if necessary. Mix together the breadcrumbs, parsley, garlic, cheese, and pepper to taste. Add enough olive oil to make a paste.

4. Cover the mortadella with this mixture and lightly sprin-

kle with salt. Roll up and secure with toothpicks if necessary. Slide onto double skewers so they fit tightly.

5. Grill for 8 minutes a side, basting with melted lard or butter.

Serves 4.

Cheese Rolls Stuffed with Veal

INVOLTINI DI TUMA

½ pound chopped veal
1 tablespoon olive oil
Salt and pepper
4 tablespoons chopped parsley
1 pound fresh or whole-milk
    packaged mozzarella, sliced
    ⅛ inch thick
1 cup breadcrumbs
Flour
2 eggs, beaten
Olive oil, for deep frying

This is a wonderful dish but a bit tricky to make. The difficulty is in flattening the mozzarella slices for stuffing and rolling. Choose a large firm ball of fresh mozzarella, one that doesn't unravel when removed from the water. Buy a little more than called for in case some of the slices fall apart.

1. Sauté the veal in the tablespoon of olive oil over low heat. Add salt and pepper to taste and stir. Add half the parsley and 2 tablespoons water. Cover and simmer for 10 minutes. Drain and set aside.

2. Bring a pot of water to a boil. Using a slotted spoon, plunge 1 slice of mozzarella at a time into the boiling water for 5 seconds maximum. Drain. Working very quickly so the cheese doesn't harden, flatten it with the side of a cleaver by pressing, not hitting, or use your hand or fingertips. Be careful not to break apart the cheese. You can patch tiny breaks later with the flour and breadcrumbs.

3. Divide the meat stuffing among the mozzarella slices. Roll them up and pinch the sides closed. Mix the remaining parsley into the breadcrumbs and add salt and pepper to taste. Dredge the rolls in flour, dip in the eggs, then coat with breadcrumbs. Refrigerate for 30 minutes before frying.

4. Heat the oil for deep frying to 360°F. Deep-fry the cheese rolls until just before they turn golden. If any cheese begins to

escape from the breadcrumb coating, remove immediately. Drain on paper towels. Serve warm.

Serves 6.

Fried Skewered Meatballs and Bread

Spitini Fritti

1 ¼ *pounds ground beef*
3 *tablespoons grated parmesan*
3 *tablespoons breadcrumbs*
4 *eggs*
Salt and pepper
¾ *pound fresh* primu sale *or* *mozzarella*
½ *long loaf crusty Italian or French bread*
Flour
Breadcrumbs
Olive oil, for frying

These fried brochettes are said to come from the small town of Piana degli Albanesi near Palermo. The town was founded by Greek Catholic Albanians fleeing Turkish rule in the Balkans in the sixteenth century.

1. Mix together the beef, the parmesan, the breadcrumbs, 1 of the eggs, and salt and pepper to taste. Knead well, and with wet hands, form meatballs about 1 inch in diameter.

2. Cut the *primu sale* into 1-inch cubes. Slice the bread 1 inch thick and remove the crust on the sides, leaving it on top and bottom, to form rectangles. Using 2 wooden skewers side by side and about ½ inch apart, skewer a meatball, a slice of bread, a piece of cheese, another meatball, and so on until the skewer is full. Continue in this manner until all the ingredients are used up.

3. Lightly beat the remaining eggs in a shallow bowl. Spread out some flour on a sheet of wax paper and some breadcrumbs on another. Coat the brochettes with flour, dip into the eggs, and roll in the breadcrumbs, shaking the skewers so that all surfaces are breaded.

4. Pour olive oil into a 10- to 12-inch frying pan to a depth of 1 inch and heat over medium heat for at least 6 minutes before frying. Preheat the oven to 150°F.

5. Fry 1 or 2 brochettes at a time for 4 minutes, turn carefully with tongs, and fry for another 4 minutes. Remove and place on paper towels to drain. Keep warm in the oven while you fry the others.

Serves 6.

Sweet-and-Sour Lamb

AGNELLO IN AGRODOLCE

4 pounds leg or shoulder of
    lamb
1 garlic clove, peeled and
    very thinly sliced
Fresh rosemary leaves
1 onion, sliced
¼ cup olive oil
1 pound tomatoes, crushed
Salt and pepper .
½ cup red wine vinegar
3 tablespoons sugar

Sicilians are fond of dishes prepared in *agrodolce* (literally sour-sweet) sauce. The combination of sweet and sour comes from the Arabs, who believed that it had a dietetic importance. The Arab philosopher Avicenna even wrote a treatise on it. *Agrodolce* dishes from Sicily also entered other European cuisines. In *The Forme of Cury*, a 1390 cookbook compiled by the master chefs of King Richard II of England, there are scores of recipes for *egurdolce*, mostly using rabbit or kid.

Egyptian cuisine had a high reputation in the Middle Ages, similar to the reputation of French food today. Egyptian women cooks were employed even in distant places, such as in the kitchens of Frankish knights. In this recipe I bake the lamb in the long and slow manner I learned from a contemporary Egyptian woman cook, Ameena Ghattas. The lamb will fall off the bone.

1. Preheat oven to 300°F.
2. With a sharp knife or larding needle, puncture the lamb in numerous places and stuff each with a sliver of garlic and some rosemary needles.
3. Sauté the onion in the olive oil in a casserole with a cover over medium heat for 6 minutes. Brown the roast on all sides in

the casserole with the onions. Add the tomatoes and season with salt and pepper to taste. Spread evenly over the meat. Roast, covered, for 2½ hours.

4. Add the wine vinegar and continue roasting, uncovered, for 20 minutes. Stir in the sugar. Reduce the heat to 275°F. and cook, covered, for another 2½ hours or until the meat is tender and falls off the bone.

5. Remove the meat from bone and cover with sauce. Serve immediately.

Serves 4 to 6.

Lamb with Sweet Citrus Sauce

AGNELLO CON AGRUMI

4 pounds boneless lamb, cut
    into 1-inch pieces
3 tablespoons olive oil
1 onion, peeled
Salt and pepper
Juice of 2 lemons
Juice of 2 oranges
¼ cup red wine vinegar
¼ cup sugar
3 orange slices, cut in half
3 lemon slices, cut in half
1 tablespoon finely chopped
    parsley

This marriage of spring lamb with orange and lemon is another Sicilian dish of Arab inspiration. Although they are not traditional, roast potatoes are wonderful with this dish.

1. Brown the lamb in the olive oil over high heat for 5 minutes. Add the onion and continue browning for 3 minutes. Reduce the heat to medium-low and sprinkle on salt and pepper to taste. Cover and cook for 20 minutes. Add a little water from time to time if needed.

2. Transfer the lamb, using a slotted spoon, to another skillet. Set the sauce aside. Stir together the lemon and orange juice, vinegar, and sugar until the sugar is dissolved. Sprinkle over the lamb.

3. Sauté the lamb over medium heat for 5 minutes. Add the reserved sauce and cook for 8 minutes. The juices should be nearly evaporated. Serve hot on a platter decorated with half slices of orange and lemon and a sprinkling of parsley.

Serves 6 to 8.

Kid with Almonds

CAPRETTO CON LE MANDORLE

1½ pounds leg of kid or
   lamb, cut into 2-inch pieces
2 tablespoons olive oil
1 small onion, finely chopped
2 plum tomatoes, peeled and
   seeded
1 teaspoon salt
¼ teaspoon pepper
¼ cup blanched almonds

The mingling of almonds and kid or lamb in this rustic stew is so natural you'll wonder why you didn't think of it before.

1. Brown the kid in olive oil in a large pan with high sides over high heat with the onion, tomatoes, salt, and pepper. After 5 minutes, lower the heat and cook for 1½ hours, turning every once in a while and adding water if necessary.

2. Meanwhile, crush the almonds in a food processor until nearly "creamed." This should take about 3 minutes. Once the meat is tender, pour the almonds into the frying pan, bring to a boil, and remove from the heat. Serve hot.

Serves 4.

Kid with Mint Sauce

CAPRETTO ALLA MENTA

2½ pounds kid or lamb, one
   boneless piece from the leg
2 ounces pancetta, cut up
1½ tablespoons finely
   chopped parsley

Here roast kid or lamb is coated with a flavorful mint sauce that many Sicilians will tell you is an Arab heritage. The dish is served at room temperature. The idea for this recipe came from La

3 scallions, finely chopped
⅔ cup breadcrumbs
3 tablespoons (⅜ stick)
   butter, cut into 10 thin
   slices
Salt and pepper
1⅓ cups white wine
15 mint leaves, chopped
Juice of 1 lemon
2½ teaspoons sugar
⅓ cup red wine vinegar

Cucina Siciliana Nobile e Populare, by
N. Sapio Bartelletti.

1. Preheat the oven to 375°F.
2. Lard the meat by puncturing it with a sharply pointed knife and inserting the pieces of pancetta. Mix together the parsley, scallions, and breadcrumbs, and sprinkle the mixture over the meat. Place it in a baking pan and cover with the slices of butter. Sprinkle with salt and pepper to taste and pour the white wine over the meat. Roast for 1½ hours.
3. Meanwhile, prepare the sauce. Put the mint in a small bowl and add the lemon juice, sugar, and vinegar and ⅓ cup water. Mix and let stand until the meat is done.
4. Remove the meat from the pan. Add a few tablespoons of pan gravy to the sauce and pour the sauce over the meat. Let stand for 1 hour. Slice and serve.
   Serves 4.

Poor Man's Veal Roulade

BRACIOLONE DEL POVERELLO

2 pounds spinach
4 tablespoons butter
¾ cup freshly grated
   parmesan
4 eggs
Salt
1¾ pounds shoulder of veal,
   butterflied
2 tablespoons olive oil
½ cup dry white wine
½ cup veal or chicken stock

Spinach was introduced to Sicily by the Arabs, but today this stuffed veal recipe is one of the very few dishes in which it is used.

1. Wash the spinach and place it in a pot. Add no extra water, since some water will remain on the leaves. Cover and bring to a boil. When it wilts completely, in about 5 minutes, drain. Place the spinach in a strainer or colander and with the back of a wooden spoon, squeeze all the water out by pressing down. Chop the spinach.

2. Sauté the spinach in 2 tablespoons of the butter until the remaining water evaporates, about 3 minutes. Mix in half the parmesan and set aside.

3. Beat the eggs well in a bowl with a pinch of salt. Bring the remaining butter to a sizzle in an omelet pan. Pour in the eggs, sprinkle with the remaining cheese, and make an omelet. Be careful not to overcook it; it should take less than thirty seconds.

4. Place the veal between 2 pieces of wax paper and flatten it with a mallet or the side of a cleaver. Place the omelet on the top, trimming any sides that overlap. Cover evenly with the spinach. Roll the meat into a cylinder and tie it with kitchen twine. Close the two ends with toothpicks.

5. Brown the roulade in the olive oil in a casserole over high heat, about 5 minutes. Add the wine and salt to taste. Cover and cook on low heat until the wine evaporates, about 20 minutes. Add the stock and continue cooking on low heat, covered, for 10 minutes. Uncover and cook for another 10 minutes.

6. When the meat is cooked, remove it from the casserole and let it cool. Slice it, place it on an ovenproof serving platter, and pour the gravy over it. Reheat it in a slow oven before serving.
    Serves 4.

Beef Croquettes with Pistachios

POLPETTE DI MANZO

1 pound lean ground beef
1 egg, beaten
2 tablespoons crumbled
  amaretto cookie
3 tablespoons pine nuts
12 unsalted pistachio nuts,
  coarsely ground
1½ tablespoons golden raisins
1 teaspoon salt
Pinch of ground cinnamon

These beef croquettes, with their flavor of nuts, cinnamon, and amaretto, are both exotic and typically Sicilian.

Pepper
Flour, for dredging
1 cup olive oil

1. Combine the meat, egg, cookie, pine nuts, pistachios, raisins, and salt in a large bowl. Mix well with your hands. Let rest for about 30 minutes. Add the cinnamon and pepper to taste, working them in for a minute. Form the meat into croquettes about 3 x 1½ inches in the middle. Roll them in flour.
2. Heat the olive oil and fry the croquettes until golden, about 15 minutes. Serve warm.
    Serves 4.

Veal Croquettes with Sweet-and-Sour Tomato Sauce

POLPETTE DI VITELLO ALL'AGRODOLCE

¾ cup dry breadcrumbs
6 tablespoons milk
1½ pounds ground veal
2 eggs, beaten
½ cup grated caciocavallo or
*   pecorino*
5 tablespoons chopped parsley
1 teaspoon salt
½ teaspoon pepper
¼ cup olive oil
1 tablespoon flour
2 cups Smooth Tomato Sauce
*   (page 82)*
3 tablespoons red wine
*   vinegar*
3 tablespoons sugar

The Arab influence of sweet and sour is more pronounced in these croquettes than in some others. My favorite way to eat these meatballs is slightly warm with a full-bodied red wine and crusty Italian bread.

1. Preheat the oven to 375°F.
2. Moisten the breadcrumbs with the milk. The mixture should look like little pellets. Squeeze out the liquid if they seem too wet. Combine the breadcrumbs, meat, eggs, cheese, parsley, salt, and pepper. Form into croquettes about 3 x 1 inch. Brown in

the olive oil, shaking the pan occasionally to make sure they don't stick.

3. Dissolve the flour with several tablespoons of tomato sauce in a baking pan, mixing well. Add the remaining tomato sauce, the vinegar, and the sugar. Mix well again.

4. Add the croquettes and bake for 15 minutes. Or cook on top of the stove on medium–high heat for 20 minutes, shaking almost constantly.

Serves 4.

Meat Croquettes with Almonds

POLPETTE CON LE MANDORLE

2/3 cup breadcrumbs
1/4 cup milk
1 1/4 pounds ground beef or
  veal
1 egg, beaten
5 tablespoons finely chopped
  parsley
1/4 cup grated caciocavallo or
  pecorino
4 tablespoons olive oil
1 small onion, sliced very
  thin
4 tomatoes, peeled, seeded,
  and ground
3/4 cup blanched almonds
Salt and pepper

These beef croquettes are simmered with tomatoes and the sauce is thickened with finely ground almonds, reminiscent of Arab and Persian cuisine.

1. In a large mixing bowl that will hold all the ingredients, soak the breadcrumbs in the milk. Add the meat, egg, parsley, and cheese and knead for 2 minutes, until thoroughly mixed. Form the meat into croquettes about 3 x 1 inch. Sauté in 2 tablespoons of the olive oil in a large frying pan over low to moderate heat.

2. In another frying pan, sauté the onion in the remaining olive oil until it turns translucent, about 6 minutes. Set aside. Meanwhile, gently shake the croquettes so they don't stick and continue cooking for 5 minutes. Push the tomatoes through a sieve, colander, or food mill.

3. Add the tomatoes to the pan with the meat. Add the on-

ions to the sauce. Turn the heat up to medium and cook for 10 minutes.

4. In a food processor grind the almonds until they look like coarse powder. Pour the almonds into the frying pan with the meat and turn the flame up high. When it reaches a boil, take it off the heat. Add salt and pepper to taste and serve hot.

Serves 4.

Caul Stuffed with Parsley and Sage

STIGGHIOLE

8 pieces of lamb, kid, mutton, or pork omenta (about ¾ pound, cut in 12 x 8-inch pieces)
1 lamb or veal heart
8 scallions
40 parsley sprigs
8 sprigs fresh sage
Salt and pepper

Stigghiole consist of omentum layers wrapped around a bunch of fresh parsley, sage, scallions, and veal heart or lung. Better known as caul, the omentum is a netlike, nearly transparent membrane, which covers the viscera. *Stigghiole* have what the Italians call a "Homeric" taste. Don't let that deter you—this really is an extraordinary dish.

Stigghiole are street food, and I remember fondly their smell and smoke wafting through an outer road of Palermo. They were sold by *u stigghiularu*, street vendors who sell *stigghiola* for a pittance.

Finding lamb omenta may be difficult, so ask your butcher for pork caul fat, which is more readily available. The Sicilians call the omenta "handkerchiefs." They are very fragile and must be handled with care. They are self-basting and fatty, so don't enfold the ingredients in more than one layer. Since the sale of lung is banned, you will have to substitute veal heart.

1. If the omenta are not already cleaned, wash them and soak in cold salted water in a large bowl.

2. Prepare a charcoal fire or preheat a gas grill.

3. Slice the heart into 8 strips and skewer lengthwise onto the wooden skewer. Unfold the caul fat carefully and place a skewer on one edge. Lay 1 scallion, 5 parsley sprigs, stems and all, and the sage on top of the skewered heart. Sprinkle with salt and pepper. Wrap up the ingredients with the caul fat, making sure it is tight and firmly closed. Continue until all the ingredients are used up.

4. Grill for 30 minutes, not too close to the flame. Keep a close eye on the grill. The *stigghiole* are done when they are brown and firm when pinched. They look like a thick sausage. Pull the skewer out and slice off pieces to eat, including the now crisp caul fat.

Serves 8.

Stuffed Caul in Tomato Sauce

STIGGHIOLE 'O SUCU

8 stigghiole *(page 139)*
½ medium onion, chopped
3 garlic cloves, peeled
3 tablespoons olive oil
¾ cup (6-ounce can) tomato paste
6 mint leaves, chopped

In Sicily, as in the Arab countries, lamb and goat offal are very popular. In an ancient Sicilian preparation called *turtiduzza* all the entrails are used and cooked in a tomato sauce. In this variation, *stigghiole* are used instead.

1. Prepare and grill the *stigghiole*. Remove the skewers and slice the *stigghiole*.

2. Sauté the onion and garlic in olive oil over medium heat until translucent, about 7 minutes. Dissolve the tomato paste in 1 cup water and add to the onions along with the mint. Add the sliced *stigghiole* and cook on low heat for 30 minutes.

3. Serve warm with some of the sauce in which they cooked. Save the rest for pasta.

Serves 4.

Stuffed Caul

STIGGHIOLE CHINE

2 lamb or pork casings, in
  four 16-inch lengths
2 pieces of lamb or pork
  omentum (caul fat) (about
  6 ounces)
12 scallions, trimmed
½ pound fresh pecorino or
  fresh mozzarella, cut into
  strips (2 cups)
30 parsley sprigs
2 bay leaves
Salt and pepper
2 tablespoons olive oil
½ cup red wine

This recipe was described to me by the Sicilian food writer Tommaso d'Alba. He discovered the recipe in a locally printed cookbook on the cuisine of Enna, which is located in the center of Sicily. Lamb omenta and intestine will be hard to find, but you can use pork instead. Make sure you wash the intestines thoroughly. Use the intestines as you would twine to wrap each *stigghiola* tightly.

1. Rinse and soak the casings. Slip one opening of the casing over a faucet and turn the water on gently. Once the water has gone through the length of casing, wash the outside in water.

2. Soak the omenta in cold water. Spread one omentum on a flat surface. Arrange half the scallions, half the cheese, half the parsley, and one of the bay leaves on top. Sprinkle with salt and pepper to taste. Roll it up tightly and tie a 16-inch length of casing. Make a second *stigghiola* with the remaining ingredients.

3. Brown the *stigghiole* in olive oil and sprinkle with salt and pepper. Add 1 cup water and cook over low heat for 45 to 50 minutes. If there is still some liquid left in the pan, remove the *stigghiole* and pour out the excess. Add the wine and cook over high heat for 4 to 5 minutes to make a creamy sauce. Cut each *stigghiola* in half and serve warm.

Serves 4.

Beef Tongue in Sweet-and-Sour Sauce

LINGUA ALL'AGRODOLCE

Fresh beef tongue (3 to 3½
   pounds)
½ cup olive oil
½ onion, chopped
1 carrot, peeled and chopped
1 celery stalk, chopped
1¼-inch slice salt pork
½ clove garlic, finely chopped
2 teaspoons chopped parsley
Salt
Pepper
1¼ cups red wine
1 cup Beef Broth (page 86)
3 tablespoons sugar
1 garlic clove, peeled
1 bay leaf
¼ cup red wine vinegar
2 tablespoons grated
   unsweetened chocolate
½ cup pine nuts
1 tablespoon chopped orange
   peel
3 orange slices, halved
   (optional)

This sweet-and-sour tongue is an old baronial recipe from Còmiso, an agricultural center west of Ragusa, according to Pino Correnti and Giuseppe Coria. It has a sophisticated taste that reminds me of the finest nouvelle cuisine recipes.

1. Place the tongue in a large casserole with the oil, onion, carrot, celery, salt pork, chopped garlic, and parsley. Add salt and pepper to taste and brown well over moderate heat for 20 minutes. Add the wine and continue cooking until it has evaporated, about 20 minutes.

2. Add the broth and lower the heat. Cook, covered, for 2 hours, or until the tongue is well done, turning it over every half hour.

3. Remove and set aside until it is cool enough to handle. Strain the sauce and reserve in a saucepan on the side. Skim with a spoon any scum that remains on top of the sauce. Once the tongue is cool enough to handle, make a cut in the skin and peel it off. Slice the tongue and keep it warm on the side.

4. Place the sugar, garlic, and bay leaf in a small saucepan, and let the sugar melt over low to medium heat. Mix frequently (do not add water), and when the sugar is light brown in color, about 10 minutes, add the vinegar. The sugar will immediately congeal in a somewhat alarming manner. Continue stirring for another 2 to 3 minutes, scraping the bottom and sides of the pan, until the sauce thickens and the sugar dissolves. Add the chocolate and cook for another 2 minutes.

5. Add this sauce to the strained pan sauce. If it is too thin, reduce it. Add the pine nuts, orange peel, and a pinch of salt, and stir.

6. Reheat the tongue and sauce, if necessary, and arrange the slices of tongue on a platter. Cover with the sauce and decorate the edges of the platter with orange slices if you wish.

Serves 4.

POULTRY

To Sicilians, the only good thing about a chicken is its eggs, which are important in festive baked pasta dishes and pastry. Many Sicilian cookbooks don't even have poultry sections. When I was doing the research for this book I came across a chicken dish made with rice and saffron that Goethe described having tasted on a visit to Catania in the eighteenth century. But I never found an actual recipe—probably a good thing, because Goethe hated it.

Small birds are commonly prepared in Sicily. The Italians and Sicilians, like the Arabs, love such small birds as the thrush, snipe, warbler, pigeon, and lark. Waterfowl are also popular. In Enna one such preparation is called *Polli Sultanti*. It is made with stilt, an avocet-like water bird that lives near ponds.

Chicken with Almonds

GALLETTO CON LE MANDORLE

1 chicken, cut into 8 pieces (3 to 3½ pounds)
6 tablespoons olive oil
1 tablespoon tomato paste
4 tablespoons white or red wine vinegar

(Ingredients continued)

This chicken preparation, typical of Sciacca on the southern coast of Sicily, is coated with the almonds grown throughout the area.

2 tablespoons sugar
1 teaspoon salt
½ teaspoon pepper
¾ cup blanched almonds,
    crushed
¼ cup blanched whole
    almonds, toasted

1. Brown the chicken in 2 tablespoons of the olive oil over low heat. This will take about 15 minutes. Drain the chicken and set aside.

2. Pour the remaining olive oil into the pan with the tomato paste dissolved in 1 cup warm water. When the sauce begins to boil, add the vinegar, sugar, salt, pepper, and crushed almonds. When the sauce returns to a boil, add the chicken pieces, lower the heat, and cook, uncovered, for 45 to 50 minutes, adding a little water if the sauce starts to get too thick. Turn the pieces of chicken over at least once.

3. Arrange the chicken on a platter covered with some sauce. Sprinkle the toasted almonds on top. Serve warm in winter and at room temperature in summer.

Serves 4.

Sweet-and-Sour Chicken

POLLO ALL'AGRODOLCE

1 chicken (3½ to 4 pounds)
3 tablespoons olive oil
1 large onion, finely chopped
1 celery heart, cut into small
    pieces, including some
    leaves (2 cups)
2 tablespoons sugar
⅔ cup red wine vinegar
9 large green Sicilian olives,
    pitted and chopped
2 tablespoons capers, rinsed
½ teaspoon salt
Pepper
½ cup blanched almonds,
    toasted and coarsely crushed

This is particularly nice served at room temperature on a hot summer day.

1. Remove the skin and fat from the chicken. Cut it up into small pieces, dividing the breast in 4 parts and each thigh in 2 parts.

2. Pour 1 tablespoon of the oil into a large skillet and heat over medium-high heat. Add the chicken and cook until golden brown, about 15 minutes. Turn the pieces of chicken so all sides are browned.

3. Remove the chicken from the skillet with a slotted spoon and set aside. Pour in 2 tablespoons of olive oil and heat. Add the onion and celery and sauté over moderate heat, stirring constantly, until soft, about 5 minutes.

4. Add the drained chicken pieces, turn the heat up to high for 1 minute, and add the sugar, vinegar, olives, capers, salt, and pepper to taste. Let the vinegar evaporate, cooking for 3 to 4 minutes while turning the chicken in the sauce.

5. Correct the seasoning, cover the skillet, turn the heat down to medium-low, and cook until the chicken is done, about 30 minutes. Turn off the heat and mix in half of the almonds. Cover and let the chicken sit for 1 hour. Serve at room temperature with the remaining almonds sprinkled on top.

Serves 4.

The Chicken Pie of Mohammed ibn ath-Thumna

PASTICCIO DI MOHAMMED IBN ATH-THUMNA

1 chicken, cut into 8 pieces
   (3½ pounds)
¼ cup olive oil
2 cups chicken broth
Salt and black pepper
3 tablespoons blanched
   almonds, toasted
3 tablespoons pistachios
1 tablespoon capers, rinsed
1 tablespoon chopped parsley
2 eggs
Juice of 1 lemon
1 large round loaf crusty
   Italian bread (about 9
   inches in diameter)

This unique chicken pie is made from a hollowed-out loaf of bread stuffed with a combination of chicken, almonds, pistachios, and capers bound with eggs. I love serving it because its noble and magical taste bespeaks a history all its own.

Mohammed ibn ath-Thumna, Emir of Catania in the eleventh century, allied himself with the Normans invading Sicily. We don't know how the dish originated exactly but a thirteenth-century cookery book written in Baghdad has a similar recipe, called Egyptian chicken. Claudia Roden has adapted the recipe, which she calls Chicken Aw-sat; it consists of a loaf of bread with the inside removed and replaced with a chicken filling.

Felice Cùnsolo, a noted Sicilian culinary researcher, considers this dish to be a very typical example of *cucina arabo-sicula.*

1. In a heavy ovenproof skillet, sauté the chicken in the oil over medium heat until it is brown on all sides. Pour in the chicken broth and salt and pepper to taste. Cook over low to medium heat for 1½ hours, or until the meat falls off the bone.

2. While the chicken is cooking, grind the almonds, pistachios, capers, and parsley together. Set aside. Beat the eggs and lemon juice together and set aside.

3. Cut the bread in half horizontally and hollow out each half of the crust, reserving what you have pulled out. Pour off 1⅓ cups of the chicken broth and soak the soft bread in it. Bone the chicken, saving the skin.

4. Preheat the oven to 350°F.

5. Push the soaked bread through a sieve, saving all the liquid. Add the nut mixture to the puréed bread and broth, along with the eggs and lemon juice.

6. Chop the boned chicken into smaller pieces and add to the bread mixture. Chop a small amount of chicken skin and add. Stuff the bottom bread crust with it, mounding it slightly. Cover with the top crust and bake for 20 minutes or until the crust is crisp and the filling is heated through. This dish can be served at room temperature, but it is very nice hot.

Serves 4 to 6.

Pie of Substance

PASTICCIO DI SOSTANZA

2 recipes Short Dough (recipe
   follows)
1 chicken, with its giblets
   except the liver (3 to 3½
   pounds)
2 tablespoons olive oil

This recipe of the *monzù,* the French-inspired grand chefs of the nineteenth century who worked for the Sicilian aristocracy, is a rich and very flavorful pie that admirably displays Arab, Spanish, and French influences all in one.

¼ cup chopped onion
2 cups peeled, seeded, and
  chopped plum tomatoes
¼ pound Italian sweet
  sausage
1 cup Smooth Tomato Sauce
  (page 82)
¾ pound sweetbreads, cooked
Ground cinnamon
¼ teaspoon ground cloves
Salt and pepper
3 hard-boiled eggs, sliced
1 egg yolk, lightly beaten
  with 1 teaspoon water, for
  glazing

Al-Maqrizi, who was a fourteenth-century Arab writer, journeyed to Sicily and described its "substantial" dishes. Hearty and filling, this one is best served in winter.

1. Prepare the dough and divide into 2 balls. Dust with a little flour, wrap in wax paper, and place in the refrigerator for 1 hour.

2. Cut the chicken into pieces and brown them in a casserole in the oil together with the giblets and chopped onion. Add the tomatoes. Cook, covered, stirring occasionally, over medium heat for 45 minutes. Remove the bones of the chicken. Cut the giblets and chicken meat into small pieces and return them to the casserole.

3. Meanwhile, cook the sausage in the tomato sauce for 30 minutes. Remove the sausage and chop. Add to the pan the sausage, sweetbreads, a pinch of cinnamon, the cloves, and salt and pepper to taste and simmer, uncovered, over low heat, for 30 minutes.

4. Preheat the oven to 350°F.

5. Roll out one of the balls of dough and place on the bottom of a well-greased deep 10-inch pie pan. Using a slotted spoon, place the chicken and some of the sauce on the dough. Cover with slices of hard-boiled eggs and sprinkle with cinnamon.

6. Roll out the other ball of dough to make a cover. Pinch down the edges and make 1-inch-long slits randomly with a knife so the pie can breathe while baking. Bake for 35 minutes. Brush the top of the pie with egg yolk glaze. Return to the oven for 10 more minutes, then remove and let the pie cool. Serve warm or at room temperature.

Serves 4 to 6.

Short Dough

PASTA FROLLA

1¼ cups all-purpose flour
6 tablespoons cold unsalted
 butter, cut into bits
2 tablespoons cold vegetable
 shortening
¼ teaspoon salt
Ice water

Blend the flour, butter, shortening, and salt together in a large, cold mixing bowl. Add 2 tablespoons of ice water. Mix again until the water is absorbed. Add more ice water if necessary to form the dough. Shape into a ball, dust it with flour, and wrap in wax paper. Refrigerate for at least 1 hour.

Baked Wild Dove

TURUNA 'NTIANATI

6 doves or squab
10 garlic cloves, peeled (6
 whole and 4 crushed)
Salt
3 tablespoons olive oil
2 cups chicken broth
Pepper

This recipe can be made with turtle-dove, thrush, wood pigeon, partridge, or squab.

Dove can be found occasionally in specialty or game butchers at astronomical prices, so I suggest you use squab. The name *turuna* is derived from the Arabic *turaniy*, a kind of dove. This dish was probably created by Arab chefs in the royal kitchens of Frederick II and popularized in the Spanish court by his granddaughter Constance when she married Peter of Aragon in 1262.

1. Clean the birds. Put a whole garlic clove in each bird along with its liver and sprinkle with salt. Truss the birds. Brown in

olive oil over medium heat together with the crushed garlic, turning often, for 15 minutes. Discard the garlic.

2. Pour the chicken broth into the pan. Bring to a boil over high heat, then reduce heat to medium and cook, uncovered, for 15 minutes. Salt and pepper the cooking liquid to taste. Turn the birds and cook for another 15 minutes. They are done when they feel firm when pushed with a finger. If the sauce is too liquid, remove the birds and keep warm on the side while you reduce the sauce. Serve hot.

Serves 6.

Snipe with Pomegranates and Marsala

BECCAZZINI 'NGRANATI 'NTO MARSALA

Seeds from 1 large
  pomegranate
1 cup Marsala
1 tablespoon chopped mint
Salt and pepper
6 snipe or quail
6 thin slices pancetta
2 tablespoons olive oil
10 tablespoons unsalted butter
12 fresh sage leaves
Peel of 2 oranges, cut into
  ¼-inch slices

This elegant dish is usually described by Sicilian epicures as an eighteenth-century dish of the nobility. But many of these baronial dishes have even older heritages. I found several similar recipes in fourteenth-century Italian cookbooks, where it is called *romania*, from the Arabic word for pomegranate. Without a doubt the nineteenth-century Sicilian chefs, the *monzùs*, added personal touches such as Marsala.

This dish can be made with any small game bird or even Cornish hen. Make it in the late fall when pomegranates are in season. Be sure the pancetta is not cut too thin or it will begin to unroll.

This recipe is adapted from Carlo Middione's *The Food of Southern Italy*.

1. Place the pomegranate seeds in a bowl with enough Marsala to cover. Sprinkle the mint on top, mix, and set aside for 1 hour.

2. Salt and pepper the birds inside and out. Drain the pomegranate seeds and mint, saving the juice, and stuff the birds. Truss the birds with a toothpick running through the body cavity opening and both legs. Wrap each bird in a slice of pancetta. If the pancetta seems to be falling off, wrap again and press tight.

3. Preheat the oven to 375°F.

4. Heat the olive oil, 2 tablespoons of the butter, and 2 sage leaves in an ovenproof sauté pan or casserole and sauté the birds over high heat for 5 minutes, or until they are very brown. Don't worry if the pancetta falls off a little. Lower the heat and add the remaining sage leaves and pomegranate seeds and a few table-spoons of leftover Marsala.

5. Cook the birds in the oven, uncovered, for 7 minutes. Drizzle the remaining Marsala on the birds and spread 4 table-spoons of the remaining butter over the birds. Stir the pan juices around and spoon over the birds to coat them. Cook for another 5 minutes.

6. Meanwhile, melt the remaining butter over low heat and sauté the slices of orange peel for 5 minutes, gently pushing them around in the pan. Remove the orange peel and set aside.

7. Transfer the birds to a serving platter and cover with the orange peel. Spoon some pan juices and any loose pomegranate seeds over the birds. Serve immediately.

Serves 4 to 6.

GAME

Wild rabbit is the most popular game in Sicilian cooking. Many rabbit recipes are made with sweet-and-sour sauces. One rabbit recipe I came across was served with a complicated sauce of honey, vinegar, eggplant, pomegranates, almonds, olives, and capers.

Near Ragusa I discovered a dish called *carmuciu*, from the Arabic word for "little mouse." It was made with baby rabbits braised with carrots, celery, and tomatoes.

Fresh rabbit is a bit hard to find, but increasingly, supermar-kets carry frozen rabbits that would work well with the recipes here.

Rabbit in Sweet-and-Sour Wine Sauce

CONIGLIO IN AGRODOLCE

MARINADE
2 cups red wine

This flavorful and rich dish from the Agrigento area on the southern coast of

1 small onion, thinly sliced
2 cloves
1 parsley sprig
1 bay leaf
1 fresh thyme sprig
5 black peppercorns
½ teaspoon salt

1 rabbit, cut into pieces
   (about 3½ pounds)
7 tablespoons olive oil
1-inch cube of salt pork, diced
1 large onion, finely chopped
Flour
Salt and freshly ground
   pepper
⅔ cup hot chicken broth or
   rabbit stock or water
2½ tablespoons sugar
½ cup wine vinegar
4 tablespoons golden raisins
4 tablespoons pine nuts
3 tablespoons finely chopped
   parsley, for garnish
   (optional)
3 tablespoons finely chopped
   red bell pepper, for garnish
   (optional)

Sicily combines the flavors of Arab Sicily—vinegar, sugar, pine nuts, and raisins—in a delicate sauce. Although it is not traditional, you can add color by sprinkling finely chopped parsley or finely chopped red bell pepper on top.

1.   Combine the marinade ingredients in a saucepan and bring to a boil over medium heat. As soon as the marinade reaches a boil, remove it from the heat. Let stand until lukewarm. Put the rabbit pieces in a casserole and pour the marinade over the rabbit to cover. Let sit for 2 hours.

2.   Heat the olive oil and salt pork together in a large skillet and sauté the chopped onion over medium heat until golden brown. Remove the pieces of rabbit from the marinade and dry well. Strain the marinade, saving 1 cup and discarding the rest. Coat the rabbit with a light dusting of flour and fry with the onion for about 10 minutes.

3.   Pour the strained marinade over the rabbit and cook, uncovered, over medium heat for 20 minutes. When the wine has almost evaporated and the rabbit is darkened, season to taste with salt and pepper. Add enough hot broth to cover the rabbit pieces.

Cover, lower the heat, and simmer for 20 minutes. The sauce will have a creamy consistency.

4. While the rabbit is cooking, dissolve the sugar with 4 tablespoons water in a small pan over a medium heat. After 5 minutes add the vinegar, stirring constantly with a wooden spoon for 5 minutes. Add the raisins and cook for 1 minute. Add this sauce to the skillet, pouring it over the rabbit pieces and scraping the bottom of the pan. Stir in the pine nuts. Sprinkle with parsley or red pepper, if desired, and serve.

Serves 6 to 8.

Rabbit, Arab-Style

CONIGLIO SARACENO

1 large onion
Pinch of saffron
1 cup Beef Broth (see page 86)
1 or 2 red chili peppers
½ cup olive oil
1 rabbit, preferably wild, cut into pieces (3½ to 4 pounds)
Salt
½ cup chopped parsley (loosely packed)

This dish, made with wild rabbit, is also known as *Coniglio alla Turca*. Wild rabbit, if you can find or catch one, will taste earthier and more authentic than farmed rabbit.

1. Soften the onion in boiling water for 10 minutes. Dissolve the saffron in the broth. Add the chili pepper, broken in half, to the broth. Drain the onion, let it cool, then slice thin with a very sharp knife.

2. In a pan large enough to hold the rabbit snugly, heat the oil and sauté the onion for 7 minutes. Add the pieces of rabbit and cook, uncovered, on low heat for 15 minutes.

3. Pour the broth over the rabbit and add salt to taste. Cook on low heat, turning the rabbit to coat all sides, until the broth is reduced to several tablespoons, about 45 to 50 minutes.

4. Remove the rabbit from the heat and sprinkle the parsley over it. The rabbit should glisten with a film of sauce. Serve hot.

Serves 4.

Rabbit in Chocolate

CONIGLIO AL CIOCCOLATO

1 rabbit, cut into pieces
  (about 3½ pounds)
Flour
4½ tablespoons olive oil
1 onion, chopped
3 celery stalks, chopped
2 parsnips, peeled and
  chopped
2 bay leaves
1 tablespoon pine nuts
1 tablespoon golden raisins
3 cloves
1 teaspoon fennel seeds
Salt and pepper
1¼ teaspoons sugar
1½ tablespoons unsweetened
  chocolate, chopped fine
½ cup white wine vinegar

Many sweet-and-sour rabbit recipes come from the interior of Sicily, mostly around Caltigirone. This recipe displays many influences besides the Arab; the chocolate flavoring is obviously a Spanish touch.

1. Roll the pieces of rabbit lightly in the flour, shaking off any excess. Heat 2 tablespoons of the olive oil in a skillet over medium-low heat and brown the rabbit pieces until golden all over, about 12 minutes.

2. In another skillet, heat the remaining olive oil and sauté the onion, celery, and parsnips over medium heat for 12 minutes. Add the bay leaves, pine nuts, raisins, cloves, and fennel seeds and continue cooking for 2 minutes.

3. Combine the onion mixture with the rabbit and add salt and pepper to taste. Sprinkle with the sugar and the chocolate and stir. Sprinkle with the vinegar. Cover and cook over low heat until the sauce is thick, about 30 to 40 minutes. Remove cloves and serve hot.

Serves 4.

EIGHT
Fish
PESCI

Because fish is so important in the Sicilian diet, I've included a large number of fish recipes, many calling for such Mediterranean fish as red mullet, sardines, and baby octopus. Thanks to advances in air transportation and distribution—and new demand—you may find these fish in your markets. Visit those neighborhood fish stores; the results will be worth it. If you live in a part of the country where Mediterranean fish are not available, use cod or red snapper as replacements. You should not have any problem getting swordfish, tuna, and shellfish.

Finding good fish means finding a good fishmonger, and finding one means doing repeat business. But don't leave everything to the fishmonger. Learn the rudiments of identifying fresh fish. In the end, the best way to tell if you have a good fishmonger and if he's selling you good fish is from the eating. The fish should taste wonderful. If not, change your purveyor.

The following glossary is meant to help you buy fish when following recipes from this cookbook and other Italian cookbooks in general. It is not a definitive statement about fish.

Amberjack, Rudderfish, or Florida Jack (ARICCIOLA)

A delicious little fish, ideal grilled and placed on top of a bowl of couscous. Butterfish or porgies could be used as a substitute.

Anchovies (ACCIUGHE)

Given the importance of preserved anchovies in Sicilian cooking, I recommend that you buy a large can of imported Sicilian whole salted anchovies, rather than the fillets. You have to wash the salt off and pull the skeleton out. Simply separate the anchovy at the top of the belly, pull apart gently with your thumbs, and peel the two fillets off. Fresh anchovies can also be found in this country, usually in Italian and Greek neighborhoods. Fresh anchovies can be used in any of the sardine recipes or you can grill them.

Babyfish (NEONATA)

Transparent and about the size of a tine of a fork, these are sometimes called fry in English. Unfortunately they are seldom found in the United States. If you find them, buy a lot and freeze them for later. You can sometimes find baby sand eels, which work very well. Use the baby fish or sand eels in *Sciabbacheddu*.

Bluefish (PESCE SERRA)

Bluefish is a good replacement fish for the oily fish used in *Cuscusù*, as well as for the *spadola* in *Spadola alla Stemperata*.

Blue-Mouth (BOCA NEGRA)

This is the closest North Atlantic fish to *rascasse*, the essential fish for a bouillabaisse.

Bogue (BOGA)

A nice fish to use in a fish broth. My fishmonger, Sal Fantasia, thinks it's the fish closest in taste to red mullet.

Bonito (BONITA)

Similar to bluefish and mackerel, bonito is very popular with the Greeks and to a lesser extent the Sicilians. It is good grilled or in a fish stew. The roe can be used as a substitute for tuna roe for *Bottarga*.

Comber (*BUDDACI*)

Occasionally found in southern U.S. waters and for sale in Portuguese communities, it is similar to wreckfish and grouper. *Buddaci*, a Sicilian name, comes from the Arabic *muddaq*.

Conch (*SCUNGILLI*)

Conch can be bought live but it will require a long time for purging and boiling. You can also buy conch in cans, which only requires reheating. Conch is more popular in Campania than in Sicily. *Scungilli* is a Campanian dialect word.

Dentex (*DENTICE*)

Although expensive, dentex has a delicate flavor that makes it a Sicilian favorite. Red snapper, *pagro dentice* in Italian, is a good substitute.

Dogfish (*GATTUCCIO*)

A very small spotted shark, dogfish is excellent in fish couscous and *Zuppa di Pesce*.

Eel (*ANGUILLA*)

Sicilians like the moray eel (*murina* in Sicilian) more than the common eel (*anguilla*). The moray is an essential ingredient in the broth for *Cuscusù*, and every effort should be made to find it. It freezes quite well. Be careful when preparing it; its teeth are very dangerous even when the eel is dead. The conger eel (*grongo*) is also used in *Cuscusù*.

It is very difficult to skin and clean an eel. Ask your fishmonger to do it for you. Save and freeze the head for a future *Zuppa di Pesce*.

Baby sand eels are sometimes found in Italian fish stores in the United States. They can be used in recipes calling for mixed tiny fish.

Garfish (*AGUGLIA*)

The bones of this fish are green. It can be found in Japanese fish stores, where it is called *sayori*. Garfish tastes a lot like mackerel or half-beak, a fish that is rare in the Mediterranean but can be found in Florida. Use garfish in *Arriciola alla Saracena.*

Grouper (CERNIA)

Grouper is fished off the U.S. coast, especially in southern waters. It has firm flesh with good flavor.

Hake (NASELLO)

A good-tasting fish that can be cooked many ways, including baked, as in *Nasello al Forno in Salsa di Semi di Sesame.* Substitute cod, halibut, or haddock if not available.

Lobster (ARAGOSTA)

The European spiny lobster (*aragosta*) lacks the large distinctive claws of its North American counterpart. Lobster is often found in dishes from western Sicily such as the pasta dishes from Pantelleria and Trapani on pages 99-100. In restaurants, lobster is sometimes used to garnish *Cuscusù.*

Mackerel (SGOMBRO)

This is a good oily fish to use in *Cuscusù* and *Zuppa di Pesce.* Because it is oily, it can be used to replace garfish and eel, even though the flavor is different.

Monkfish (ROSPO)

The tail of monkfish is good to eat; it is like lobster in texture and flavor. The head makes a good base for a fish stock.

Octopus (POLPO)

Fresh octopus can be found in ethnic fish markets; cooked octopus is often available in Japanese fish stores. The baby octopus called for in *Polipi alla Quartara* is hard to find; you will probably have to replace it with small squid.

Pompano (LECCIA STELLA)

Mostly caught off Florida, pompano can be used in recipes calling for grouper, amberjack, or red mullet.

Redfish

An excellent choice for the broth in *Cuscusù*. Also called ocean perch, it can be used to replace blue-mouth, scorpion fish, or red mullet.

Red Mullet (TRIGLIE)

Many Sicilians will tell you that this is their favorite fish. Some mullet come from the Carolinas and Florida, but most are flown to New York from the Mediterranean or even the Indian Ocean. There is no satisfactory replacement, but red snapper, redfish, or blue-mouth will do. Bogue may be closest in taste.

Red Snapper (PAGRO DENTICE)

Snapper is the fish I recommend to replace any fish I have called for that you cannot find. It is firm-fleshed, good-tasting, and readily available.

Salt Cod (BACCALÀ)

Baccalà is cod that is first salted and then dried. It is imported in Italy and Sicily from Norway, Iceland, Canada, and the United States. *Stoccafisso* (stockfish), with which it is sometimes confused, is lightly salted and air-dried cod. The Sicilian word *stoccufisu* is derived unadulterated from the Norwegian word *stokfisk*. It has been known since medieval times.

Sardines (SARDE)

The quintessentially Sicilian fish, even more so than red mullet. Sardines can be found fresh in the United States, the smaller the better. Those from Portugal are very good; those from Maine are more oily. Some writers say smelts, because they are similar in size and looks, can replace sardines when you cannot find fresh ones. This is true but unsatisfactory. I think whole Maine sardines canned in water are better than smelts.

Scorpion Fish (SCORFANO)

A delicate and flavorful fish that is excellent in a *Cuscusù* or bouillabaisse. Scorpion fish can be replaced with blue-mouth, redfish, striped bass, or rockfish.

Sea Bass (*SPIGOLA*)

Sea bass can be used to replace scorpion fish or *spadola* in *Spadola alla Stemperata*, or grouper in *Zuppa di Pesce*. It can also be used in *Pisci 'Ntammaru*.

Sea Robin or Gurnard (*COCCIO*)

The sea robin is usually used in fish broths; in Greek Sicily, it was fried in oil and pickled with vinegar and spices.

Shad (*ALOSA*)

Shad roe is so popular in American cuisine, we sometimes forget that the flesh itself is very good. In Sicilian it is also known by a number of other names, including *saracà* and *alaccia*. Try the *Saracà che Mennule* or *Alaccia 'Ncammisata*. You can replace shad with perch, cod, hake, or red snapper.

Shrimp (*GAMBERETTI*)

Shrimp are not very common in Sicilian cuisine, but there are a few dishes that appear to have some Arab provenance (pages 194–195).

Sole (*SOGLIOLA*)

Sole is commonly found in Italy and the United States. It can be used in recipes calling for grouper.

Spadola (*SPADOLA*)

This fish is very similar to scabbard fish. It has a delicious flavor and firm flesh, similar to sea bass.

Squid (*CALAMARI E SEPPIE*)

Ask your fishmonger to clean the squid for you or do it yourself. Pull the head and tentacles out of the body cavity. Pull the pointy cartilage out of the body along with the viscera. Pull off the skin or mantle under cold running water. Cut the tentacles from the head just below the eyes. Baby squid are wonderful grilled (page 62).

Swordfish (PESCE SPADA)

Because the waters around Sicily are among the world's richest for swordfishing, there are a great number of swordfish recipes, many of which can be described as Arab-Sicilian (pages 161–165).

Tuna (TONNO)

Most of the tuna in Sicily is bluefin, although yellowfin is fairly common. Tuna is becoming increasingly expensive because of heavy Japanese demand on a dwindling supply. The Japanese are willing to spend astronomical prices for belly tuna, which they call *toro* and the Sicilians call *ventresca*. Make some *Surra*, and you will see why.

The Arabs revolutionized tuna fishing in Sicily. The method of tuna fishing they introduced is still used today in the much-diminished industry centered at Trapani. The *mattanza* (tuna hunt) is today more for the tourist than the tuna. When the male tuna surface in search of a mate, they are channeled into a "hall of death," made up of increasingly smaller chambers that culminate in a death chamber, where they are slaughtered in a bloody frenzy of harpooning and clubbing upon the commands of the leader of the hunt, *il rais* (from the Arabic *al-rais*). Arabic-sounding dirges like "La Cialoma" ("The Tuna Fishermen's Chatter") or "La Sagghiata" ("The Tuna Haul") are sung by the tuna fishermen during the kill. The Sicilian chants of the tuna fishermen—*alamo, ainavo, amola*—are derived from the Arabic.

Many tuna products have entered Sicilian cuisine from the Arabs, for example, *museddu* or *musciuma*, sun-dried tuna or dolphinfish, which is sliced very thin and dressed with olive oil and lemon juice, and *Bottarga*, dried tuna roe.

Tuna Roe, Dried (BOTTARGA)

You can sometimes buy this in Italian neighborhoods. You can also make it yourself (page 185).

Grilled Swordfish

GRIGLIATA DI PESCE SPADA

1 cup olive oil
1 cup white wine
1 bay leaf, crumbled
1 medium onion, thinly sliced
Salt
8 peppercorns
6 to 8 swordfish steaks, about
  1 inch thick (3 pounds)
2 garlic cloves, finely chopped
3 canned sardines, mashed
1 tablespoon dried oregano
½ teaspoon cayenne
Juice of 1 lemon
6 to 8 lemon slices, for
  garnish
Chopped parsley, for garnish
  (optional)

This recipe probably goes back to the Greeks; the addition of red pepper can be traced to the Spaniards or recent Arabs, not Arab Sicilians.

Traditionally a Sicilian swordfish steak is about three-eighths of an inch thick and grilled about two to three minutes a side over a very hot grill. I prefer a thicker cut, about one inch, which I grill for ten minutes. Reduce the grilling time if you use thinner steaks.

1. In a large ceramic or glass dish, combine ¾ cup of the olive oil, the wine, the bay leaf, the onion, 1 teaspoon salt, and the peppercorns. Marinate the swordfish steaks for 2 hours.

2. Prepare a hot charcoal fire or preheat a gas grill.

3. Sauté the garlic in 2 tablespoons of the olive oil over low heat. Add the sardines, oregano, and cayenne and ½ teaspoon salt. With the back of a wooden spoon, mix and mash into a paste. Remove from the heat and stir in the remaining olive oil and the lemon juice. Add additional salt to taste. Mix well and keep warm.

4. Grill the swordfish for 5 minutes on one side, brush with marinade, and turn to the other side. Brush again with marinade and grill another 5 minutes.

5. Remove the swordfish and serve with the sauce. Garnish each steak with a slice of lemon and chopped parsley, if desired.

Serves 6 to 8.

Swordfish Rolls

INVOLTINI DI PESCE SPADA

10 slices swordfish (about 2½
    pounds), ¼ inch thick

FILLING
1 medium onion, finely
    chopped
2 tablespoons olive oil
1¾ cups breadcrumbs
2 anchovy fillets, chopped
1 large garlic clove, finely
    chopped
2 tablespoons pine nuts
1 tablespoon golden raisins or
    currants
2 tablespoons grated pecorino
1 tablespoon lemon juice
1 tablespoon orange juice
1 egg, beaten
Salt and pepper

1 tablespoon olive oil
1 egg, beaten
2 tablespoons olive oil
1 cup breadcrumbs
2 tablespoons grated
    caciocavallo or pecorino
½ teaspoon dried oregano
1 tablespoon finely chopped
    parsley
1 garlic clove, very finely
    chopped
Salt and pepper
3 large onions, quartered
30 large bay leaves, soaked in
    water
Olive oil, for drizzling

Swordfish are caught in the Strait of Messina, the Malta Channel, and the Sicilian Channel, and most Sicilian swordfish dishes come from the Messina area. The popularity of swordfish in Sicily goes back to the Greeks, but this dish clearly has Arab inspiration in the stuffing of pine nuts, raisins, and citrus juice. *Involtini* are found throughout Sicily; they are especially popular in Messina and Palermo. The recipe is adapted from J. C. Grasso's wonderful book *The Best of Southern Italian Cooking*.

1. Ask the fishmonger to slice the swordfish. Flatten carefully between 2 pieces of wax paper with a mallet or the side of a heavy cleaver. Each slice should be about 5½ x 3½ inches.

2. *To make the filling:* Sauté the onion in the 2 tablespoons olive oil over medium heat until translucent, about 7 minutes. Combine the sautéed onion, breadcrumbs, anchovy fillets, garlic, pine nuts, raisins, pecorino, lemon juice, orange juice, and egg. Mix well and add salt and pepper to taste.

3. Divide the filling among the swordfish pieces and roll up tightly, securing with a toothpick. Roll the *involtini* in 1 tablespoon of the olive oil and refrigerate until ready to grill, but not more than 4 hours. Freeze any remaining stuffing.

4. Prepare a hot charcoal fire or preheat a gas grill.

5. Stir the beaten egg and the 2 tablespoons olive oil together and set aside. Combine the breadcrumbs, grated cheese, oregano, parsley, garlic, and salt and pepper to taste. Dip the swordfish rolls in the egg mixture and then roll them in the breadcrumb mixture to coat lightly.

6. Thread the rolls onto double skewers, alternating with onion slices and bay leaves. Drizzle olive oil over the *involtini*. Grill for 6 minutes a side.

Serves 5.

Layered Swordfish

PESCE SPADA ALLA SFINCIONE

2 pounds swordfish, cut into 6
   steaks, ½ inch thick
12 anchovy fillets
10 tablespoons olive oil
⅔ cup breadcrumbs
3 tablespoons dried oregano
Salt and pepper

This unusual recipe can also be made with tuna. The anchovies and oregano give the dish a wonderful flavor. Serve directly from the casserole you cook it in.

1. Soak the swordfish slices in water for 2 hours. Chop the anchovies and soak them in 2 tablespoons of the olive oil.

2. Drain the fish and dry thoroughly. Pour 2 tablespoons of the olive oil into a casserole with high sides and swish each piece of fish in it, oiling the sides too. Use 3 slices to form a bottom layer. Spread half the breadcrumbs on top, then half the anchovies

with half the olive oil they have been soaked in. Sprinkle with half the oregano and salt and pepper, and 3 tablespoons olive oil.

3. Cover with the remaining swordfish. Spread the remaining breadcrumbs, anchovies, and oregano on top; add salt and pepper to taste. Pour the remaining olive oil over the top. Cover the pan and cook over high heat for 3 minutes. Remove the lid and lift the fish with a spatula so the pieces don't stick. Do not turn over. Cover again and cook for another 3 minutes. Remove from the pan carefully and serve very hot.

Serves 4 to 6.

Swordfish Rolls in Ghiotta

INVOLTINI DI PESCE SPADA ALLA GHIOTTA

8 slices swordfish (about 2 pounds), ¼ inch thick

FILLING
1 medium onion, chopped
½ cup olive oil
⅔ cup chopped swordfish (½ pound)
1 celery stalk, finely chopped
1½ teaspoons capers, rinsed and chopped
¼ cup green Sicilian olives, pitted and left whole (optional)
Salt and pepper
½ cup breadcrumbs
2 eggs, beaten
2 tablespoons grated pecorino
2 basil leaves, coarsely chopped

1 medium onion, thinly sliced
2 tablespoons olive oil
1 celery stalk, cut in half
2 tablespoons golden raisins or currants

Ghiotta literally means "delicious fish soup" in Sicilian. As a fish sauce it is the essential broth for Cuscusù (page 121). "Ghiotta," which in Italian refers to the pan it marinates in, is believed to come from the Arabic word ghatta, meaning dishes that are soaked or immersed in a sauce or liquid. In Tunisia today there is a fish broth known as guiotta. This recipe is typical of Messina, where one will find many variations of this preparation. Any sauce that is left over can be used over pasta.

2 tablespoons pine nuts
¼ cup green Sicilian olives,
  pitted and chopped
1½ teaspoons capers, rinsed
  and chopped
2 pounds plum tomatoes,
  peeled and passed through a
  large-holed sieve or
  colander
Salt and pepper

1. Ask the fishmonger to slice the swordfish. Flatten the pieces carefully between 2 pieces of wax paper with a mallet or the side of a heavy cleaver. Each slice should be about 5½ x 3½ inches.

2. *To make the filling:* Sauté the chopped onion in ½ cup of olive oil over medium heat until translucent, about 7 minutes. Add the chopped swordfish, chopped celery, 1½ teaspoons capers, and the whole olives, if using. Sauté gently for 10 minutes, stirring every once in a while. Remove from the pan and add salt and pepper to taste. Mince the mixture until very fine. Blend in the breadcrumbs, eggs, pecorino, and basil. Divide the filling among the pieces of swordfish and roll them up. Freeze any leftover stuffing.

3. In another pan, sauté the sliced onion in the 2 tablespoons olive oil over medium heat for 5 minutes. Add the celery, raisins, pine nuts, chopped olives, and 1½ teaspoons capers. Sauté on a medium heat for 10 minutes. Add the tomatoes and cook, covered, for 30 minutes. Taste the sauce and add salt and pepper if needed.

4. Place the swordfish rolls in the sauce and cook for 6 to 7 minutes. Using 2 spoons, carefully turn the rolls and cook for another 6 to 7 minutes. Serve immediately.

Serves 4 to 6.

Red Mullet with Orange Sauce

TRIGLIE ALLA SICILIANA

Peel of 2 oranges, cut into
*   strips*

MEAT GRAVY
2 cups Beef Broth (page 86)
¼ cup white wine
1 tablespoon flour
1 tablespoon butter
Juice of 1 orange
Juice of 1 lemon
10 tablespoons butter, cut into
*   small pieces*
Salt and pepper

12 red mullet, cleaned and
*   gutted, with heads and tails*
*   (3½ to 4 pounds)*
Salt and pepper
5 tablespoons olive oil

Fresh red mullet is an exquisitely delicate fish of the Mediterranean. It is wonderful whether grilled or oven-baked. In *Arrosto di Triglie*, also called *Triglia al Forno*, the fish is covered with a mixture of breadcrumbs, pine nuts, and raisins and baked. Ada Boni, the noted Italian cookbook author, adapted the recipe, grilling the fish instead of baking it, and the dish became widely known as *Triglie alla Siciliana*. This is my version of her recipe. The original oven-baked dish follows in the variation.

You can substitute red snapper, redfish, blue-mouth, or bogue for red mullet.

1. Prepare a hot charcoal fire or preheat a gas grill.
2. Boil the orange peel in water to cover for 1 minute. Drain the peel and set aside.
3. Reduce the broth over high heat to ¼ cup. Stir in the wine. Blend the flour and butter together into a smooth paste and beat into the broth mixture. Bring to a simmer and cook for 1 or 2 minutes, or until thick enough to coat a spoon.
4. Marinate the fish for 10 minutes in salt, pepper, and olive oil. Place the fish directly on the grill for 6 minutes per side, turning once. If the fish are ready before you complete Step 5, keep warm in a 150°F. oven.
5. Meanwhile, finish the sauce over low heat, stirring constantly. Add the orange juice and lemon juice. Add the butter and keep hot after it melts. Taste and add salt or pepper as needed. Pour the sauce over the fish and serve.
   Serves 6 to 8.

Preheat the oven to 425°F. Place the fish in a baking pan. Combine 1 cup breadcrumbs, ¼ cup golden raisins, ¼ cup pine nuts, 2 tablespoons very finely chopped parsley, the finely chopped peel of 1 orange, and salt and white pepper to taste. Mix well and spread over the fish and bake for 10 minutes. Serve with the sauce from Step 3.

Fennel-Flavored Red Mullet

TRIGLIE CON AROMA DI FINOCCHIO

10 red mullet, cleaned and
   gutted, with heads and tails
   (3 pounds)
Juice of 1 lemon
Juice of 1 orange
4 teaspoons fennel seeds
Salt and pepper
3 tablespoons bacon fat or lard
3 tablespoons chopped parsley
4 tablespoons olive oil

This may be a baroque dish. Its roots undoubtedly go back to the Greeks, but the use of citrus juices is Arab in inspiration. A similar dish is found in Provence in the south of France.

If you can't find red mullet, substitute red snapper.

1. Place the fish in an enameled or glass baking dish that will hold them all flat; or use 2 pans. Mix together half the lemon juice, half the orange juice, 1 teaspoon of the fennel seeds, and salt and pepper to taste. Pour over the fish and marinate for 2 hours.
2. Prepare a hot charcoal fire or preheat a gas grill.
3. In a mortar with a pestle or in a small, deep bowl, pound the remaining fennel seeds until well cracked. Add the bacon fat or lard and parsley and continue pounding until the mixture is almost homogenous. Stuff each fish with some of this mixture, and press the opening closed. Moisten the fish with the remaining juice, the olive oil, and salt and pepper to taste. Grill for about 5 minutes a side on a hot grill, turning carefully.
4. Remove from the grill with care. Serve very hot.
Serves 6.

Red Mullet with Mint Sauce

TRIGLIE CON SALSA ALLA MENTA

¾ cup breadcrumbs
3 tablespoons white wine
  vinegar
1 tablespoon finely chopped
  parsley
2 tablespoons mint leaves,
  chopped finely
1 heaping tablespoon capers,
  rinsed
2 anchovy fillets
1 cup olive oil
1 tablespoon sugar
Olive oil, for deep frying
Flour
8 red mullet, cleaned and
  gutted, with heads and tails
  (1½ to 2 pounds)

This red mullet preparation from western Sicily is a splendid summer dish. It is served at room temperature with a fragrant and delicious whipped-cream-like dressing of fried breadcrumbs infused with mint, parsley, capers, sugar, and vinegar. You can use porgies or small red snappers instead of red mullet in this dish.

1. Moisten the breadcrumbs with 2 tablespoons of the vinegar and mix in the parsley and mint. In a mortar with a pestle, pound the capers together with the anchovies, adding 3 tablespoons olive oil a little at a time until the mixture is fluid. Combine the 2 mixtures in a frying pan over low heat. Add the sugar, the remaining vinegar and the remaining oil, about a tablespoon at a time to make a soft, homogenous mixture with the consistency of thick whipped cream.

2. Heat the oil for deep frying to 370°F.

3. Flour the fish, shake off the excess, and fry the fish until a crispy golden brown. Remove and drain on paper towels. When the fish are cool, spread each side with the sauce and leave for ten minutes before serving.

Serves 4.

Grouper Rolls

SPITINI DI CERNIA

8 grouper fillets (about 1¾
    pounds)
Juice of 1 lemon
Juice of 1 orange
1 teaspoon sugar
Pinch of cinnamon
¾ cup breadcrumbs
⅓ cup grated pecorino
2 tablespoons finely chopped
    parsley
2 tablespoons golden raisins,
    soaked
2 tablespoons pine nuts
Salt and pepper
8 large bay leaves
Extra-virgin olive oil, for
    drizzling

This is a delicate dish I heard about from Tommaso d'Alba. The mixture of citrus juices with cheese, sugar, and cinnamon marries well with grouper or really any kind of fish fillet.

1. Cut each fillet in half and gently pound between 2 pieces of wax paper until each slice is about 2½ x 3½ inches. Mix the lemon and orange juices together and stir in the sugar. Measure out 4 tablespoons of the juice, sprinkle with a pinch of cinnamon, and set aside.

2. Mix together ½ cup of the breadcrumbs, the cheese, parsley, drained raisins, pine nuts, the 4 reserved tablespoons citrus juice, and salt and pepper to taste. Place a tablespoon of filling on each fish slice, roll it up, and secure with a toothpick.

3. Preheat the oven to 350°F.

4. Double-skewer the fish rolls, inserting a bay leaf between each roll, placing 2 rolls on each set of double skewers. Place the skewers in an oiled baking dish, sprinkle the remaining breadcrumbs on top, and drizzle with olive oil. Bake for 35 to 45 minutes, sprinkling with some more lemon and orange juice seasoned with the sugar and cinnamon.

Serves 4.

Fish Stew, Arab-Style

ZUPPA DI PESCE ALLA SARACENA

3 garlic cloves, chopped
1 large onion, chopped
¼ cup parsley leaves
2 dried red chili peppers,
    crumbled
3 tablespoons olive oil
3 pounds grouper fillets, with
    the head if possible
1 fish head, monkfish if
    possible
2 pinches of saffron
1 pound squid, cleaned and
    cut into rings
1 large yellow pepper,
    roasted, peeled, and sliced
    into strips
2 tablespoons sea salt
6 red mullet, cleaned and
    gutted, or 1½ pounds
    porgies or red snapper
1 teaspoon dried oregano
Black pepper
½ cup dry white wine
½ pound shrimp, with heads
    if possible, peeled
1 pound sole fillets
6 to 8 slices Italian bread,
    fried in olive oil

I love *zuppe di pesce* because they have a lustiness of taste all their own. This Arab-style Sicilian version is flavored with garlic, saffron, oregano, and red pepper. Make sure you get a good mix of fish even if you can't get the ones called for here. Use a deep flameproof and ovenproof terra-cotta casserole that you can bring to the table.

1. Sauté the garlic, onion, parsley, and chili peppers in the olive oil over low to medium heat for 10 minutes, stirring once in a while. Add the fish heads and cover with 3 to 4 quarts water. Bring to a boil, then reduce the heat to medium and add the saffron. Cook for 15 minutes, then add the squid and cook another 15 minutes.

2. Remove the fish heads and discard. Add the yellow pepper and salt and cook for 10 minutes. Add the grouper, red mullet,

oregano, pepper to taste, white wine, and shrimp. Cook for 12 minutes over medium heat. Add the sole and cook for 5 minutes.

3. Shake the casserole so that the flavors mix gently. Taste the broth and add more salt and pepper if needed. Serve with the fried bread.

Serves 6 to 8.

Stuffed Sardines, Palermo-Style

SARDE A BECCAFICO ALLA PALERMITANA

12 fresh sardines
½ cup breadcrumbs
1 tablespoon olive oil
1 garlic clove, finely chopped
1 tablespoon golden raisins or currants
1 tablespoon pine nuts
1 tablespoon grated pecorino
1 tablespoon finely chopped parsley
Salt and pepper
Bay leaves
½ teaspoon sugar
Juice of 1 lemon or 1 orange

The name of this famous dish is controversial among Sicilians. Some believe it comes from a kind of bird, the *beccafico*, that eats ripe figs and is considered a gourmand. The Italian is similar to the French *bec fin*, a reference both to a warbler and a gourmand. Perhaps both words derive from the Sicilian *bufisisu*, a word from Pantelleria derived from the Arabic *bu fassiyuah*, which means "a small warbler-like bird that is a gourmand."

1. Clean the sardines but leave the heads on. Take the backbone out by spreading the fish open and holding the backbone where it meets the head. Slowly and carefully pull the bone toward the tail until it comes out. Pat dry with a paper towel.

2. Sauté the breadcrumbs in olive oil over medium-high heat, stirring constantly, for 3 to 4 minutes. Remove and let cool for 15 minutes. Combine half the breadcrumbs with the garlic, raisins, pine nuts, cheese, parsley, and salt and pepper to taste. Spread about 1 tablespoon of stuffing in each sardine and pinch closed. Lightly oil a baking pan and place the sardines next to one another with a bay leaf between each.

3. Preheat the oven to 350°F.

4. Combine the remaining breadcrumbs with the sugar and lemon or orange juice and sprinkle over the sardines. Bake, uncovered, for 20 to 30 minutes. Serve hot or at room temperature.

Serves 4.

Grilled Sardine Sausages

SASIZZEDDI DI SARDE ARRUSTUTI

2 pounds fresh sardines
½ cup white wine vinegar
2 tablespoons olive oil
¾ cup breadcrumbs, toasted
⅓ cup finely diced
   caciocavallo
1½ tablespoons currants,
   soaked
1 garlic clove, finely chopped
1½ tablespoons chopped
   parsley
1 tablespoon pine nuts
Salt and pepper
2 eggs
Flour, for coating
3 oranges
1 long loaf crusty Italian or
   French bread
Olive oil, for drizzling
Lemon wedges, for garnish
Parsley sprigs, for garnish

This recipe is typical of western Sicily—Palermo in particular. *Sasizzeddi* is the Sicilian word for "little sausage."

1. Remove the heads of the sardines and pull out the backbones and entrails. Wash each sardine with cold water, inside and out, pat dry, and set aside in the vinegar.

2. In a small pan, cook 3 of the sardines in olive oil until they disintegrate. Add the breadcrumbs, stirring with a wooden spoon, until they are moistened. Add the cheese, drained currants, garlic, parsley, and pine nuts. Season to taste with salt and pepper. Mix for about 2 minutes.

3. Stuff each sardine with a teaspoon of the breadcrumb mixture. Squeeze closed, holding the sardine in your hands as if you were praying. Don't worry if they don't pinch shut. Set aside. Or lay the sardines flat, spread some stuffing on them, and roll up from head to tail.

4. Beat the eggs in a shallow bowl. Spread some flour on a piece of wax paper and carefully coat each sardine in egg, then in

flour. Try not to handle the sardines too much. Shake the tray once to shake off excess flour from the sardines.

5. Prepare a hot charcoal fire or preheat a gas grill.

6. Slice the oranges in rectangular shapes, about 1 x 3 inches, leaving the peel on. Slice the bread into the same size and shape. Thread a sardine onto double skewers, then add a slice of bread and a slice of orange. Continue in that order, placing 2 sardines on each set of double skewers. Keep the split part of the sardine up so the stuffing doesn't fall out. When you lift the sardines from the tray to the skewers, use 2 hands and squeeze them a bit. Once they are on the skewer, squeeze them with the bread and orange slices so all the pieces are tight together.

7. Drizzle olive oil over the skewers and place on the grill for 5 minutes a side or until some of the bread begins to blacken. Serve with lemon wedges and parsley. Don't discard the oranges and their peel. You eat everything!

Serves 4 to 6.

Sardine Croquettes

POLPETTE DI SARDE

1¼ pounds fresh sardines
½ cup breadcrumbs
¼ cup grated pecorino or parmesan
1 tablespoon very finely chopped onion
8 mint leaves, chopped
1 egg, beaten
Salt
Sunflower-seed oil, for deep frying
Flour, for coating
1 small onion, finely chopped
1 tablespoon olive oil
½ cup tomato paste

Even today in many Arab countries, fish or vegetable croquettes are prepared with great skill, which indicates that this is an ancient technique. *Edjeidjette es Serdine*, Algerian sardine croquettes, which are similar to these *polpette*, are flavored with onions, parsley, cumin, salt, and pepper. This dish is a specialty of Trapani. Use any leftover sauce with pasta.

1. Clean the sardines well and remove the head, bones, entrails, scales, and the small dorsal fin. Cut the sardines into very small pieces. Add the breadcrumbs, cheese, tablespoon of onion, mint, egg, and salt to taste. Mix thoroughly.

2. Heat the oil for deep frying to 370°F.

3. Shape the sardine mixture into small croquettes, the size and shape of your thumb. Keep your hands wet to avoid sticking. Roll the croquettes in flour and deep-fry them until deep brown, about 2 minutes. Remove and drain on paper towels.

4. Sauté the chopped onion in the olive oil until translucent, about 7 minutes. Add the tomato paste diluted in 2½ cups water. Simmer for 15 minutes. Add the croquettes and continue cooking for 30 minutes. Serve hot with some of the sauce.

Serves 4.

Baked Hake in Sesame Sauce

NASELLO AL FORNO IN SALSA DI SEMI DI SESAMO

1 whole hake, scaled, gutted,
  with as many bones as
  possible removed, and with
  head and tail (7 to 10
  pounds), or 2½ pounds
  hake or cod steaks, 1 inch
  thick
½ cup dry white wine
2 tablespoons chopped parsley
¼ cup sesame seeds, toasted
¼ teaspoon cayenne
1 teaspoon salt
1 garlic clove, peeled
¼ cup olive oil
1 medium onion, very thinly
  sliced
2 lemons, cut into wedges
Parsley sprigs, for garnish

Sesame-seed sauce on fish is typically Arab. In the Arab world the sauce called *tahina* is smoother than the Sicilian variety. A nearly identical dish, called *Samak bil Salsat al-Tahina*, is found in Egypt and the Levant.

1. Preheat the oven to 350°F.

2. Rinse the fish well with cold water and pat dry. Place the fish in an oiled shallow baking pan. If the head and tail hang over the pan cover them with aluminum foil in such a way that the juices will drip back into the pan.

3. Process the white wine, half the parsley, and the toasted sesame seeds, cayenne, salt, and garlic in a food processor until coarsely chopped. Slowly pour in the olive oil. Cover the fish with

this sauce. Lay the sliced onion on top and sprinkle with the remaining parsley.

4. Bake, basting the fish from time to time, until it flakes at the touch of a fork, about 30 to 45 minutes for whole fish, 20 to 30 minutes for steaks. Arrange the fish on a heated platter. Discard the onion and parsley. Pour the sauce over the fish and garnish with lemon wedges and parsley sprigs. Serve immediately.

Serves 6 to 8.

Sweet-and-Sour Salt Cod

BACCALÀ ALL'AGRODOLCE

Olive oil, for deep frying
1½ pounds salt cod, soaked
Flour, for coating
½ cup white vinegar
¼ cup pine nuts
¼ cup golden raisins
1½ tablespoons sugar
Pinch of salt

There are several kinds of salt cod available. I prefer the bone-in or bone-out salt cod sold in ethnic fish stores. Another salt cod is a boxed product from Canada. In any case, you will need to soak the fish between two and three days in two to three changes of water a day. Some salt-cod products require only an overnight soak.

1. Preheat the oil for deep frying to 370°F. Drain the salt cod and pat dry. Cut into 4 equal pieces, coat with flour, and fry in very hot oil for about 3 minutes, or until golden. Remove and drain on paper towels.

2. Combine the vinegar, pine nuts, raisins, sugar, a pinch of salt, and ¾ cup water in a skillet. Bring to a boil and boil for 5 minutes. Add the deep-fried salt cod and cook over low heat for 5 minutes. Stir to cover all the pieces of cod with sauce. Serve hot or cool.

Serves 4 to 6.

Salt Cod Croquettes

POLPETTE DI BACCALÀ

1 pound salt cod, soaked
  (page 175)
4 eggs
1 tablespoon golden raisins
½ tablespoon pine nuts
5 tablespoons very finely
  chopped parsley
1 garlic clove, finely chopped
1 tablespoon very finely
  chopped onion
Salt and pepper
½ cup breadcrumbs, plus
  extra for coating croquettes
Olive oil, for deep frying
Flour, for coating
2 cups Smooth Tomato Sauce
  (page 82) (optional)

These croquettes make a great snack.

1. Bring a large pot of water to a boil and add the cod. Boil for 15 minutes. Drain and remove the bones, cartilage, and skin. Mash the flesh. Beat 2 of the eggs and add to the fish. Mix in the raisins, pine nuts, parsley, garlic, onion, and salt and pepper to taste. Add up to ½ cup of breadcrumbs, 1 tablespoon at a time, until the mixture has a doughy consistency.

2. Heat the oil for deep frying to 370°F.

3. Form the fish mixture into croquettes, about 3 x 1½ inches. Beat the remaining eggs in a shallow bowl. Spread flour on one piece of wax paper, breadcrumbs on another. Roll the croquettes in flour, dip them in egg, and roll them in breadcrumbs. Deep-fry for 2 minutes. Drain on paper towels and serve with tomato sauce, if desired, or without.

Makes 10 to 12 croquettes.

St. Joseph's Pie

Pasticcio di San Giuseppe

Dough
2¼ cups flour
¾ cup sugar
10 tablespoons lard, cut into
    bits
Peel of 1 lemon, grated
3 eggs, beaten

Stuffing
Salt
2 bulbs fennel, bulbs only, cut
    into eighths
1 small cauliflower, florets
    only
¾ pound asparagus, trimmed
    and cut into 1-inch lengths
2 fresh artichoke hearts,
    quartered
Olive oil, for deep frying
Flour

1 pound lean fish steaks, cut
    into silver dollar-size
    rounds, ½ inch thick,
    preferably cod
Flour
1 medium onion, chopped
2 tablespoons olive oil
2 anchovy fillets, rinsed and
    chopped
1 tablespoon capers, rinsed
1 cup pitted and chopped
    large green Sicilian olives
1 tablespoon golden raisins
¼ cup sugar
½ cup white wine vinegar
2 eggs
Salt

Many extravagant dishes in Sicilian cuisine are named after saints and are devotional food for holy days. This fish pie, from Sciacca on the southern coast, may very well have originated as a feast meal for the Muslim *'Aid al-Fitr* (or *al-Kebir*), the holiday that ends the holy month of Ramadan. Al-Maqrizi, an Arab writer of the fourteenth century, describes Easter and Christmas dishes of medieval Christian Sicily as being similar to the Muslim devotional dishes of the Cairo of his day. The outstanding characteristic of these dishes, according to al-Maqrizi, is that they are "substantial," like this one.

1. Work together the flour, sugar, lard, and lemon zest with your fingers until pebbly-looking. Add the eggs and knead to form a smooth, soft dough. Divide into 2 balls, wrap each in wax paper, and refrigerate for 1 hour.

2. Bring a large pot of water to a rolling boil and add salt. Parboil the fennel, cauliflower, asparagus, and artichoke hearts for 5 minutes. Drain and cool.

3. Preheat the oil for deep frying to 370°F.

4. Roll the vegetables in flour and deep-fry, in batches, for 2 to 3 minutes, or until golden. Drain on paper towels and set aside. Roll the fish in the flour and deep-fry for 3 to 4 minutes, or until golden. Set aside.

5. In a large sauté pan that will hold all the ingredients, sauté the onion in 1 tablespoon of the olive oil over medium heat until translucent, about 7 minutes. Combine the anchovies, capers, olives, raisins, and sugar. Add to the onion, along with the vinegar, and cook over medium heat for 6 to 7 minutes, or until the vinegar evaporates. Add the vegetables and fish to the sauce. Mix by lifting with a spatula or large spoon; don't stir or shake. Beat the eggs with a little salt and mix carefully into the vegetables. Lift once more with a spatula and remove from the heat.

6. Preheat the oven to 350°F.

7. Sprinkle the work surface with flour. Roll out 1 ball of dough ⅛ inch thick and place in an oiled 10-inch deep-pie dish. Spoon in the vegetables, fish, and sauce. Roll out the second ball of dough and cover the top, pinching the edges closed. Make several 1-inch-long cuts in the top crust for the pie to breathe. Bake for 30 minutes, or until the top shows some brown spots. Serve hot or warm.

Serves 6.

Stockfish, Messina-Style

STOCCAFISSO ALLA MESSINA

1½ pounds stockfish or salt
  cod, soaked (page 175)
1 medium onion, sliced
½ cup olive oil
2 pounds plum tomatoes,
  peeled, seeded, and chopped

Harald Hardraade, King of Norway from 1045 to 1066, whose adventures are chronicled in the *Heimskringla Saga*, arrived in Sicily as head of the Varingian Guard to fight the Arabs with his Byzantine allies. Harald proved to be a

1½ tablespoons pine nuts
1½ tablespoons golden raisins
2 tablespoons capers, rinsed
12 black olives, pitted and
  chopped
2 large potatoes, peeled and
  sliced ⅛ inch thick
¼ teaspoon salt
¾ teaspoon pepper
1 cup dry white wine

clever and dangerous adversary. To subdue one of the heavily fortified Arab castles, Harald caught some of the small birds whose nests were inside the castle. He tied small splinters of sulfur-coated wood to the birds and set them afire. The flaming birds returned to their nests and the fire spread throughout the castle. The Arabs surrendered. It is thought that the castle is at Abbazia di Maniace, about forty miles west of Taormina.

Could Harald be the source for this wonderful dish? *Stoccafisso* is Norwegian *stokfisk,* and Harald did fight around Messina. But the dish itself is clearly Arab-influenced; witness the pine nuts and golden raisins. The potatoes, of course, were added much later. Salted and dried fish were a staple of the Vikings in the eleventh century and it would not be far-reaching to assume that Harald brought large quantities with him on his travels. Could this dish be the only example of Arab-Sicilian-Norwegian cooking? Try it and pass off the story on your guests.

1. Drain the fish, remove the bones, and cut into small pieces.
2. Preheat the oven to 350°F.
3. Sauté the onion in olive oil in a baking casserole until translucent, about 7 minutes. Add the tomatoes. Continue cooking over low to medium heat for 5 minutes. Add the fish, pine nuts, raisins, capers, olives, potatoes, salt, and pepper. Pour in the wine, cover, and bake for 1 hour. Test the potatoes. If they are still a bit resistant, add some water or wine and continue cooking until done. Serve hot.

Serves 4.

Eel in Sweet-and-Sour Sauce

ANCIDDA A PICCHI-PACCHIU ALL'AURUDUCI

Pinch of saffron
1¼ tablespoons sugar
¼ cup white wine vinegar
2 tablespoons dry white wine
1 tablespoon fresh tarragon
  leaves
1 eel, about 2½ to 3 pounds,
  cleaned and skinned
1 clove garlic, peeled and
  crushed
1 large onion, chopped
½ cup olive oil
2 pounds plum tomatoes,
  peeled, seeded, and chopped
12 fresh basil leaves, chopped
  fine
¼ cup finely chopped parsley
Salt and pepper

Picchi-Pacchiu refers to various sauces made with tomatoes. I was told that the word has no meaning. I was also told that it is a corruption and diminutive of pacchiuni, a coarse Sicilian word for the vagina. Here is another example of the Sicilian penchant for attributing sexual connotations to food.

Tarragon is a key flavoring in this dish. Even though the Arabs introduced tarragon to Sicily (the word comes from the Arabic tarkhoun), it is not in common use.

1. Dissolve the saffron in ¼ cup hot water and set aside. Combine the sugar with the vinegar, wine, and tarragon and set aside. Cut the eel into 2-inch pieces and set aside.

2. Brown the garlic and onion in the olive oil over medium heat for 8 minutes, stirring often so that the garlic doesn't burn. Add the tomatoes and cook over medium–high heat for 8 minutes. Stir in the saffron water, then add the basil and parsley and stir again to mix well. Cover and cook over medium–high heat for 8 minutes.

3. Put the pieces of eel into the sauce, sprinkle with salt and pepper to taste, cover, and cook over medium–high heat for 10 minutes. Add the sugar-and-vinegar mixture and continue to cook for 10 minutes. Remove from the heat, transfer to a serving platter, and serve.

Serves 4 to 6.

Shad Baked in Puff Pastry

ALACCIA 'NCAMMISATA

1 pound frozen puff pastry
4 shad fillets (about 2
   pounds)
Salt and pepper
2 tablespoons olive oil
1 garlic clove, finely chopped
1 tablespoon finely chopped
   parsley
½ tablespoon fennel seed
½ teaspoon red pepper flakes
   (optional)
12 very thin slices of lemon
   (2 peeled lemons)
1 egg beaten with 1 teaspoon
   water, for coating

The making of puff pastry, called *pasta sfoglia* in Italian and known as *millefoglie* in Sicily, is thought to have been taught to the medieval Sicilians by the Arabs and to the French by the Italians, although its roots may also be in medieval Spain. The Italian *camicia* and Sicilian *cammisa* are words for "shirt." Wrapping food in puff pastry, 'ncammisata in Sicilian, is to "enshirt" the food, so to speak. This preparation is from Cattolica Eraclea near Agrigento.

Excellent commercially made puff pastry is available in the frozen-food sections of most supermarkets. Cod is a versatile substitute for shad. For other suitable fish, see page 159.

1. Follow the package directions for thawing the pastry. There are usually 2 sheets to a 1-pound package. Roll each sheet out on a floured countertop to 14 x 11 inches, and divide each sheet in half, to get 4 sheets.

2. Preheat the oven to 350°F.

3. Lay each of the 4 fillets on each of the 4 sheets of puff pastry. Salt and pepper to taste and season with the olive oil. Mix together the garlic, parsley, salt, pepper, fennel seeds, red pepper (if using), and the slices of lemon. Wrap up the puff pastry, pinching the sides with a fork so the fillets are enclosed.

4. Brush the egg on top of each pastry. Bake on a lightly oiled baking sheet until golden brown, about 35 to 45 minutes.

Serves 4.

VARIATION

Add 1 cup chopped green or black olives in Step 2.

Shad with Almonds

SARACÀ CON MENNULE

1 pound shad fillets
2 cups milk
Olive oil, for deep frying
Salt and pepper
Flour, for coating
½ cup blanched and very
  finely chopped almonds
¼ cup olive oil
¼ finely chopped parsley
Juice of 1 lemon

In Sicilian dialect shad is called *alaccia* but also *saracà*, from the Arabic. Shad has many small bones; fortunately it is almost always sold already filleted. This dish is also good made with perch, cod, hake, or red snapper.

1. Cut the fish into bite-size pieces. Place in a bowl and cover with the milk. Leave to soak for 1 hour.

2. Heat the oil for deep frying to 370°F. Preheat the oven to 150°F.

3. Drain the fish and sprinkle with salt and pepper. Roll the pieces in flour until they are well coated. Deep-fry until golden, 2 to 3 minutes. Place in an oven-proof serving platter and keep warm in the oven while you make the sauce.

4. Sauté the almonds in the ¼ cup olive oil over moderate heat until they turn color, 3 to 4 minutes. Add the parsley, lemon juice, and salt and pepper to taste. Stir vigorously for a few seconds, then pour over the fish. Serve immediately.

Serves 4.

Amberjack in Ghiotta

ARICCIOLA ALLA GHIOTTA

1 medium onion, thinly sliced
¼ cup olive oil
2 celery stalks, finely chopped

This preparation is probably from *cucina pantesca*, the cuisine of the island of Pantelleria. Dotted with Moorish-

2 tablespoons pitted and
   chopped green Sicilian
   olives
2 tablespoons capers, rinsed
   and chopped
¾ pound plum tomatoes,
   peeled, seeded, and chopped
Salt
4 amberjack fillets (about 1½
   pounds)

style villas called *dammuso*, Pantelleria is a serene summer vacation destination and famous for its capers. The sautéing of celery, olives, tomatoes, and capers provides the clue to this extraordinary cuisine. The best alternative to amberjack, also called rudderfish or Florida Jack, in this recipe is cod, although you could use red snapper, pompano, or striped bass as well.

1. In a skillet large enough to hold all the fish, sauté the onion in the olive oil over medium heat until golden, about 8 minutes. Add the celery, olives, and capers and continue cooking for 4 minutes. Add the tomatoes, lower the heat to a simmer, and cook for 35 minutes, or until the sauce has thickened. Add salt to taste.

2. Place the fish in the pan and cover. Simmer for 8 minutes. Using a spatula, delicately turn the fish over. Continue cooking for 8 minutes. Serve the fish hot, covered with sauce.
   Serves 4.

Baked Amberjack, Arab-Style

A*RICCIOLA ALLA* S*ARACENA*

1 tablespoon finely chopped
   garlic
1 tablespoon finely chopped
   parsley
2 tablespoons pitted and
   chopped black olives
2 tablespoons capers, rinsed
   and chopped
6 tablespoons olive oil
6 amberjack fillets (2 to 2½
   pounds)
1 tablespoon dried oregano
Salt and pepper
6 ripe tomatoes, peeled
½ cup dry white wine

This recipe provides powerful flavor in a short amount of time; it is extremely easy to prepare. Nearly any fish will go well with this sauce.

1. Preheat the oven to 350°F.

2. Mix together the garlic, parsley, olives, and capers. Pour 2 tablespoons of the olive oil into a baking casserole and arrange the fish fillets. Sprinkle the fish with oregano and salt and pepper to taste. Cut the tomatoes in half and remove the seeds and pulp. Divide the caper mixture among the tomato halves. Turn each tomato half upside down on top of the fish fillets. Pour 2 tablespoons of the olive oil over the tomatoes.

3. Bake for 15 minutes, then sprinkle the wine over the fish and baste with the pan juices and the remaining olive oil. Bake for another 15 minutes and serve.

Serves 6.

Melting Bluefish

SPADOLA ALLA STEMPERATA

1½ pounds bluefish fillets
Flour, for coating
¾ cup olive oil
1 garlic clove, crushed and peeled
2 tablespoons white wine vinegar
1 cup fresh mint leaves, finely chopped
Salt and black pepper
Mint sprigs, for garnish

Chef Pasqualino Giudice's restaurant in Syracuse, the Jonico 'a Rutta 'e Ciauli (literally, The Ionian by the Crow's Nest), sits high above the azure sea below. Preparations for *alla stemperata* are typical of Syracuse. Pasqualino, who gave me the recipe for this dish, uses *spadola*, a long, flat, silver fish that looks like a shovel; it is related to the bluefish family. He is convinced that this dish is Arab-influenced.

If bluefish is not in season, use sea bass.

1. Cut the fish into 2-inch pieces, wash them, and dry with paper towels. Coat with flour.

2. Heat all but 2 tablespoons of the oil until smoking hot. Fry the fish 2 to 3 minutes a side. Turn with tongs. Drain on paper towels and set aside.

3. In another skillet, heat the remaining olive oil; brown the garlic and discard. Add the fried fish to the pan and sprinkle with the vinegar, ½ cup water, the mint leaves, and salt and pepper to taste. Cover the pan and cook over low to medium heat for 5 minutes. Serve immediately with the juices and mint sprigs. This dish is also good at room temperature.

Serves 4.

Salted Dried Tuna Roe

BOTTARGA

About 1 to 2 pounds roe,
    preferably tuna
Olive oil
2 to 4 cups sea salt

Originally *bottarga* was made from mullet roe and its production has been known since Pharaonic Egypt. In western Sicily it is now made from tuna roe, dried, salted, and pressed into a tight sausage shape. As with so many tuna products, *bottarga* comes from the innovations introduced by the Arabs. The method of preparation is identical in Sicily and Egypt.

Bottarga is nearly impossible to find in the United States, which is a great shame. In fact, it is nearly impossible to find tuna roe to make it yourself. That is why I suggest other kinds of roe. Ask your fishmonger to get for you the roe from a tuna, albacore, bonito, cod, or bluefish. The roe should still be in the ovarian membrane. Examine the roe to make sure there are no breaks in the membrane. When cooking with *bottarga*, cut off a piece and rinse the salt off. It is a powerful flavor and you will never need more than a cup at a time.

1. Rinse the roe and dry well with paper towels. Brush the roe carefully with olive oil and then gently roll it in about 1 cup of sea salt. Arrange the roe on a wooden board on top of several layers of paper towels and put in a warm place, such as inside a turned-off oven. Change the paper towels as soon as they become saturated. Add more salt, turning the roe on all sides. Continue for about 2 days, or until the roe is dry and hard. It should be stiff and hard, but not rock hard.

2. With the salt still on, wrap the *bottarga* in wax paper. Wrap in plastic wrap. Keep in the refrigerator for 4 months or in the freezer for even longer.

Makes about 1 pound.

Marinated Tuna

Tunnina Ammarinata

2 large onions, thinly sliced
⅓ cup olive oil
Salt and pepper
3 tablespoons vinegar
3 tablespoons sugar
2 pounds fresh tuna, cut into
  1- to 2-inch pieces
Finely chopped mint, for
  garnish (optional)

Nearly all tuna recipes come from western Sicily, where the tuna industry is based. The ancient Greeks had established *tunnare*, tuna-processing plants, in Messina, but today that city does not provide many tuna recipes.

Sicilians never eat their tuna raw or rare. Nor do they overcook it. Don't be tempted to cut this recipe in half: Part of the pleasure is to serve it the next day for lunch or as an appetizer.

1. Cook the onions in ½ cup water over high heat for 5 minutes, or until the water evaporates. Reduce the heat to medium and pour in ¼ cup of the olive oil. Cook for another 7 minutes.

2. Season the onions with salt and pepper to taste. Add the vinegar and sugar. Cook for 2 minutes. Add the tuna and the remaining olive oil. Simmer over lower heat until the tuna is cooked but not dry, about 4 minutes. Check the tuna: The inside should be pink. If it's purple, cook for 1 or 2 minutes longer. It will continue to cook after you take it off the heat. Sprinkle with mint if you like. Serve hot immediately or at room temperature the next day.

Serves 6.

Tuna and Orange al Cartoccio

Tunnu 'Ncartatu

4 tuna steaks, ½ inch thick
  (about 2 pounds)
Juice of 1 lemon
Olive oil or butter
Salt and pepper

Even in Sicily it is common to use aluminum foil for steaming *al cartoccio* (literally, in a paper bag). This will work, but for guests it seems to me more elegant to use parchment paper. When

1 cup finely chopped parsley
8 thin slices orange
4 tablespoons orange juice

punctured, it will puff its aroma of tuna, orange, and parsley. This recipe is probably not very old, but the marriage of fish with citrus is definitely Arab in inspiration.

1. In a ceramic or glass dish, marinate the tuna in lemon juice for 20 minutes. Cut 8 pieces of aluminum foil or cooking parchment paper, 12 x 12 inches (see Note), and grease 4 of them with the olive oil or butter.

2. Preheat the oven to 350°F.

3. Drain the tuna and place 1 steak on each half of the greased pieces of foil or paper. Sprinkle with salt and pepper to taste and the parsley and place 2 orange slices on top of each steak. Pour 1 tablespoon orange juice over each tuna steak. Fold the other half of the heart over and crimp the edges tight so no liquid or steam can escape. Bake for 10 minutes.

Serves 4 to 6.

Note: To cut the parchment paper or aluminum foil, fold the paper in half. With the fold on your left, trace half of a heart with a pencil. Make sure the top part of the heart touches the top of the paper or foil and that the right side of the heart touches the right of the paper or foil. Cut out with scissors.

Sweet-and-Sour Tuna

Tonno in Agrodolce

1 tuna steak, 1 inch thick
   (about 1 pound)
Flour, for coating
3½ tablespoons olive oil
1 large onion, thinly sliced
¼ cup white wine vinegar
1 teaspoon sugar
5 tablespoons finely chopped
   mint
Salt

I first read about this savory and simple dish in Mimmetta Lo Monte's first book on Sicilian cuisine, *La Bella Cucina*. I finally tasted it in a trattoria in Trapani while watching Sicilian stevedores load a ship for Tunis.

1. Preheat the oven to 150°F.

2. Dredge the tuna in the flour and shake off any excess.

Sauté in 2½ tablespoons of the olive oil over medium heat, for 2 minutes a side. Set aside in a warm oven.

3. In the same skillet, heat the remaining olive oil and sauté the onion for 3 minutes, stirring occasionally. Pour in the vinegar and sprinkle with the sugar, the mint, and salt to taste. Mix well.

4. Return the fish to the skillet. Cover and simmer for 5 minutes over medium heat, shaking the pan every minute to avoid sticking or burning. Transfer the tuna to a plate and let stand 10 minutes before serving.

Serves 2 to 4.

Baked Tuna Rolls

INVOLTINI DI TONNO ARROSTITI

2 large tomatoes, peeled,
   chopped, and seeded
2 garlic cloves, peeled
1 cup parsley leaves
6 tablespoons olive oil
1 tablespoon white wine
   vinegar
1 teaspoon dried oregano
1 teaspoon pepper
Salt
1½ pounds tuna, sliced ¼
   inch thick
1 tablespoon crumbled dried
   sage
1 tablespoon crumbled bay
   leaf
1 tablespoon dried rosemary
   leaves
1 teaspoon red pepper flakes

This piquant tuna dish is covered with a refreshing tomato-and-parsley pesto, which contrasts with the hot spicing.

1. Prepare a pesto by pounding the tomatoes, garlic, and parsley together in a mortar or in a heavy deep ceramic bowl. Or process them in a food processor, using 8 to 10 short bursts of 2 seconds each. Add 3 tablespoons of the olive oil, the vinegar, oregano, and pepper, and salt to taste. Set aside.

2. Flatten the pieces of tuna carefully between 2 pieces of wax paper with a mallet or the side of a heavy cleaver. Each piece

should be about ¹⁄₁₆ inch thick. Spread out the sage, bay leaf, rosemary, and pepper flakes on a piece of wax paper or small plate. Season each slice of tuna with a pinch of each. Sprinkle each lightly with salt. Roll up the slices and secure with a toothpick if necessary.

3. Preheat the oven to 375°F.

4. Grease the bottom of a baking dish with 1 tablespoon of the olive oil. Place the tuna rolls in the dish and cover with the remaining olive oil. Bake for 10 minutes. Pour the sauce over the tuna, roast for 3 to 4 minutes, and serve.

Serves 4.

Fried Tuna Rolls with Wine and Onions

INVOLTINI DI TONNO IN TEGAME

1½ pounds tuna, sliced ¼
  inch thick
½ cup breadcrumbs
¼ cup grated caciocavallo or
  pecorino
2 tablespoons golden raisins
2 tablespoons pine nuts
2 large onions, thinly sliced
⅓ cup olive oil
Salt and pepper
1 cup white wine

In this preparation, slices of tuna are rolled with raisins and cheese.

1. Flatten the pieces of tuna carefully between 2 pieces of wax paper with a mallet or the side of a heavy cleaver. Each piece should be about ¹⁄₁₆ inch thick.

2. Mix together the breadcrumbs, cheese, raisins, and pine nuts. Place 1 to 2 tablespoons of the mixture on one end of the tuna slice, roll it up, and secure with a toothpick if necessary.

3. Sauté the onions in olive oil over medium heat until translucent, about 7 minutes. Add the tuna rolls, season with salt and pepper to taste, and pour in the wine. Cook uncovered, over moderate heat for 8 to 10 minutes. Turn the rolls over several times and watch closely, since they easily overcook. I like the center of the tuna a little pink, although it is not traditional among Sicilians.

4. Transfer the tuna rolls to a platter and spoon the onions on top with a slotted spoon. Serve immediately.

Serves 4 to 6.

Poached Tuna, the Captain's Way

Tunnu Squadatu d'u Capu Rais

1½ pounds fresh tuna, in 1 piece (about 2 inches thick)
Cold water, salted with sea salt
½ cup milk
2 large lemon slices, peeled and seeded
1 cup finely chopped parsley
¼ cup olive oil
Juice of ½ lemon
Salt and pepper

In Trapani, on the western side of the island, a small tuna industry remains. The tuna hunt, the *mattanza*, is now something of a tourist attraction since the tuna have diminished. The captain of the hunt is known as *il rais*, an Arabic word meaning chief. Supposedly, this is the way he likes his tuna prepared, very simply.

1. Place the tuna in a sauté pan and almost cover with the salted water. Add the milk and one slice of the lemon. Bring to a boil, then reduce to a simmer. Cook for 20 minutes. Drain and set aside.

2. While the tuna is cooking, combine the parsley, olive oil, lemon juice, and salt and pepper to taste. Mix well. Pour the sauce over the tuna. Carve the tuna at the table, cutting with the grain to get thin slices. Serve with the other slice of lemon.

Serves 4.

Tuna Croquettes

Polpette di Tonno

1 pound tuna, preferably from the belly
3 tablespoons breadcrumbs
1 egg, beaten

These tuna croquettes are a specialty in Trapani. They are fried, then simmered in a fresh tomato sauce, which can also be used over pasta.

1 tablespoon grated pecorino
1 teaspoon golden raisins
1 teaspoon pine nuts
Salt and pepper
Flour, for coating
1 cup olive oil
1 garlic clove, crushed and
   peeled
1½ pounds plum tomatoes,
   peeled, seeded, and chopped
2 tablespoons chopped parsley

1. Mash the tuna in a bowl with the back of a wooden spoon, removing any sinews or skin. Add the breadcrumbs, egg, cheese, raisins, and pine nuts. Mix thoroughly until you have a doughy paste. Lightly salt and pepper the mixture. Form it into oval croquettes, about 3 x 1½ inches.

2. Roll the croquettes in flour and shake off the excess. Heat the oil until very hot. Fry the croquettes, in batches, until golden. Remove with a slotted spoon and drain on paper towels. Set aside. The croquettes can be frozen at this point if you wish.

3. Remove half the cooking oil and discard. Fry the garlic in the remaining oil until light golden. Remove and discard the garlic. Pour the tomatoes into the oil. They will spurt, splatter, and bubble while cooking. Add salt and pepper to taste. Cook, uncovered, over medium heat, stirring and breaking up the tomatoes from time to time, until dense, about 20 minutes.

4. Place the croquettes in the sauce and cook for about 10 minutes. Remove, sprinkle with parsley, and serve very hot.

Makes 12 croquettes.

VARIATIONS

Moisten the breadcrumbs in milk. Simmer the croquettes in wine instead of tomato sauce.

Sicilian Seviche

SCHIBBECI

2 pounds tuna, preferably in
    2 pieces, one from the belly
    and one from another part,
    cut not more than 1 inch
    thick
6 tablespoons extra-virgin
    olive oil
3 tablespoons red wine
    vinegar
2 cloves garlic, finely chopped
10 mint leaves, finely
    chopped
2 red chili peppers, crumbled
½ teaspoon salt

Schibbeci, a Sicilian dialect word meaning, roughly, "every which way," comes from the Arabic *iskebeg*, which means marinated. This method of cooking is sometimes called *a scapece*. The famous nineteenth-century Sicilian lexicographer Antonino Traina describes the fish used as being flavored with olive oil, onions, and raisins.

Schibbeci is served at room temperature; it makes a wonderful summer plate. The marinade of extra-virgin olive oil, red wine vinegar, fresh mint, and red chili peppers brings out all the tastiness of fresh tuna.

1. Cut the tuna in cubes. If using a tuna steak, unravel the meat: Find the seam and pull apart until you have one long spiral.

2. Bring a pot with lightly salted cold water to a boil and add the tuna pieces. Immediately turn the heat to medium, so the water is just under a boil. Cook for 3 to 4 minutes. Drain quickly and set aside on a serving platter to cool, spreading the tuna pieces so they do not cover one another.

3. Mix together the olive oil, vinegar, garlic, mint, and chilies. Pour over the tuna. Salt tuna to taste and serve at room temperature.

Serves 4 to 6.

Marinated Fish

PISCI 'NTAMMARU

Olive oil, for deep frying
4 garlic cloves, peeled and
mashed
¼ cup olive oil
½ cup white wine vinegar
Peel of 1 lemon, sliced very
fine
1½ pounds fish, cut into
pieces
Flour, for coating
Salt

The Sicilian dialect word for "marinated," *'ntammaru*, comes from the Arabic word *ta'm*, meaning "appetizing flavor" or "immersed," as in a marinade. Even though Apicius, writing in first-century Rome, described fried fish preserved in vinegar, I believe this cold marinated fish dish of the Arabs is the ancestor to *Sfogi in Saor*, which is traditionally served in Venice on the night of the Feast of the Holy Redeemer in July. The Venetian specialty includes pine nuts, golden raisins, and cinnamon—the classic ingredients of *cucina arabo-sicula*. The dish probably traveled north by virtue of Venice's role as a great trading and banking city in the thirteenth and fourteenth centuries.

Sole, cod, red snapper, grouper, and perch all work well in this recipe.

1. Heat the oil for deep frying to 360°F. Sauté the garlic in the ¼ cup olive oil over medium heat, stirring, for 3 to 4 minutes. Be careful not to burn the garlic. Add the vinegar and lemon peel and remove from the heat immediately.

2. Roll the pieces of fish in flour and deep-fry until golden, 4 to 5 minutes. Salt the fish while it is still hot and pour on the sauce. Serve at room temperature.

Serves 2 to 4.

Shrimp Croquettes

POLPETTE DI GAMBERONI

1 small onion
4 garlic cloves
1 egg
1½ teaspoons ground cumin
2½ teaspoons salt
1 teaspoon pepper
5 mint leaves, finely chopped
2½ tablespoons lemon juice
2 pounds shrimp, peeled
½ cup breadcrumbs
Olive oil, for basting
Chopped mint, for garnish

Carlo di Napoli Oliver, whose mother, Fiammetta di Napoli Oliver, has written extensively on Sicilian cuisine, recommended al-Duari, an Arab-Sicilian restaurant in Palermo, near the port on the Via Emerico Amari. It was too good to be true, for al-Duari reflected the influence of Sicily's newest Arabs, Tunisian and Libyan laborers who arrived in the 1970s and 1980s with recipes like this one.

1. Combine the onion, garlic, egg, cumin, salt, pepper, mint leaves, and lemon juice in a food processor and process for 2 minutes. Transfer to a bowl. Process the raw shrimp in batches, using 10 one-second pulses.

2. Combine the shrimp with the onion mixture. Add the breadcrumbs and mix well. Refrigerate for at least 1 hour.

3. Prepare a hot charcoal fire or preheat a gas grill.

4. Form the shrimp mixture into croquettes the shape of thick fingers, dipping your hands in water as you work so the mixture doesn't stick. Double-skewer the croquettes, 3 at a time, and brush with olive oil. Grill for 5 to 7 minutes a side. Garnish with chopped mint.

Makes 18 to 24 croquettes.

Shrimp with Tomatoes

GAMBERETTI AL POMODORO

¼ cup sea salt
1 pound medium shrimp,
   peeled
1 onion, chopped
1 celery stalk, chopped
½ cup olive oil
1 pound ripe tomatoes,
   peeled, seeded, and chopped
1 tablespoon pine nuts
1 tablespoon golden raisins,
   soaked
1 tablespoon capers, rinsed
Salt and pepper
2 bay leaves

This exquisite shrimp preparation is typical of a style of cooking found around Marsala and Pantelleria, an island halfway between Sicily and Tunisia. Pantelleria is noted for its capers. Its cuisine owes much to the Arabs; it is fresh and simple and features excellent fish. This dish is delicious the next day as a cool and piquant salad.

1. Bring 4 quarts water to a rolling boil and add the sea salt. Boil the shrimp for 1 to 2 minutes. Drain immediately. Cut the shrimp into thirds.

2. In a flameproof and ovenproof casserole, sauté the onion and celery in olive oil over medium heat for 10 minutes, stirring very often. Add the tomatoes, pine nuts, raisins, and capers. Add salt and pepper to taste. Cook for 10 minutes. Stir in the shrimp and bay leaves and cook for 1 minute. Remove the casserole from the heat.

3. Preheat the oven to 375°F.

4. Put the casserole in the oven, uncovered, to bake for 10 minutes. Discard the bay leaves and let stand for 10 minutes, then serve.

Serves 4.

Fresh Snails

BABBALUCI D'U FISTINU

2 pounds fresh snails, in the
  shell, or 10 ounces canned
  snails, or 2 pounds limpets,
  in the shell
½ cup baking soda
Vinegar or lemon juice
Salt
4 garlic cloves, finely chopped
4 tablespoons very finely
  chopped parsley
1¼ cups olive oil
Pepper

This recipe comes from Pino Correnti and Enzo Siena. Enzo is the head of the Syracuse delegation of the Accademia Italiana di Cucina. He says that the snails used can be either *latine* or *saracene*—that is, "Latin" or "Arab." The *saracene* are coarser and grayer than the *latine*.

This dish figures in a Sicilian proverb: *Babbaluci a sucari e donni a vasari 'un ponnu mai saziari* (Snails to suck out and women to kiss, that's all one needs to be satisfied). According to Pino, this proverb comes from the Arab era in Sicily. The name *babbaluci* derives in fact from the Arabic, and the Arabs borrowed the word from the Persians, who use it to refer to curly-toed slippers. Today in Tunisia the snails are called *babbouch*.

This particular species of snail will be impossible to get in the United States, although you can find fresh snails in ethnic groceries. Otherwise use the less satisfactory canned snails. You could also replace the snails altogether with another single-shelled mollusk, such as murex, periwinkle, or limpet. I have used limpets for this recipe and they worked quite well. Be sure not to cook them more than two minutes.

1. Wash the fresh snails or limpets under cold water. Let stand in 4 quarts cold water with baking soda for 24 hours to expunge waste. Wash them under running water and soak for 2 hours in cold water acidulated with vinegar or lemon juice and salt. Drain and put the snails in clear water. Keep changing the

water until it stays perfectly clear for 1 hour. Discard any snails that have not pushed themselves out. Pull off any beards. This step is not necessary with canned snails.

2. Marinate the snails with the garlic and parsley and 1 cup of the olive oil for 2 to 6 hours.

3. In a deep terra-cotta or enameled casserole, heat the remaining olive oil. Sauté the snails with the marinade and salt and pepper to taste over medium heat, stirring or lifting gently so that they don't break, for 2 minutes. Remove from the heat and check one. If necessary, put back on the heat for another 2 minutes. Serve immediately.

Serves 4.

Snails in Pic-Pac

BABBALUCI A PIC-PAC

2 pounds fresh snails, in the
   shell, or 10 ounces canned
½ cup baking soda
Vinegar or lemon juice
Salt
4 garlic cloves, finely chopped
3 tablespoons olive oil
1½ cups chopped parsley
1 pound ripe tomatoes,
   peeled, seeded, and chopped
Pepper
1 pound penne (optional)

Pic-pac is short for *picchi-pacchiu*, a kind of tomato sauce. If you are unable to find fresh snails, use the canned. I have made this dish with fresh conch, which Italian-Americans call *scungilli*.

1. If using live snails, let stand in 4 quarts cold water with baking soda for 24 hours so they can purge themselves. Wash them under running water and soak for 2 hours in cold water acidulated with vinegar or lemon juice and salt. Drain and put the snails in clear water. Keep changing the water until it is perfectly clear after one hour. Discard any snails that have not pushed themselves out. Drain and set aside. This step is not necessary for canned snails.

2. Brown the garlic in the olive oil over medium heat for 2 minutes. Add the parsley, tomatoes, and salt and pepper to taste. Stir well, lower the heat, cover, and cook for 20 minutes. Add fresh snails and continue cooking for another 6 minutes. If using

canned snails, cook for 1 minute. Serve hot in a bowl or as a topping to penne.

Serves 4.

VARIATION

Substitute 10 ounces canned conch for the snails. Add the conch to the sauce in Step 2 and cook 2 minutes.

Baby Octopus Cooked in a Quartara

POLIPI ALLA QUARTARA

2 pounds baby octopus or
  small squid, cleaned
4 garlic cloves, finely chopped
5 tablespoons finely chopped
  parsley
2 tomatoes, peeled, seeded,
  and chopped
¼ cup extra-virgin olive oil
1 teaspoon freshly ground
  black pepper
1 teaspoon salt

This specialty of Arab origin comes from the town of Gela. It was prepared for me by the Syracusan chef Pasqualino Giudice.

This dish was made originally in a *quartara*, a kind of narrow-necked Sicilian earthenware jug derived from the Arabs. The *quartara* would be filled with octopus and sealed, with a tube poking through the seal. The *quartara* would then be placed in the embers of a wood fire. When the octopus was cooked, the neck of the jug would be broken and the octopus served directly from it. You can fashion a makeshift *quartara* with a large pot and aluminum foil. The rim of the pot can also be sealed with ropes made from flour and water.

If you think this dish is not for you, please read on. I invited some friends and their children when I tested this recipe. Several parents declined a taste but the children, not noted for their adventurous palates, tried it and loved it. "Try it, it's really good!" they said to their amazed parents.

1. Rinse and dry the octopus or squid. Chop the garlic and parsley together. Mix all the ingredients and put them into a heavy

enameled baking pan. Cover with a tight-fitting layer of aluminum foil, leaving a small opening. Cover with another sheet of
foil, tightening all the edges so no steam escapes except through
the small opening. Marinate for 2 hours or more in the refrigerator.

2. Preheat the oven to 425°F.

3. Bake for 40 minutes, shaking the pan every 10 minutes.
Serve hot.

Serves 4 to 6.

NINE

Vegetables and Side Dishes

VERDURE E CONTORNI

In both the Arab world and Sicily you will find a great love for vegetables whether raw, cooked in olive oil and eaten at room temperature, or stuffed. Many Sicilian vegetable preparations owe their beginnings to Arab cuisine: dishes of artichokes, fennel, and eggplant.

Medieval chroniclers tell us that Sicilians liked their vegetables dressed with olive oil and lemon juice. This is still true today. Long before we became concerned about healthful foods, the Sicilians were making vegetable dishes that were low in calories and cholesterol, filled with vitamins, easy to prepare, and delicious.

Caponata

CAPONATA

2 medium eggplants, unpeeled
  (2½ pounds)
Salt
Olive oil, for deep frying
Celery stalks, without the
  leafy tops, cut into 1-inch
  pieces
½ cup extra-virgin olive oil
1 large onion, sliced
¾ cup tomato paste or 3 ripe
  plum tomatoes, peeled,
  seeded, and finely chopped
4 teaspoons sugar
1 cup red wine vinegar
2 tablespoons capers, rinsed
½ cup green Sicilian olives
Freshly ground black pepper
½ teaspoon unsweetened
  cocoa powder (optional)

Caponata is a vegetable medley relish served at room temperature; the main ingredient is eggplant.

Most Sicilians think caponata is Spanish. Alberto Denti di Pirajno believes the dish was born on shipboard as a mariners' breakfast, because of the large amount of vinegar, which would have acted as a preservative. Giuseppe Coria, on the other hand, thinks caponata was originally inn food, since the word derives from the Latin *caupo* (taverna). Whichever it is, the sweet-and-sour influence surely derives from the Arabs.

1. Cut the eggplant into ¾-inch cubes. Spread on paper towels and sprinkle with salt. Let stand for 1 hour or more, then pat dry with paper towels.

2. Heat the oil for deep frying to 360°F.

3. Deep-fry the eggplant in batches until brown and crisp and set aside. Dry the celery and deep-fry until edges are brown.

4. Take ½ cup of the oil for deep frying and mix with the extra-virgin olive oil. Sauté the onion in the mixed oil until it changes color, about 6 minutes. Add the tomato paste diluted with a little water. Stir and cook over moderate heat for 15 minutes. Gently stir in the sugar, vinegar, capers, olives, eggplant, and celery. Sprinkle with pepper and salt if necessary. Add the cocoa, if desired. Cook for 10 minutes. Remove from the heat and let cool to room temperature.

Serves 8.

Sweet-and-Sour Eggplant

MELANZANE IN AGRODOLCE

*1 large eggplant, peeled and
  cut into 1-inch cubes (2
  pounds)*
Salt
Olive oil, for deep frying
*1 large onion, cut in half
  vertically and separated*
1 cup extra-virgin olive oil
2 tablespoons wine vinegar
1 tablespoon sugar
*6 fresh mint leaves, finely
  chopped*

This eggplant dish, also served at room temperature, is seasoned with mint.

1. Spread the eggplant pieces on paper towels and sprinkle with salt. Let stand for 1 hour or longer, and then pat dry with paper towels.
2. Heat the oil for deep frying to 360°F. Fry the eggplant in batches, drain, and set aside.
3. Fry the onion in the cup of olive oil on medium-high heat, stirring often until translucent and almost golden, about 15 to 20 minutes. Now return the reserved fried eggplant to the pan with the onions. Cook for 1 minute then add the vinegar and sprinkle the sugar over all. Stir and add half of the chopped mint and salt to taste. Remove from the heat.
4. Transfer to a serving platter, draining off some of the oil. Let cool, sprinkle with the remaining mint, and serve at room temperature.
   Serves 4 to 6.

VARIATION

Add 2 celery stalks, chopped and fried, in Step 3.

Eggplant Croquettes

POLPETTE DI MELANZANE

2 large eggplants (about 4
   pounds), peeled and cut
   lengthwise into eighths
Salt
1 egg, beaten
½ cup freshly grated pecorino
¼ cup fresh basil leaves,
   finely chopped
1 garlic clove, finely chopped
Pepper
1⅓ cups breadcrumbs
Flour, for coating
Sunflower-seed oil, for deep
   frying

There are many different recipes for this popular dish. Some cooks add nutmeg; others serve the *polpette* with tomato sauce. If you like, you can add half a cup more pecorino cheese.

1. Spread the eggplant pieces on paper towels and sprinkle with salt. Let stand for 1 hour or longer, then pat dry with paper towels. Bring a large pot of lightly salted water to a boil. Add the eggplant pieces and simmer for 20 minutes. Drain.

2. When the eggplants are cool, mash them with a fork or food processor together with the egg, cheese, basil, garlic, and salt and pepper to taste. Add enough breadcrumbs to obtain a soft paste, starting with ¾ cup all at once, then a little at a time. Shape into croquettes the size of a walnut. Dip your hands into cold water so that the paste doesn't stick. Roll the croquettes in flour and place them on a tray in the refrigerator for 15 minutes.

3. Heat the oil for deep frying to 360°F.

4. Fry the croquettes until golden. Drain on paper towels and serve.

Makes about 36 croquettes.

Farmhand's Balls

CUGGHIUNE DELL'ORTOLANO

*9 baby eggplants (about 2½
 pounds)*
Salt
2½ cups olive oil
1 cup breadcrumbs
*¼ cup fresh mint leaves,
 finely chopped*
*2 garlic cloves, peeled and
 finely chopped*
*3 tablespoons capers, rinsed
 and chopped*
Pepper
*6 tablespoons red wine
 vinegar*
*2 garlic cloves, peeled and
 crushed*
3 tablespoons sugar

The ribald name for these stuffed baby eggplants is a play on words, since *cugghiuni* is the Sicilian word for testicles. But when used figuratively, it also means idiot or jerk.

The *ortolani* (farmhands) worked for the *gabelotti* (farmers) in the medieval Sicilian kitchen gardens, an Arab innovation of the tenth century.

You need small baby eggplants for this dish.

1. Slice off the tops of the eggplants with the stem and carve out the interior pulp, being careful not to break the skin. Start with a paring knife, then continue with an apple corer or a long-handled spoon such as an iced-tea spoon. Salt the inside of the eggplants and let them drain, upside down, for 1 hour. Salt and drain the pulp too for 1 hour. Chop the pulp. Save the top parts for a decorative cover if you wish. Dry the eggplants, inside and out, with paper towels.
2. Sauté the eggplant pulp in ½ cup of the olive oil over medium heat for 12 minutes. Meanwhile, stir together the breadcrumbs, mint, chopped garlic, capers, and salt and pepper to taste. Moisten with 2 tablespoons of the vinegar, breaking up any lumps.
3. When the eggplant pulp is ready and looks mushy, stir in the breadcrumb mixture, mixing well. Sauté over high heat for 2 minutes. Immediately remove the mixture from the heat and transfer it to a strainer resting over the bowl you used to mix the stuffing. Let cool for 10 minutes.
4. Stuff the eggplants loosely with this mixture. If you want to plug the openings, use the tops, carving to fit if necessary.

5. Pour the remaining olive oil into a pot that will hold 3 to 4 eggplants at a time and heat over medium–high heat until just before the oil starts smoking, about 8 minutes (360°F.). Sauté the crushed garlic until it begins to turn brown. Remove from the oil and discard. Fry the eggplants for 4 to 5 minutes. Remove and drain on paper towels.

6. Mix 3 tablespoons of the oil you used to cook the eggplants with the sugar and the remaining vinegar in a small sauté pan over low heat. Cover for a minute, then stir to dissolve the sugar. Cover again for a minute, then raise the heat to high. When the sauce begins to bubble vigorously, remove and pour 3 tablespoons of it over the eggplants. Serve at room temperature.

Serves 4 to 6.

Baked Eggplant Rolls

MELANZANE AL BECCAFICO

1 large eggplant (about 2
  pounds), unpeeled
Salt
4 tablespoons olive oil
1 medium onion, finely
  chopped
2 garlic cloves, finely chopped
1 tablespoon finely chopped
  parsley
5 tablespoons breadcrumbs
1 tablespoon golden raisins,
  soaked
1 tablespoon pine nuts
1 tablespoon freshly grated
  pecorino
Pepper
2 bay leaves
3 tablespoons lemon juice

This recipe is the eggplant version of the famous stuffed-sardine dish, *Sarde a Beccafico alla Palermitana.*

1. Cut the eggplant crosswise in ¼-inch slices. Spread on paper towels and sprinkle with salt. Let stand for 1 hour or longer, then pat dry with paper towels.

2. Heat 3 tablespoons of the oil and sauté the onion and garlic until translucent, about 7 minutes. Add the parsley, breadcrumbs,

raisins, pine nuts, cheese, and salt and pepper to taste. Stir and remove from the fire.

3. Bring a large pot of water to a boil and blanch the eggplant until soft, 3 to 5 minutes. Drain.

4. Preheat the oven to 350°F.

5. Place a small amount of stuffing on each slice and roll up tightly, securing the roll with a toothpick. If the slices are not large enough to roll, fold them over the stuffing to form half moons.

6. Arrange the eggplant rolls in an oiled baking pan. Lightly drizzle olive oil on top. Crumble the bay leaves over all and moisten with lemon juice. Bake for 30 minutes. Serve from the baking dish.

Serves 4.

Stuffed Eggplant Rolls

INVOLTINI DI MELANZANE

1 large eggplant (about 2
  pounds)
Salt
Olive oil, for deep frying
1 cup breadcrumbs
1 garlic clove, finely chopped
2 tablespoons finely chopped
  mint
1 tablespoon capers, rinsed
  and chopped
¼ cup olive oil
2 tablespoons white wine
  vinegar

Filling and rolling eggplant slices, as in this recipe, is an ancient method of preparation. Mimmetta Lo Monte showed me a rare nineteenth-century Sicilian cookbook that has an interesting recipe for *Involtini di Melanzane* called *Frittura di Molignane Ripiene*. The stuffing was made with fresh provola cheese, candied orange peel, and cinnamon.

1. Peel the eggplant and cut lengthwise into ¼-inch slices. Spread on paper towels and sprinkle with salt. Let stand for 1 hour or longer, then pat dry with paper towels.

2. Heat the oil for deep frying to 360°F. Deep-fry the eggplant until brown. Drain on paper towels.

3. Mix together the breadcrumbs, garlic, mint, and capers and add salt to taste. Moisten with the olive oil and wine vinegar by slowly pouring in and mixing at the same time. The stuffing should look like wet sand.

4. Place a small amount of stuffing on each eggplant slice and

roll up carefully. Arrange the eggplant rolls in a pattern on a serving platter. Serve at room temperature.

Serves 4.

Eggplant Seviche

MULINCIANA A SCHIBBECI

2 large eggplants (about 4
  pounds), unpeeled
Salt
Olive oil, for deep frying
2 tablespoons olive oil
1 large onion, thinly sliced
1 tablespoon sugar
½ cup white wine vinegar
2 cups Tomato Sauce (page
  82)
10 mint leaves, finely
  chopped
1 teaspoon freshly ground
  black pepper
½ cup finely diced
  caciocavallo or provolone

Schibbeci or a scapece refers to a method of preserving that employs wine vinegar. Originally associated with fish, it is used with vegetables too. This humble dish is one of my favorites and may well outshine your main course.

1. Slice the eggplants crosswise ¼ inch thick, then cut each slice in half. Spread on paper towels and sprinkle with salt. Let stand for 1 hour or longer, then pat dry with paper towels.

2. Heat the oil for deep frying to 360°F.

3. Fry the eggplants until golden. Drain and set aside.

4. Heat the 2 tablespoons olive oil in a large pan and sauté the onion until golden, about 10 minutes. Add the eggplant. Mix very gently, using a spatula to lift. Dissolve the sugar in the vinegar and add. Let it evaporate for 5 minutes, then add the tomato sauce. Simmer over low to medium heat for 15 minutes. Add the mint, pepper, and cheese. Mix well in the pan and cook for 1 minute more. Remove from the heat and transfer to a serving platter. Add salt to taste.

5. Let the dish come to room temperature and serve.

Serves 6 to 8.

Tomatoes Stuffed with Breadcrumbs and Anchovies

POMODORI RIPIENI CON MOLLICA E ACCIUGHE

4 large ripe but firm tomatoes
¼ cup finely chopped onion
5 tablespoons olive oil
4 tablespoons breadcrumbs
1 tablespoon finely chopped
  parsley
1½ tablespoons capers, rinsed
5 anchovy fillets, chopped
2 tablespoons golden raisins,
  soaked
Freshly grated nutmeg
Salt and pepper

Stuffing tomatoes is popular in Sicily and the Arab world. This preparation is a nice amalgam of the earthy and tangy. The mixture of fried breadcrumbs, capers, raisins, and nutmeg will surprise you with its lightness.

1. Slice the tomatoes in half and scoop out the pulp and seeds. Turn the tomatoes upside down on paper towels to drain.

2. Meanwhile, sauté the onion in 2 tablespoons of the olive oil until golden, about 7 minutes. Remove from the heat and add 2 tablespoons of the breadcrumbs, the parsley, capers, anchovies, raisins, and nutmeg, and salt and pepper to taste. Mix thoroughly. Cook for 1 minute over medium heat.

3. Preheat the oven to 375°F.

4. Stuff the tomatoes loosely with the breadcrumb mixture. Combine the remaining breadcrumbs with the remaining olive oil and mix until it looks like bulgur. Spoon over each stuffed tomato. Bake for 35 minutes and serve hot.

Serves 8.

Tomatoes Stuffed with Ground Beef, Rice, and Mint

POMODORI RIPIENI CON CARNE E RISO ALLA MENTA

4 large ripe and firm tomatoes
4 tablespoons finely chopped
  onion
2 tablespoons olive oil
½ cup cooked ground beef
½ cup cooked Arborio rice
1 tablespoon chopped mint
Salt and pepper

This filling preparation from western Sicily resembles Middle Eastern stuffed-tomato dishes.

1. Slice the tomatoes in half and scoop out the pulp and seeds. Turn the tomatoes upside down on paper towels to drain.
2. Meanwhile, sauté the onion in the olive oil until translucent, about 7 minutes. Remove from the heat and add the meat, rice, and mint, and salt and pepper to taste. Mix thoroughly. Taste and correct the seasoning.
3. Preheat the oven to 375°F.
4. Stuff the tomatoes loosely with the mixture. Bake for 35 minutes and serve hot.
Serves 8.

Tomatoes Stuffed with Shrimp and Olives

POMODORI RIPIENI ALLA MARSALESE

4 large ripe and firm tomatoes
4 tablespoons finely chopped
  onion
2 tablespoons olive oil
½ pound small shrimp,
  peeled
(Ingredients continued)

These stuffed tomatoes are typical of the Marsala area; the stuffing sometimes includes *bottarga*, dried tuna roe.

¼ cup green Sicilian olives,
   pitted and chopped
2 tablespoons chopped celery
2 tablespoons chopped parsley
1 tablespoon washed and
   chopped Salted Dried
   Tuna Roe (page 185)
   (optional)
Salt and pepper

   1. Slice the tomatoes in half and scoop out the pulp and seeds.
Turn the tomatoes upside down on paper towels to drain.
   2. Meanwhile, sauté the onions in olive oil until golden,
about 7 minutes. Add the shrimp, olives, celery, parsley, and tuna
roe, if using, and salt and pepper to taste. Sauté for 1 minute on a
high flame. Remove immediately from the heat and spread on a
platter to cool.
   3. Preheat the oven to 375°F.
   4. Stuff the tomatoes loosely with the mixture. Bake for 35
minutes and serve hot.
   Serves 8.

Sweet-and-Sour Summer Squash

CUCUZZA ALL'AGRODOLCE

1½ pounds summer squash,
   such as zucchini or yellow
   squash, peeled and sliced
   very thin
Salt
1 cup olive oil
1 very large onion, chopped
3 large garlic cloves, finely
   chopped
3 tablespoons golden raisins,
   soaked
3 tablespoons red wine
   vinegar
Pepper
¼ cup pine nuts

Sicilians call both summer and winter
squash cucuzza. This dish can be made
with pumpkin, but I prefer zucchini or
yellow summer squash.

1. Place the zucchini slices in a colander or on paper towels, sprinkle with salt, and let drain for 30 minutes, if desired.

2. Heat about ¾ cup of the olive oil in a wide skillet over medium heat. Sauté the onion until translucent but not browned, about 7 minutes. Add the garlic.

3. Pat the zucchini slices dry. Add and cook for 2 minutes, stirring to mix well. Add the raisins, vinegar, and salt and pepper to taste. Cook over low heat for 10 minutes.

4. Meanwhile, sauté the pine nuts in 2 to 3 tablespoons of the remaining olive oil. Add the pine nuts to the zucchini and remove from the heat immediately. Stir well. Serve warm or at room temperature, using a slotted spoon.

Serves 6.

Sweet-and-Sour Summer Squash with Smoked Herring

CUCUZZA BAFFA

*4 yellow summer squash
    (about 2 pounds), julienned
½ cup olive oil
4 garlic cloves, finely chopped
1 pound smoked (kippered)
    herring, cut into ½-inch
    pieces (2 cups)
Salt and white pepper
3 tablespoons vinegar
3 tablespoons sugar
2 basil leaves, chopped*

The Arabs grew summer squash in great abundance in Sicily, and they introduced the sweet-and-sour treatment. Some say smoked herring is an introduction of the Normans in the twelfth century, although it was known by the Romans. This recipe is a modern interpretation given to me by that tireless promoter of Sicilian food, Pasqualino Giudice.

Pino Correnti writes about a similar dish that includes a piece of vanilla bean and cinnamon. He argues that *Cucuzza all'Agrodolce* is a Spanish, not Arab, dish as testified by the saying *a cucuzza vinni cauda d'a Spagna* (pumpkin came warm from Spain), used also in making fun of people who resemble ignorant Spanish aristocrats, meaning that their head is empty inside like a pumpkin.

1. Preheat the oven to 350°F.

2. Spread the squash evenly around in a baking pan. Drizzle with half the olive oil and cover with half the garlic, all the herring, and salt and pepper to taste. Place in the oven and bake for 30 minutes.

3. Meanwhile, combine the remaining olive oil and garlic, the vinegar, and the sugar in a small pan over moderate heat and bring to a boil, stirring constantly. Lower the heat immediately and simmer for 5 minutes, stirring.

4. Remove the baking pan from the oven and pour the sweet and sour sauce over the squash. Before serving, sprinkle with basil. Serve hot or at room temperature.

Serves 8.

Fried Pumpkin Seven Spouts (with Mint and Pepper)

FEGATO AI SETTE CANNOLI

2 pounds pumpkin or hard
   squash, peeled and sliced
12 garlic cloves, peeled and
   lightly crushed
1 cup olive oil
2 tablespoons sugar
¼ cup red wine vinegar
Salt and pepper
2 tablespoons mint leaves,
   chopped

Many writers have told the story of this dish. There once was a street vendor who stood near the Seven Spouts of the Garrafello fountain near Palermo's Vucciria market. He sold sweet-and-sour pumpkin with veal liver, but when veal became too expensive he dropped the costly ingredient but kept the fountain's name.

During the Arab era there was a spring at that spot. Garrafello comes from the Arabic *gharaf*, abundant in water.

This is a subtle dish, so be careful not to overdo the pepper.

1. Clean, peel, and thinly slice the pumpkin. Lightly brown the garlic in ¾ cup of the olive oil. Remove and reserve. Use the same oil to fry the pumpkin slices, in batches if necessary, making sure all the pieces are covered with oil.

2. Return the garlic to the pan, add the remaining olive oil,

the sugar, and the vinegar, and bring to a boil. Remove from the heat.

3. Arrange the pumpkin in a lipped serving platter. Sprinkle each layer with salt and pepper, and toss all the garlic cloves on top. Decorate with the mint. Leave to mellow, covered, in the refrigerator, but serve at room temperature.

Serves 4 to 6.

Fried Cauliflower

CAVOLFIORE A VASTEDDA

1 cauliflower head (about 2
   pounds), trimmed
Salt
Olive oil, for deep frying
½ pound (2 sticks) unsalted
   butter
6 anchovy fillets
Flour, for coating
Pepper

Vastedda or guastedde means a loaf of bread. The meaning here is unclear, but this dish may be related to 'arnabeet ma'ly, the fried cauliflower of Egypt and the Levant, which is similarly prepared.

1. Boil the cauliflower in salted water until slightly resistant when pierced in the center with a sharp knife. Drain, cool, and break up into bite-size florets.

2. Preheat the oil for deep frying to 370°F.

3. Melt the butter with the anchovies. Remove from the heat. Dip the cauliflower florets into the anchovy-butter mixture, then roll in flour. Deep-fry until golden, about 30 seconds. Sprinkle with salt and pepper to taste and serve hot.

Serves 4.

Stuffed Escarole

SCAROLA RIPIENA

2 escarole heads (about 2½
  pounds)
Salt
½ cup breadcrumbs
2 anchovy fillets, chopped
1 tablespoon pine nuts
1 garlic clove, finely chopped
1 teaspoon capers, rinsed
1 tablespoon golden raisins,
  soaked
Black pepper
¼ cup olive oil
½ cup chicken broth

In Sicily a whole head of escarole is stuffed with a typically Arab-Sicilian mixture: raisins, pine nuts, and breadcrumbs.

1. Wash the escarole well in cold water and leave to soak briefly. Drain and blanch in boiling salted water for 45 seconds. Drain and let cool in a colander.

2. Mix together the breadcrumbs, anchovies, pine nuts, garlic, and capers. Drain and add the raisins and salt and pepper to taste. Mix well.

3. Carefully open the escarole by resting it on its stem and peeling the leaves gently apart, without pulling them off, so that it opens like a flower. Push half the stuffing mixture into the center of each escarole and close up again by folding the leaves back to their original position. The escarole can be prepared several hours ahead up to this point.

4. Place both escarole in an oiled pan. Pour the olive oil and broth over, sprinkle lightly with salt and pepper, and cook, covered, for 15 minutes. Transfer to a serving platter and cut each head in half lengthwise. Serve immediately.

Serves 4.

Roasted Onions

CIPOLLE ARROSTITE

6 large sweet onions,
  preferably Vidalias,
  unpeeled
Olive oil
Salt and pepper
⅓ cup red wine vinegar

This recipe is adapted from Carlo Middione. I include it not only because it is delicious but to describe some Arab-Sicilian onion lore.

The great Arab agronomist Ibn al-Awwam, whose work has come down to us as *Kitab al-Filahah (The Book of Agriculture)*, describes the unique Sicilian method of planting onions. Ibn Hawqal, the Arab traveler who voyaged for thirty years, visited Sicily toward the end of the tenth century. He said that Arab Sicilians were lazy because they ate lots of onions, day and night, which damaged their brains. Yaqut, another famous medieval Arab chronicler, observed in his *Mu'gam 'al-buldan* that the citizens of Palermo drank water from wells, despite all the rivers and ponds of the city, because they were stupid from eating too many onions.

Yaqut writes that the Arab doctor Yusuf ibn Ibrahim, in his book *'Ahbar 'al 'atibba'*, concluded that Palermitans ate onions so as not to taste the saltiness of the water. A famous doctor of the time claimed that onions have the peculiar feature of damaging the brain and consequently the senses. "For this reason," the doctor said, "in Sicily there are no intelligent men nor learned scientists; on the contrary it is common to find stupidity, cowardice and lack of wit and religion." Enjoy this dish—but remember what they said a thousand years ago!

1. Preheat the oven to 375°F.
2. Rub the onions lightly with olive oil all around. Season with salt and pepper to taste. Place the onions in a baking pan with high sides, so that they are held close but do not touch. Bake until done, 1 to 1½ hours. The onions should still be a bit firm. Cut them in half, leaving the outer brown skin in place, or make an incision and the inside of the onion will pop out.
3. Place the roasting pan over moderate heat. Add the vinegar, stirring and scraping the pan for about 4 minutes, or until reduced to a thick sauce.
4. Remove from the heat and drizzle the sauce on the onion. The onions can be kept warm in an oven for 30 minutes. Serve warm or hot.
Serves 6.

Sweet-and-Sour Pearl Onions

CIPOLLINE IN AGRODOLCE

1 pound pearl onions
2 tablespoons white wine
   vinegar
½ cup white wine
2 tablespoons butter
Pinch of black pepper
¼ cup sugar

This recipe preparation is very popular. Another version achieves the sweet-and-sour taste with honey and a splash of Marsala wine.

1. To peel the pearl onions, drop them in a pot of boiling water with their skins on. When the water returns to a boil, boil the onions for 10 minutes. Drain and cool. Cut a small tip off the root end and pinch off the skin.
2. Place all of the ingredients in a heavy saucepan, cover, and bring to a boil. Reduce the heat and simmer for 30 to 40 minutes, stirring occasionally. Test the onions by piercing with a paring knife. If the knife goes in easily, the onion is done.
3. Uncover the pan, and shake it for about 5 minutes to caramelize. Remove the pan from the heat.
4. If there is any liquid left in the pan, remove the onions with a slotted spoon and keep warm on the side. Raise the heat and reduce the onion juices. Add the onions and stir. Serve hot or at room temperature.
Serves 4.

Peppers Stuffed with Cheese, Salami, and Raisins

PEPERONI IMBOTTITI CON FORMAGGIO E UVA PASSA

¾ cup breadcrumbs, toasted
¼ pound soppressata, cut into
   tiny pieces
¾ cup grated caciocavallo
¼ pound fresh primu sale or
   mozzarella, diced
¾ cup golden raisins, soaked
¾ cup pine nuts
Salt and pepper
4 to 6 green bell peppers
4 tablespoons olive oil
2 cups Smooth Tomato Sauce
   (page 82)

This Arab-influenced dish is from the Palermo region.

1. Mix together the breadcrumbs, soppressata, caciocavallo, *primu sale,* raisins, and pine nuts, and salt and pepper to taste.

2. Cut a ring around the top of the peppers. Pull out the lid and remove all the seeds. Stuff the peppers loosely with the breadcrumbs-and-soppressata mixture. Put the tops back on.

3. Preheat the oven to 350°F.

4. Pour 1 tablespoon olive oil over each pepper, then stand them side by side in a baking pan. Cover with tomato sauce and bake for 50 minutes, adding water to the baking pan, if necessary, to prevent burning. Transfer the peppers to a platter and serve warm or at room temperature.

Serves 4 to 6.

Peppers Stuffed with Sardines, Caciocavallo, and Capers

PEPERONI IMBOTTITI DI SARDE, CACIOCAVALLO, E CAPPERI

4 green bell peppers
2 cups grated caciocavallo
¾ cup mashed canned
   sardines (two 4-ounce cans,
   water-packed)
2 tablespoons capers, rinsed
   and chopped
Salt and pepper
4 tablespoons breadcrumbs
4 tablespoons olive oil

The pepper was brought back from the New World by Christopher Columbus. In Sicily, as in the Arab world, it was stuffed with aromatic ingredients and baked as in this recipe from the Marsala area.

1. Slice the tops off the peppers and discard. Remove all the seeds. Mix together the cheese, sardines, and capers. Add salt and pepper to taste. Stuff the peppers with this mixture.
2. Preheat the oven to 350°F.
3. Over each pepper sprinkle 1 tablespoon breadcrumbs and drizzle 1 tablespoon olive oil. Place in an oiled baking dish. Bake for 30 minutes. Serve hot.
   Serves 4.

Roasted Peppers with Breadcrumbs

PEPERONI CON LA MOLLICA

1 pound red bell peppers
1 pound yellow bell peppers
1 small onion, very thinly
   sliced
1½ tablespoons olive oil
2 tablespoons golden raisins,
   soaked
2 tablespoons pine nuts
½ cup breadcrumbs

Not only is this aromatic preparation a classic vegetable dish of cucina arabo-sicula, it is also radiant with color.

¼ *cup grated caciocavallo or*
  pecorino
Salt and pepper

1. Preheat the oven to 400°F.
2. Place the peppers on a baking sheet and leave in the oven until the skin blisters, about 20 to 30 minutes. Remove the peppers from the oven, and once they are cool, peel away the skin. Remove the seeds. Cut the peppers into strips and set aside.
3. Sauté the onion in olive oil until it begins to turn translucent, about 6 minutes. Add the peppers and cook over moderate heat for about 10 minutes.
4. Mix together the raisins, pine nuts, breadcrumbs, and cheese. Pour into the frying pan with the peppers and onion, mixing well. Season to taste with salt and pepper. Cook for 2 minutes over moderate heat. Transfer to a serving platter and serve hot or at room temperature.
    Serves 4.

Sweet-and-Sour Peppers

PEPERONI ALL'AGRODOLCE

3 pounds bell peppers
3 tablespoons sugar
3 tablespoons vinegar
¼ *cup olive oil*
Salt and pepper
1 cup Smooth Tomato Sauce
  (page 82)
Pinch of dried oregano
  (optional)

Here's another sweet-and-sour dish that Sicilians love so much. This one is cooked with tomato sauce.

1. Preheat the oven to 400°F.
2. Place the peppers on a baking sheet and roast until the skin blisters, 20 to 30 minutes. Remove the peppers from the oven and once they are cool, peel off the skin. Remove the seeds. Cut the peppers into strips, and set aside. Dissolve the sugar in the vinegar and set aside.
3. Sauté the peppers in the oil, add salt and pepper to taste, cover, and cook over low heat for 20 minutes. Add the tomato sauce and season with the sugar-vinegar mixture. Simmer for 10

minutes, uncovered. With a slotted spoon transfer the peppers to a serving platter and serve hot. Sprinkle with oregano, if desired.
Serves 6 to 8.

Stuffed Artichokes

CARCIOFI RIPIENI

3 medium artichokes, cut in
   half, chokes and inner
   bracts removed
Salt and pepper
Olive oil
⅔ cup breadcrumbs, toasted
1 tablespoon very finely
   chopped onion
1 tablespoon grated
   caciocavallo or pecorino
1 tablespoon very finely
   chopped parsley
½ tablespoon pine nuts
½ tablespoon currants, soaked

This typical preparation is from Agrigento. Another version from Agrigento has the artichokes stuffed with breadcrumbs, garlic, parsley, pecorino, salami, salted sardines, olive oil, and lemon juice. In the Arab world, stuffed artichokes, *ardishawki mahshi*, are often stuffed with ground meat, onions, pine nuts, and lemon juice.

1. Lay the artichoke halves in one layer, cut side up, in a large skillet. Sprinkle with salt and pepper and drizzle with olive oil. Add ½ cup water. Cover and simmer over very low heat until al dente, about 12 minutes. Test for doneness by pushing the tip of a sharp knife into the artichokes. There should be slight resistance.

2. Mix the breadcrumbs with the onion, cheese, parsley, pine nuts, and currants and set aside.

3. Preheat the oven to 375°F.

4. When the artichokes are done, remove from the pan and place them, side by side, cut side up, in a lightly oiled baking pan. Spoon several tablespoons of the pan liquid over the artichokes. Divide the breadcrumb mixture over the artichokes and push it into them. Bake for 10 to 15 minutes until the tops look crisp. Serve hot or at room temperature.
Serves 6.

Almond Artichokes

CARCIOFI ALLE MANDORLE

8 artichokes or 16 baby
  artichokes
Salt
1 cup blanched almonds
½ onion, very finely chopped
5 tablespoons extra-virgin
  olive oil
2 tablespoons flour
4 anchovy fillets
3 tablespoons white wine
  vinegar
2 tablespoons sugar
1 teaspoon lemon juice
2 tablespoons capers, rinsed
8 sweet gherkins (optional)

Baby artichokes are ideal for this recipe. They have not yet formed the
tough outer bracts and will melt in
your mouth. You may find them in
specialty or gourmet vegetable markets.

The sauce for this dish is also good
with cold meats. This recipe makes one
cup of sauce.

1. Peel off the outer leaves of the artichokes and cut off the
top inch. Boil the artichokes for 15 minutes in salted water, then
cut them into quarters (or halves if they are small). Let drain
upside down.

2. Chop the almonds in a food processor until they look like
coarse flour, about 3 to 4 minutes.

3. Sauté the onion in 2 tablespoons of the olive oil over moderate heat, stirring constantly, for 5 minutes. Add the almonds and
cook, stirring constantly, for about 3 minutes. Dissolve the flour
in 2 cups water and stir in. Cook, stirring every once in a while,
over moderate heat, for 15 to 20 minutes. Remove from the heat.
Mash the anchovies in 1 tablespoon of the oil and add to the sauce.

4. Stir together the remaining oil, the vinegar, sugar, and
lemon juice, and 1 teaspoon salt.

5. Pass the onion sauce through a sieve 2 times. Whip with a
whisk, slowly adding the oil-and-vinegar mixture.

6. Place the artichokes on a serving dish. Pour the sauce over
the artichokes. Decorate with capers and gherkins, if desired.
Serves 4.

Sweet-and-Sour Artichoke Hearts

CARCIOFI IN AGRODOLCE

5 to 6 large artichokes or 12
  to 14 baby artichokes
Juice of 2 lemons
3 tablespoons olive oil
1 onion, chopped
Salt
2 tablespoons vinegar
3 tablespoons sugar
2 tablespoons pine nuts

This is a very quick, simple preparation that brings out the full flavor of
artichoke hearts.

1. Pull off all the bracts and remove the hearts of the artichokes along with the stems. Cut the hearts into sixths if large, in
half if small. Place the hearts and stems in a shallow bowl with the
lemon juice and cover with water and salt to taste.
2. Heat the oil in a frying pan, add the onion, and cook over
medium heat until translucent, about 7 minutes. Drain the artichoke hearts and add. Stir, cover with 2 cups water, and cook over
low to medium heat until the water is nearly all reduced, about 20
minutes. Add the vinegar, sugar, and pine nuts. Stir and continue
cooking for 5 minutes. Serve hot or at room temperature.
    Serves 4.

Fennel Croquettes

POLPETTE DI FINOCCHIO

1 bulb fennel (preferably
  wild), trimmed of the top
  half of its stalks
Salt
⅔ cup breadcrumbs
⅓ cup grated pecorino
  pepato (page 41)
1 egg, beaten

In Sicily, as in Tunisia, vegetable croquettes are often served as a side dish or
as an appetizer with various vegetable
salads.

*Sunflower-seed oil, for deep
  frying
1 cup Smooth Tomato Sauce
  (page 82)*

1. Boil the fennel in salted water until tender, about 45 minutes. Drain and chop well, making sure as little water as possible is left; the fennel should be completely dry. Add the breadcrumbs, cheese, egg, and salt to taste. Shape into small balls.

2. Preheat the oil for deep frying to 360°F.

3. Deep-fry the croquettes until brown. Drain on paper towels. Cook in the tomato sauce over low heat for another 5 minutes. Serve hot.

Makes 36 small croquettes.

The Priest's Mistresses' Potatoes

PATATE ALLO SFINCIONE O STICCHIU 'I PARRINU

*½ cup olive oil
2 pounds potatoes, peeled and
  cut into ½-inch cubes
2 red sweet onions, chopped
1 pound tomatoes, peeled,
  seeded, and chopped
3 tablespoons dried oregano
Salt and pepper*

When I asked the noted Sicilian culinary historian Pino Correnti what his latest project was, he told me *cucina erotica*. Knowing how fond the Sicilians are of naming culinary dishes after sexual vulgarities, I asked him to give me an example. He mentioned this dish, apparently named by a famous anticlerical Sicilian poet. In Sicilian, *sticchiu* is a sexual vulgarity and a reference to the popular notion of the lack of celibacy among priests.

When this dish is made with meat its name changes to *sciarabbaddazzu* or *sciarbuzzia*. *Sciarabbaddazzu*, an old Sicilian word for a kind of *focaccia* made into the shape of the female pudendum, is related to *carbuciu* (see page 70). Both words, *sciarabbaddazzu* and *carbuciu*, derive from the Syrian Arabic *karbusa*, which itself comes from the root Arabic word for bread, *khubz*.

1. Preheat the oven to 350°F.

2. Oil a baking casserole with some of the olive oil. Cover the bottom of the baking casserole with half the potatoes, add a layer of half the onion, and then half the tomato. Sprinkle with half the oregano, and salt and pepper to taste. Drizzle with 3 tablespoons of the olive oil, making sure all the potatoes are covered with a thin film of oil. Cover with the remaining potatoes, onions, and tomatoes. Sprinkle with the remaining oregano and more salt and pepper. Drizzle with 3 tablespoons more olive oil.

3. Bake for 1 hour to 1 hour and 20 minutes. Check to see if the potatoes are done by tasting. Drizzle more olive oil over the potatoes if you like and serve.

Serves 4 to 6.

Vegetable Medley with Eggs

CHACHICHOUKA

1 eggplant, peeled and cut
   into ½-inch cubes
Salt
Olive oil, for deep frying
1 medium onion, chopped
1 carrot, peeled and chopped
⅓ cup extra-virgin olive oil
1 large green bell pepper,
   chopped
1 large red or yellow bell
   pepper, chopped
1 garlic clove, chopped
2 large tomatoes, peeled,
   seeded, chopped, and
   drained
Pepper
10 basil leaves, chopped
1 whole dried red chili pepper
4 eggs

Chachichouka is a typical dish of the cuisine of the island of Pantelleria. It is a purely North African specialty popularized by recent Tunisian immigrants in such towns as Sciacca. It is known by the same name in Algeria and Tunisia.

1. Spread the eggplant pieces on paper towels and sprinkle with salt. Let stand for 1 hour or longer, then pat dry with paper towels.

2. When you are almost ready to fry the eggplant, preheat the oil for deep frying to 360°F.

3. Deep-fry the eggplant until golden. Drain on paper towels and set aside.

4. Sauté the onion and carrot in the extra-virgin olive oil over high heat until the onion is translucent, about 5 minutes. Add the peppers and garlic and cook, stirring over high heat, for 5 minutes. Add the tomatoes and cook for 4 to 5 minutes. Add salt and pepper to taste and the basil, chili, and eggplant. Cover, reduce heat to a simmer, and cook for 5 minutes, stirring every once in a while.

5. Uncover and correct the seasoning. Simmer 5 to 10 minutes longer to evaporate any liquid. Break the eggs into the pan and stir everything together. Cover and cook 3 minutes to set. Remove the hot pepper and serve.

Serves 4 to 6.

TEN

Desserts and Drinks

DOLCI E BEVANDE

The glorious orange groves of Biancavilla near Mount Etna are like beacons when you drive through the arid Sicilian countryside in summer. A thousand years ago the Arab-Sicilian poet Ibn Zaffir wrote, "In Sicily the trees have fire in their leaves and water in their roots." And indeed the oranges of Sicily are dazzling in flavor and beauty.

For many Sicilians, there is no dessert more satisfying than ripe fruit plucked fresh off the tree, accompanied perhaps by espresso and some *Mazarisi,* the madeleine-like pistachio cakes from Mazara del Vallo. In most Sicilian homes a bowl of fruit bobbing in ice water is placed on the table after a meal. The most common fruits are apricots, peaches, oranges, blood oranges, mandarins, tangerines, clementines, apples, pears, plums, cherries, and pomegranates. Prickly pears, azaroles, medlars, sorbs, figs, dates, strawberries, and blackberries are also popular. Sweets are eaten at any time of the day, not typically as a dessert course to end a meal.

Sweets are often endowed with mystical connotations, ritual

roles, and deep religious significance. Appropriately, the convents and monasteries of Sicily are the great repositories of Arab-influenced desserts, the so-called *dolci di badia* (abbey sweets). *Crispelle di Riso alla Benedettina*, delicate rice fritters covered with orange-blossom honey, or the heart-shaped *Cuoriccini* were made by the Benedictines. And as late as the nineteenth century, the street cries of Palermo's fruit vendors contained the same phrases one heard in Cairo.

Filled pastries are very popular in Sicily. *Mecucke*, for example, are made from nut flours and filled with a ricotta pastry cream or pistachio preserves. *Nucatuli* are filled with nuts or figs.

The single most famous Sicilian dessert is probably cannoli, which has an Arab heritage. Tubes of fried pastry made with sugar and sweet wine are stuffed with fresh sheep's-milk ricotta, sugar, candied orange peel, pistachios, chocolate bits, and grated orange peel.

Cassata is another famous Sicilian cake with an Arab heritage. "Cassata" comes from the Arabic word *qa'sat*, a kind of large baking pan. Sicilian folklore dates cassata to the fourteenth century. But the very first mention of it is in the Paris manuscript of the *Riyad an-Nufus*, a tenth-century chronicle attributed to al-Maliki. He reports that Abu al-Fadl, an orthodox jurist from the Aghlabid capital in Tunisia, refused to eat a sweet cake called a *ka'k* because it was made with sugar from Sicily, then ruled by unorthodox Shiites.

Over the centuries, cassata became a richly decorated cake of aristocratic proportions. *Pan di Spagna* (a sponge cake) is sprinkled with sweet liqueur and filled with a mixture of ricotta, sugar, cinnamon, candied fruit, and chocolate. The cake is covered with a sugar icing or marzipan, and baroque decorations are added, including candied fruits, such as pears and cherries, and slices of citron twisted into bows.

Sfince, or *Zeppole di San Giuseppe*, a fried-dough specialty for the festival of St. Joseph of Enna, are beloved throughout southern Italy. The word *zeppole* (*zippula* in Sicilian) comes from the Arabic *zalabiyah*, meaning fried soft dough.

Sicilian sweets are often made for the religious celebrations around Easter, Christmas, Lent, and countless saints' days. Al-Maqrizi, a fourteenth-century Egyptian writer, in his book *Al-Mawa'iz*, observed that the banquets of sweets provided during the religious holidays of Christian Sicily resembled exactly the ones made for Ramadan in the Cairo of his day.

Many Arab-influenced Sicilian sweets are not suitable for American home cooking, so I will just describe them. Some sweets survive today with their Arabic names, such as *cubbaita,* a kind of nougat with honey, sesame seeds, almonds, and orange peel, or *calia,* a toasted chick-pea. *Cuccia* or *chicchi* is a sweet wheat dish made for St. Lucia's day. The Sicilian names come from the Arabic *kiskiya,* which is still served today in Egypt, where it is called *kisik.*

Other candies and brittles are often found in the marketplace rather than fancy confectioneries. *Petrafennula,* a hard candy, is made with honey and orange and citron peel mixed with almonds and cinnamon. *Torrone* are almond sweetmeats made with sugar, lemon juice, and vanilla.

Marzipan, called *pasta reale* in Sicily, a paste of sugar, almonds, and egg whites, is another well-known Sicilian sweet. Marzipan, from the Arabic *mahsaban,* a kind of sweet, may have roots in Persia or India. In the fourteenth century, Ibn Battuta, the famous Arab traveler, used the word to refer to a box or vase containing sweets.

The expert confectioners of Sicily used to sculpt marzipan into fantastically real shapes such as pears, apples, and prickly pears. Nowadays special molds are used. Once the marzipan sculptures are dry, they are colored to resemble real fruit. Then they are brushed with liquid gum arabic to make them shine.

Trionfi di Gula, another category of desserts, are usually in the form of layered tarts. They began as sugar sculptures in eleventh-century Islamic North Africa and went on to Sicily and Italy. The Origlione monastery in Palermo makes a famous *trionfu* of sponge cake, pistachio preserves, and pastry cream mixed with pistachio bits. The cake is collared in a thin layer of marzipan and is sometimes doused with a sweet liqueur.

Couscous can also be a dessert. In his book *Great Italian Desserts,* Nick Malgieri tells the story of the origin of *Cuscusù di Pistacchi.* It was created by an Arab cook in the thirteenth-century abbey of the Santo Spirito monastery in Agrigento.

There are many other sweets, such as *Mostarda,* a kind of pudding made from grape juice, cinnamon, almonds, and walnuts. The original recipe can be found in the twelfth-century book *Al Qasd wa'al Bayan,* by Ibn Basal. In Agrigento it is called *tibu,* an Arabic name.

Cucuzzata is a candied squash used in many Sicilian desserts, such as *Cucchiteddi,* a famous dessert of Sciacca and a specialty of the nuns of the cloister of the Santa Maria of Itra monastery. It is made with almonds, sugar, flour, eggs, and *Cucuzzata.* Another of their specialties is *Uova Murine,* egg crêpes filled with a pastry cream and *Cucuzzata,* then sprinkled with confectioners' sugar and cinnamon.

There are so many wonderful Sicilian sweets—enough to fill

a book—it was hard for me to choose among them. So I picked the ones I think you will love.

Pasta Threads with Orange-Blossom Honey

PASTA A VENTO BARBA DI SAN BENEDETTO

Pinch of saffron
1 cup all-purpose flour
1 cup fine semolina flour
Pinch of salt
2 egg yolks
1 tablespoon orange water
⅓ cup orange-blossom honey
Olive oil, for deep frying
¼ cup unsalted finely
  chopped pistachios
⅓ cup diced candied orange
  peel

Honey goes back to antiquity, but using it with pistachios and saffron, as in this delightful dessert, is purely Arab. This is an old, nearly forgotten, specialty of the nobility of Catania and the Enna region. Little pyramids of fried pasta are arranged in a large pyramid, drizzled with honey, and sprinkled with pistachios and orange peel.

This dessert is a kind of *ziriddu*, a confectionery pasta made with honey. The Sicilians learned how to make orange water and essences from the Arabs, and that fact is reflected in the Italian and Sicilian words for orange blossom, *zagara* (*zahar* in Arabic), and the Sicilian word for orange water, *nanfia* (*nafhah* in Arabic).

1. Dissolve the saffron in ½ cup tepid water and let stand for 15 minutes.
2. Combine the flour and semolina in a bowl with the salt. Add the egg yolks and saffron water and knead for 15 minutes until the dough is a smooth ball. The dough will be sticky and crumbly at first. Roll the dough out in a pasta machine or with a rolling pin until ⅛ inch thick. Lightly dust the dough with flour and wrap in wax paper or plastic wrap. Place in the refrigerator to rest for at least 1 hour.
3. Dissolve the orange water in the honey in a small bowl. Heat by setting the bowl in a larger bowl of hot water.
4. Roll the dough into a thin sheet and cut into linguine-size strips. Form the pasta into 8 pyramids.
5. Heat the oil for deep frying to 360°F.

6. Deep-fry the pasta pyramids for 20 seconds, then turn and fry for another 20 seconds. Remove and drain on paper towels. Arrange the little pyramids into a big pyramid on a platter.

7. Drizzle the warm honey sauce over the pyramid. Sprinkle with the pistachios and candied peel and serve immediately. Let each person pull a little pyramid off the big pyramid.

Serves 8.

Whitecaps

NIDI DI SCUMA

¾ pound capellini
Olive oil, for deep frying
½ cup orange-blossom honey
Ground cinnamon
½ cup chopped candied
    orange peel
1 orange, cut in half and
    sliced

In this dish, capellini is shaped into nests and deep-fried, and the crunchy pasta is then covered with orange-blossom honey. Serve this dessert warm as a midday treat or after dinner with espresso.

Scuma is a Sicilian word derived from the Arabic; it means whitecap, and indeed, the angel hair is like the crest of foam on a wave. Sometimes these pasta doughs are called liccumia, from the Arabic rahah al-halqumi, which means literally "treat for the throat."

1. Cook the capellini in boiling water until al dente, and drain. While the capellini is still wet and hot, twirl a large bunch on a table fork. Remove the fork and with your hands form the twirled pasta to resemble a little bird's nest. Make 6 nests. Place the nests on an oiled tray and let stand for 30 minutes.

2. Heat the oil for deep frying to 360°F. Preheat the oven to 150°F.

3. Warm the honey in a small pan. Deep-fry the nests, in batches, for 2 minutes. Drain and place on an ovenproof serving platter. Keep warm in the oven while you continue deep-frying. When all are cooked, drizzle the honey over all the nests and sprinkle with cinnamon and candied orange peel. Garnish the border of the platter with orange slices.

Serves 6.

Sweet Fried Rice Balls

ARANCINE DOLCE

2 cups Arborio rice, washed
1 teaspoon salt
2 tablespoons butter
6 eggs
1/3 cup chopped assorted
  candied fruit
1½ cups ricotta
1 cup sugar
2 ounces canned chocolate
  frosting (optional)
Olive, vegetable, or seed oil,
  for deep frying
Flour, for coating
Breadcrumbs, for coating
Confectioners' sugar, for
  dusting

These deep-fried rice balls are filled with sugar, chocolate, and ricotta cream. They look just like *arancine*. Serve them a while after dinner with coffee or fresh fruit.

1. Bring a quart of water to a boil and add the rice, salt, and butter. Reduce the heat to medium and cook, uncovered, stirring often, for 15 minutes or until the rice has absorbed the water. Remove from the heat. Beat 3 of the eggs and stir in. Add the candied fruit and mix thoroughly. Spread on a platter to cool, breaking up any lumps.

2. Sieve the ricotta into a bowl, pushing through with the back of a wooden spoon or pestle, and mix with the sugar and chocolate frosting, if using.

3. Place some of the rice in the palm of your hand and place 1 teaspoon of the ricotta in the middle. Fold over and form into a ball about the size of a tangerine. Continue until all are formed. Store leftover ricotta in the refrigerator.

4. Heat the oil for deep frying to 360°F.

5. Beat the remaining eggs in a shallow bowl. Spread some flour on a piece of wax paper and breadcrumbs on another. Roll the *arancine* in flour, dip in egg, and roll in breadcrumbs to coat. Let the *arancine* rest in the refrigerator for 30 minutes. Deep-fry the *arancine* until golden, about 4 to 5 minutes. Remove the rice balls and drain on paper towels. Dust on all sides with confectioners' sugar while still hot. Serve immediately.

Makes 10 to 15 balls.

Sicilian Rice Pudding

Risu Ammanticatu

1 cup short grain rice,
 preferably Vialone, washed
3 cups milk
1⅓ cups sugar
1 tablespoon butter
1 tablespoon unsweetened
 cocoa
⅓ cup chopped candied fruit
 or peel
2 cups almonds, blanched,
 toasted, and finely chopped
Pinch of cinnamon
½ tablespoon grated lemon
 peel

This rice pudding, with its almonds, candied fruit, and cinnamon, is reminiscent of Arab puddings and a favorite with children.

    1. Combine the rice, milk, sugar, and butter in a pot, bring the mixture to a boil, then lower the heat to a simmer and cover. Simmer for 25 minutes to 1¼ hours, depending on the kind of rice. Check the rice occasionally. Remove from the heat when the liquid has been absorbed and the rice is fluffy. Let cool.
    2. Stir in the cocoa, half the candied fruit and almonds, and all the cinnamon and lemon rind. Mix thoroughly. Spoon the rice into individual serving dishes. Decorate with the remaining almonds and candied fruit. Serve cold.
    Serves 6.

Rice Fritters

Crispelle di Riso alla Benedettina

½ cup Vialone rice, washed
1⅓ cups milk
½ tablespoon butter
¼ teaspoon salt
1 teaspoon yeast

These *crispelle* are a specialty of the Benedictine monastery in Catania. Traditionally they are made for the feast of San Giuseppe, patron saint of the family—and of pastry chefs.

½ tablespoon grated lemon
  peel
Vegetable or seed oil, for deep
  frying
Flour, for coating
Orange-blossom honey,
  warm, for drizzling

1. Combine the rice, milk, butter, and salt in a heavy pot and bring to a boil. Reduce the heat to low, cover, and simmer until the rice has absorbed all the milk (about 10 to 15 minutes), adding more if necessary. The rice should be creamy but without any liquid. Remove from the heat.

2. Dissolve the yeast in 2 tablespoons tepid water. Let stand for 5 minutes. Add the yeast and lemon peel to the rice. Mix well and let stand, covered, for 1 hour.

3. Heat the oil for deep frying to 360°F.

4. Shape the rice into croquettes, 1 x 3 inches. Roll in flour. Deep-fry for 5 minutes. Serve immediately with honey. Makes 8 to 10 fritters.

St. Joseph's Fritters

SFINCE DI SAN GIUSEPPE

1½ teaspoons yeast
⅔ cup milk, lukewarm
2 cups flour, sifted
¼ teaspoon vanilla extract
3 tablespoons granulated sugar
Confectioners' sugar, for
  dusting
Pinch of ground cinnamon
Vegetable or seed oil, for deep
  frying

This Sicilian kind of doughnut reminds me a lot of New England fried dough. *Sfince* is a Sicilian word derived from the Arabic *sfang*, meaning "fried pastry." In the Arab world today, particularly in Tunisia and Algeria, a kind of fried dough is called *sfenaj*. These *sfince* are also called *zeppole*.

1. Dissolve the yeast in the milk and let stand for 5 minutes. Add the flour, vanilla, and granulated sugar. Form the dough into a ball and work well, kneading until it is soft and smooth, about 12 minutes. Cover the bowl and let the dough rise in a warm spot in the kitchen. Mix together the confectioners' sugar and cinnamon and set aside.

2. Heat the oil for deep frying to 370°F.

3. Form either balls of dough or flat pieces. For balls, pull off about a tablespoon of dough at a time and drop it in the oil. For flat pieces, pull off a handful of dough and flatten it between your palms. Fry them 1½ minutes a side. Remove when golden and drain on paper towels. Sprinkle with the cinnamon sugar.

Makes 8 fritters.

Honey Fritters

SFINCE CON MIELE

2 teaspoons yeast
2 egg whites
1⅓ cups flour
½ teaspoon salt
1 tablespoon melted butter
Olive or sunflower-seed oil,
   for deep frying
Confectioners' sugar, for
   dusting
Honey, warm, for drizzling

This fried dough is particularly light.

1. Dissolve the yeast in ½ cup lukewarm water and let stand for 5 minutes. Beat the egg whites until stiff. Combine the flour, salt, butter, and dissolved yeast. Fold in the egg whites. Cover with a cloth and let rise until the dough doubles in volume. It should look like an extremely thick pancake batter.

2. Heat the oil for deep frying to 360°F.

3. Drop the dough into the hot oil by the spoonful. Deep-fry until golden, turning once, about 90 seconds. Remove and drain on paper towels.

4. Place the *sfince* on a serving dish and dust with confectioners' sugar until they are covered. Serve with honey.

Makes about 16 fritters.

Watermelon Pudding

GELO DI MELONE

1 very ripe watermelon
1 cup sugar
¾ cup cornstarch
¼ teaspoon ground cinnamon
1 teaspoon rose water
⅛ teaspoon vanilla extract
½ cup semisweet chocolate
   bits
½ cup candied orange peel,
   diced very small
¼ cup unsalted pistachio
   nuts, chopped
Jasmine flowers, for garnish
   (optional)

What an exquisite summer dessert! The main ingredients were all introduced by Arab agronomists and traders of medieval Sicily—watermelon, cinnamon, jasmine, candied orange, and pistachios. It is often served at the festival of Santa Rosalia, patron saint of Palermo. The traditional recipe calls for jasmine water and *cucuzzata* (candied squash), and the pudding is decorated with jasmine flowers.

1. Remove the pulp from the melon and take out seeds. Liquefy the pulp in a food processor or cut it into small pieces and force them through a sieve twice. Measure 5 cups of watermelon juice and set aside.

2. Stir the sugar and cornstarch together in a saucepan over low to medium heat. Slowly add the watermelon juice, stirring constantly, until the sugar and cornstarch are dissolved. Cook, stirring, until the pudding begins to boil, about 15 minutes. Remove from the heat and stir in the cinnamon, rose water, and vanilla. The pudding should be thick and velvety.

3. Let cool completely. Add the chocolate bits and candied peel. Wet 8 to 10 individual dessert bowls or molds and pour the mixture in. Chill in the refrigerator overnight. Unmold or leave in the bowls or molds and serve garnished with chopped pistachios and a jasmine flower, if available.

Serves 8 to 10.

VARIATION

Pour the watermelon pudding into a large serving bowl for a spectacular effect.

Zabaglione

ZABAIONE

4 egg yolks
¼ cup sugar
½ cup Marsala
4 small strawberries
   (optional)
4 mint leaves (optional)

Zabaglione, a delicious foam of Marsala wine, egg yolks, and sugar, must be one of Italy's most famous desserts. It is usually served warm, but I prefer this chilled version.

All kinds of theories have been advanced about the origins of zabaglione—that it comes from the Greeks, or from the French word *sabayon*, or from the seventeenth-century chef of Carlo Emanuele I of Savoy. But I believe it might have its roots with the Arabs. The Sicilian word *zabbina* comes from the Arabic word *zabad*, meaning "foam of water and other things." *Zabbina* means to whip while cooking, which is what you do to make zabaglione.

1. Combine the egg yolks, sugar, and Marsala in the top of a double boiler. Bring the water to a boil, whisking the egg mixture all the while. Continue until well blended, thick, and frothy, about 4 minutes after the water starts to boil. Remove from the heat immediately.

2. Pour into 4 large wineglasses and place in the refrigerator for a few hours. Decorate with strawberries and mint leaves, if desired.

Serves 4.

Pistachio Cakes

MAZARISI

⅔ cup unsalted shelled and
   peeled pistachio nuts
½ cup sugar
1 potato or 1 teaspoon potato
   starch

This is a typical dessert made for festivals in Mazara del Vallo. These delicious madeleine-like cakes are delightful served with a dessert wine.

½ teaspoon salt
¼ cup plus 2 tablespoons
  flour
11 egg yolks
Grated peel of 1 orange
3 egg whites
Butter

1. Grind the pistachios in a food processor with the sugar. Peel and grate the potato. Let stand, covered with cold water, for 1 hour. The sediment at the bottom of the bowl is the starch. Pour off the water and spoon out the starch.

2. Pour the pistachio-and-sugar mixture into a mixing bowl. Add the salt, flour, and potato starch, and the egg yolks, one at a time, mixing gently after adding each one. Stir in the orange peel. Beat the egg whites until stiff and gently fold into the batter.

3. Preheat the oven to 325°F.

4. Grease small oval molds with butter and fill them with batter. Bake for 30 minutes, or until firmly set. Remove from the molds while still hot and let cool on a greased cake rack.

Makes 24 cakes.

Almond Pastries

NUCATULI

FILLING
½ pound almonds, blanched
8 small dried California figs,
  finely chopped (optional)
1 cup sugar
¼ teaspoon cinnamon
½ teaspoon rose water

DOUGH
2 cups flour
2 egg yolks
3 tablespoons butter or lard
4 tablespoons sugar
½ tablespoon vanilla extract
⅓ cup Marsala or other sweet
  dessert wine

This filled Sicilian pastry is a typical Christmas sweet found throughout western Sicily. Its name derives from the plural of the Arabic *nuqulat*, meaning "confectionery" or "dried sweet." For those of you familiar with Arabic sweets, it is very similar to *karabeej*. In Sicily, when it is made into one huge pastry it is called *La Luna di Maometto* (Mohammed's Moon).

1. Chop the almonds in a food processor until almost powdery. Combine the almonds, figs, if using, sugar, cinnamon, and rose water and knead together.

2. Prepare the dough by kneading the flour with the egg yolks, butter, sugar, and vanilla. After you have worked the dough well, add the dessert wine and knead the dough into a ball. Wrap in wax paper or plastic wrap and refrigerate for 1 hour. Remove, and when the dough is pliable, roll it out into a thin sheet, about ⅛ inch thick. Cut out 3½-inch rounds.

3. Preheat the oven to 350°F.

4. Put 1 tablespoon of filling on each piece of dough. Raise the sides of each piece of dough and fold and pinch together with your fingers.

5. Grease 2 baking sheets with butter and place the pastries on the sheets without crowding. Bake for 25 to 30 minutes, or until golden. Remove and cool on a cake rack.

Makes 20 pastries.

VARIATION

Add 2 teaspoons grated lemon peel to the dough. Roll out a large circle and place the filling on half. Fold over the other half for a large half moon. Continue as in Step 4.

Nut Pastries

MECUCKE

3 cups almonds
1¼ cups peanuts
1¼ cups hazelnuts
3 cups sugar, or more, to taste
Grated peel of 1 lemon
2 egg whites
1 cup ricotta
2 tablespoons candied fruit or
    peel
2 tablespoons chopped sweet
    chocolate
Butter
Confectioners' sugar

These nut pastries are named after the shape of a dry measure.

1. Preheat the oven to 375°F.
2. Shell the nuts, keeping them separate. Blanch the nuts by plunging in boiling water for 7 minutes. Drain, peel, and toast in the oven until most of the moisture has evaporated. Chop the nuts separately in a food processor until they are like coarse flour. You should have 1¼ cups almond flour, ⅓ cup peanut flour, and ⅓ cup hazelnut flour. This nut flour will feel wet because of all the natural oils. If it feels too wet, or clumps together, toast it for a few minutes more.
3. Combine the nut flours in a mixing bowl. Knead in 2 cups of the sugar and the lemon peel. Beat the egg whites until stiff and fold in. Form into a well-kneaded ball of dough. If the dough is too soft, add a bit of flour.
4. Sieve the ricotta through a strainer, pushing with the back of a wooden spoon or a pestle, into a mixing bowl. Add the remaining sugar, the candied fruit, and the chocolate. Blend well. The filling should be thick. If not, add more sugar.
5. Butter a baking sheet. Take a small piece of dough, roll it in the palm of your hand, make an indentation, fill with the ricotta cream, and close the ball. Place the balls on the baking sheet, leaving plenty of room between them. Bake for 10 minutes, or until light brown on top. Remove from the oven and let cool on the baking sheet. Transfer to a platter and sprinkle with confectioners' sugar.

Makes about 12 pastries.

VARIATION

Fill with *Conserva di Pistacchi* (pistachio preserves). Chop 1¼ cups shelled and blanched pistachios in a food processor until very fine. Dissolve 1¼ cups sugar in a scant ½ cup of water in a saucepan over low heat. Add the pistachios and simmer until a thick toffeelike consistency is reached. Remove from the heat and let cool. This makes 2½ cups of preserves. Use some to fill the *mecucke* as in Step 4. Store the rest in glass jars in the refrigerator.

Azarole Jam

LAZZERUOLE SCIROPPATE

1½ pounds azaroles or crab apples
2 cups sugar

The azarole is a small medlar tree that produces fruit similar to crab apples. The English and Italian words both come from the Arabic *al-za'roor*. The azarole is a common fruit in Sicily, small, round, and red or yellow. This jam has the consistency of applesauce and is served in the same way.

1. Cut the azaroles or crab apples in half and remove the pits and stems. Bring a large pot of water to a boil and boil the azaroles. Just before they are done, about 10 minutes, drain, and purée them in a food processor.

2. Dissolve the sugar in ½ cup water in a saucepan over low heat, about 10 minutes. Stir in the fruit pulp. Simmer until the mixture reaches a jam consistency, about 6 to 8 minutes. Let cool. Store in glass jars in the refrigerator.

Makes 2 cups.

Candied Peel

SCORZETTA CANDITA

Peel of 1 orange
*Peel of 1 lemon, citron, or
   lime*
½ cup sugar

Many Sicilian desserts are based on candied fruit and peel, particularly orange, citron, and lemon peel. The same method lends itself nicely to fruit like cherries. The art of candying peel was brought to Sicily by the Arabs.

1. Bring 2 pots of water to a boil. Drop the orange peel in one and the lemon peel in the other. Boil for 1 minute, drain, and let dry. Cut the peel into thin strips.

2. Bring the sugar and 3 tablespoons water to a boil in a heavy saucepan over moderate heat, stirring constantly. When it begins to foam, remove from the heat. Add the peels, mixing well so that all the pieces are thoroughly coated.

3. Lightly oil a sheet of aluminum foil and pour the peel onto it, separating all the pieces. Let cool completely. Store in a jar in the refrigerator.

Makes 1 cup.

Lemon Sherbet

SORBETTO DI LIMONE

8 lemons
2 cups sugar
3 lemon slices, for garnish
6 mint sprigs, for garnish

Another delightful sherbet of the Arab Sicilians, *Scursunera*, can be found today in western Sicily. It is made with jasmine water and flowers. Since jasmine is the sign of hospitality, the Arabs often used it to flavor foods, tea, and coffee. Sherbet was invented, so the legend goes, by the Arabs, using snow from Mount Etna. The word comes from the Arabic *sciarbat*.

1. Grate the peel of all the lemons and soak in 1 quart water for 2 hours. Be careful not to grate the white part of the rind. Squeeze all the lemons, strain the juice, and set aside. Filter the water through a cheesecloth-lined strainer and discard the peel. Add the strained lemon juice to the water. Add the sugar and stir to dissolve.

2. Place in a bowl in the freezer for 3 hours, stirring every 15 minutes, until creamy and rather dense. Serve in glasses garnished with a half slice of lemon and a sprig of fresh mint.

Serves 6.

VARIATION

Replace 2 of the lemons with unripe (green) lemons if you can find them. Steep 2 or 3 handfuls jasmine flowers that have not been sprayed in 1 quart water for 24 hours. Strain through a cheesecloth and mix with the sugar in Step 1 until the sugar is dissolved. Add a pinch of cinnamon and 2 tablespoons lemon juice. Proceed as in Step 2.

Lemon Ice

GRANITA DI LIMONE

8 lemons
1 cup sugar, or more, to taste
4 lemon slices, for garnish
   (optional)

Granita is more granular than *sorbetto*. The three most popular *granita* flavors are lemon, coffee, and almond. *Granita di mandorla* (almond ice) is made with *latte di mandorla* (almond milk), an Arab infusion of crushed almonds in water.

1. Grate the peel of 2 of the lemons. Squeeze all the lemons and strain the juice. Add the peel to the juice. Stir the lemon juice with 1 cup sugar in a saucepan over low heat until the sugar is dissolved. Taste the juice. If you would like it sweeter, add more sugar. Pour the juice into an ice-cube tray and place in the freezer until frozen.
2. When ready to use, put the lemon ice cubes into a food processor or blender and crush. Serve in a glass, decorated with a slice of lemon, if desired.
   Serves 4.

VARIATION

Replace 2 of the lemons with unripe (green) lemons.

Coffee Ice

GRANITA DI CAFFÉ

¾ cup brewed Italian-roast
   coffee
1 cup sugar

The Arabs brought coffee to Sicily from Yemen. Later I read that the Qays and Quraysh tribes of the Yemen, part of the ninth-century Arab invasion force, had settled in Palermo. Then I began to wonder whether the cuisines of Sicily and Yemen had some connection—but no, I had been in the sun too long. A cool *Granita di Caffé* brought me to my senses.

1. Brew the coffee, making it strong. Let cool. Combine the sugar with 3 cups water in a saucepan over moderate heat. Stir until the sugar is dissolved. Cook until a syrup is formed.

2. Cool the syrup, then add the coffee. Pour into an ice tray without its dividers, and place in the freezer. Stir once every 30 minutes for 3 hours.

Serves 4.

VARIATION

Freeze solid, then break up in a food processor, blender, or ice crusher.

Elixir

ELISIR

1 quart 100-proof vodka
1 cinnamon stick
1 tablespoon anise seeds
5 cloves
15 mint leaves
1 vanilla bean
1 cup sugar
1¼ cups orange-blossom
  water
Pinch of saffron

I had heard about this drink from Tommaso d'Alba and later read about it in Giuseppe Coria's cookbook. I leave it to you whether you drink it as a phenomenon or as a medicine.

The Arabic word *al-iksir,* or elixir, means the medicine of long life. Alcohol, from the Arabic *al-kuhul,* was used as a disinfectant and medicine, and not as a liqueur, since Muslims were prohibited by the Koran from imbibing alcoholic beverages. Even so, some alcohol and especially wine must have been drunk by the Muslims, because Arab-Sicilian poets have written so many eulogies of wine. In Sicilian dialect a perfect wine is known as *taibbi,* which comes from the Arabic word *tayb,* meaning "just right."

Mmiscu, a liqueur made from a base of anise and *rosolio* (a spirit made from the moscatello raisin and sugar), comes from the Arabic word for musk, *miski,* because it has a musky odor.

1. Sterilize an old 2-quart juice jar and pour in the vodka. Add the cinnamon, anise, cloves, mint, and vanilla. Close tightly and let steep in a dark place for 1 week. Pour the elixir through a cheesecloth-lined strainer and discard the residue. Return the elixir to the jar.

2. Combine the sugar with 2 cups water in a saucepan and bring to a boil. Stir often, scraping down crystals clinging to the side of the pan. Cook the syrup over moderate heat for 5 minutes without stirring. Remove from the heat and let cool. You should have about 2½ cups syrup.

3. Combine the sugar syrup and the orange-blossom water with the saffron and let stand for 5 minutes, stirring occasionally. Add to the vodka and let it sit for 7 days. Store as you would any liquor.

Makes 1½ quarts.

Anise Liqueur

ZAMMÚ

1 quart 100-proof vodka
¾ cup sugar
¼ cup aniseed
Grated peel of 1 lemon

This liqueur, now quite famous as sambuca, was originally an Arab-Sicilian invention for medicinal and disinfectant purposes. The taste is similar to Pernod or ouzo.

Combine the vodka, sugar, aniseed, and lemon peel in a sterilized 2-quart juice jar or other bottle. Mix and let stand for 30 days, shaking it from time to time. Filter it and bottle it, and it is ready to use.

When serving, mix the liqueur with lots of ice water and sugar.

Makes 1 quart.

Bibliography of Cookbooks

Abdennour, Samia. *Egyptian Cooking: A Practical Guide*. Cairo: American University of Cairo, 1984.

Agnelli, Susanna, ed. *Il Grande Libro della Cucina Regionale*. Milano: Fabbri, 1979.

Agnetti, V. *La Nuova Cucina delle Specialità Regionali*. Milano: Società Editoriale Milanese, 1909.

Alberini, Massimo. *4000 Anni a Tavola: Dalla Bistecca Preistorica al Pic-Nic sulla Luna*. Milano: Fratelli, 1972.

———. *Cento Ricette Storiche*. Firenze: Sansoni, 1974.

———. With recipes compiled by Anna Martini. *Pasta & Pizza*. Translated by Elisabeth Evans. New York: St. Martin's, 1977.

Almanaccu Siciliannu. *Cucina Siciliana*. 3 vols. Marina di Patti: Pungitopo, 1988.

Apicius. *Cookery and Dining in Imperial Rome*. Edited and translated by Joseph Dommers Vehling. New York: Dover, 1977.

Apostolo, Franca Colonna Romano. *Sicilia in bocca . . . e nel cuore: Alimentazione sana-tradizione siciliana*. Palermo: FAP Grafica, 1988.

Arberry, A. J., trans. "A Baghdad Cookery Book." *Islamic Culture* 13 (1939): 21–47, 189–214.

Bartelletti, N. Sapio. *La Cucina Siciliana Nobile e Popolare: Ricette-Storia-Aneddoti-Curiosità*. Milano: Franco Angeli, 1985.

Boni, Ada. *The Talisman Italian Cook Book.* Translated by Matilde La Rosa. New York: Crown, 1950.

Bugialli, Giuliano. *Bugialli on Pasta.* New York: Simon & Schuster, 1988.

Calingaert, Efrem Funghi, and Jacquelyn Days Serwer. *Pasta and Rice Italian Style.* New York: Charles Scribner's Sons, 1983.

Cardella, Antonio. *Sicilia e le Isole in Bocca.* Palermo: Edikronos, 1981.

———. *Trapani in Bocca.* Palermo: La Nuova Edrisi, 1987.

Carluccio, Antonio. *A Taste of Italy.* Boston: Little, Brown and Company, 1986.

Carnacina, Luigi, and Luigi Veronelli. *La Cucina Rustica Regionale.* Vol. 4, *Puglia, Basilicata, Sicilia, Sardegna, Interregionali.* Milano: Rizzoli, 1978.

Cascino, Francesco Paolo. *Cucina di Sicilia.* Palermo: Misuraca, 1980.

Chines, A., and A. Pisa. *Cucina di Putiri Fari: Piccolo Breviario della Cucina Siciliana Facile e Fattibile.* Palermo: S. F. Flaccovio, 1970.

Colonna Romano, Franca. *Sicilia al Tappo.* Palermo: Il Vespro, 1975.

Consiglio, Alberto. *La Storia dei Maccheroni con Cento Ricette e con Pulcinella Mangiamaccheroni.* Roma: Moderne, 1959.

Consoli, Eleonora. *Sicilia: La Cucina del Sole.* 2 vols. Catania: Tringale, 1986.

Consoli Sardo, Maria. *Cucina Nostra.* Palermo: Flaccovio, 1978.

Coria, Giuseppe. *Il libro d'oro dei vini d'Italia.* Milano: Mursia, 1981.

———. *Profumi di Sicilia: Il Libro della Cucina Siciliana.* Palermo: Vito Cavallotto, 1981.

Correnti, Pino. *Il libro d'oro della cucina e dei vini di Sicilia.* Milano: Mursia, 1985.

———. *La Gastronomia nella Storia e nella Vita del Popolo Siciliano.* Milano: Ecotour, 1971.

La Cuisine Tunisienne. Tunis: Société Tunisienne de Diffusion; Paris: Jean-Pierre Taillandier, 1974.

Cùnsolo, Felice. *Gli Italiani a Tavola.* Milano: Mursia, 1965.

———. *Guida Gastronomica d'Italia.* Novara: Istituto Geografico De Agostini, 1975.

d'Alba, Tommaso. *La Cucina Siciliana di Derivazione Araba.* Palermo: Vittorietti, 1980.

de Stefano, Bianca. *Cucina che vai Natura che Trovi: Ricette, Tradizione e Folklore della Cucina Rustica Siciliana.* Palermo: Edikronos, 1987.

Del Conte, Anna. *Gastronomy of Italy.* New York: Prentice Hall, 1987.

De'Medici, Lorenza, and Patrizia Passigli. *Italy the Beautiful Cookbook: Authentic Recipes from the Regions of Italy.* Los Angeles: Knapp, 1988.

Denti di Pirajno, Alberto. *Il Gastronomo Educato.* Venezia: Neri Pozza, 1950.

———. *Siciliani a Tavola: Itinerario Gastronomico da Messina a Porto Empedocle.* Milano: Longanesi, 1970.

der Haroutunian, Arto. *North African Cookery.* London: Century, 1985.

di Napoli Oliver, Fiammetta. *La Grande Cucina Siciliana.* Milano: Moizzi, 1976.

Donati, Stella, ed. *Il Grande Manuale della Cucina Regionale.* Bergamo: Sogarco, 1979.

Field, Carol. *Celebrating Italy*. New York: William Morrow, 1990.

———. *The Italian Baker*. New York: Harper & Row, 1985.

Grasso, J. C. *The Best of Southern Italian Cooking*. Woodbury, NY: Barron's, 1984.

Guida Gastronomica d'Italia. Milano: Touring Club Italiano, 1931.

Guida Gastronomica e dei Vini d'Italia. "La Navicella," 1973.

Khayat, Marie Karam, and Margaret Clark Keatinge. *Food from the Arab World*. Beirut: Khayats, 1961.

Kouki, Mohamed. *La Cuisine Tunisienne d "Ommok Sannafa."* Tunis: Maison Tunisienne de l'Edition, 1971.

Lo Monte, Mimmetta. *Mimmetta Lo Monte's Classic Sicilian Cookbook*. New York: Simon & Schuster, 1990.

———. *La Bella Cucina: Traditional Recipes from a Sicilian Kitchen*. New York: Beaufort Books, 1983.

Lodato, Nuccia. *Le Ricette della Mia Cucina Siciliana*. Milano: Edizioni del Riccio, 1978.

Maffioli, Giuseppe. *La Cucina per l'Amore*. Torino: Dellavalle, 1970.

Malgieri, Nick. *Great Italian Desserts*. Boston: Little, Brown, 1990.

Mangione, Felice. *Sicilia a Tavola*. Marina di Patti: Pungitopo, 1982.

Middione, Carlo. *The Food of Southern Italy*. New York: William Morrow, 1987.

Muffoletto, Anna. *The Art of Sicilian Cooking*. New York: Gramercy, 1982.

Pisa A., and A. Chines. *Cucina d'un Putiri Fari: Piccolo Breviario di Ricette Siciliane Strane, Insolite e Divertenti*. Palermo: S. F. Flaccovio, 1970.

Platina (i.e., Bartolomeo de Sacchi di Piadena). *De Honesta Voluptate*. Vol. 5, n.p.: Mallinckrodt Chemical Works, 1967.

Pomar, Anna. *La Cucina Tradizionale Siciliana*. N.p.: Giuseppe Brancato, 1988.

Roden, Claudia. *A Book of Middle Eastern Food*. New York: Vintage, 1972.

Rousseau, Francesca. *L'Italia in 455 Ricette: La Cucina Regionale Italiana*. Firenze: Le Lettere, 1978.

Russo, Baldo. *Sapore di Sicilia*. Palermo: La Nuova ED.RI.SI., 1988.

Salaparuta, Enrico Alliata, Duca di. *Cucina vegetariana e naturismo crudo: Manuale di gastrosofia naturista con raccolta di 1030 formule scelte d'ogni paese*. Palermo: Sellerio, 1973.

Scott, David. *Recipes for an Arabian Night: Traditional Cooking from North Africa and the Middle East*. New York: Pantheon, 1983.

Simeti, Mary Taylor. *Pomp and Sustenance: Twenty-five Centuries of Sicilian Food*. New York: Alfred A. Knopf, 1989.

Tamzali, Haydée. *La Cuisine en Afrique du Nord*. Paris: Vilo, 1986.

Uccello, Antonio. *Pani e Dolce di Sicilia*. Palermo: Sellerio, 1976.

Vada, Simonetta Lupi. *The Flavors of Italy*. Tucson, Arizona: HP Books, 1986.

———. *Step by Step Cookbook: Italian Seafood and Salad and More*. Secaucus, NJ: Chartwell, 1985.

Waldron, Maggie. *Barbecue & Smoke Cookery*. San Francisco: 101 Productions, 1983.

Wolfert, Paula. *Couscous and Other Good Food from Morocco*. New York: Harper & Row, 1973.

————. *Paula Wolfert's World of Food: A Collection of Recipes from Her Kitchen, Travels, and Friends*. New York: Harper & Row, 1988.

Wright, Jeni. *The Encyclopedia of Italian Cooking*. New York: Crescent Books, 1981.

Zeitoun, Edmond. *250 Recettes Classiques de Cuisine Tunisienne*. Paris: Jacques Grancher, 1977.

Bibliography of Other Works

Abulafia, David S. H. "End of Muslim Sicily." In James M. Powell, ed., *Muslims Under Latin Rule 1100–1300*. Princeton: Princeton University Press, 1990.

———. *Frederick II: A Medieval Emperor*. London: Allen Lane, The Penguin Press, 1988.

———. *Italy, Sicily, and the Mediterranean 1100–1400*. London: Variorum, 1987.

———. "The Norman Kingdom of Africa and the Norman Expeditions to Majorca and the Muslim Mediterranean." In R. Allen Brown, ed., *Anglo-Norman Studies VII: Proceedings of the Battle Conference, 1984*. Woodbridge: Boydell & Brewer, 1985.

Ahmad, Aziz. *A History of Islamic Sicily*. Islamic Surveys 10. Edinburgh: Edinburgh University Press, 1975.

Aleppo, P. Gabriele Maria da, and G. M. Calvaruso. *Le fonti arabiche nel dialetto siciliano*. Rome: Ermanno Loescher, 1910.

Alessio, Giovanni. "Storia linguistica di un antico cibo rituale: 'i maccheroni.' " *Atti della Accademia Pontaniana*, n.s. 8 (1958–59): 261–80.

Algozina, Rosaria Papa. *Sicilia Araba*. Catania: Edizioni Greco, 1977.

Amari, Michele. *Storia dei Musulmani di Sicilia*. Vols. 1–3. Firenze: Felice Le Monnier, 1854–68.

————, ed. *Biblioteca Arabo-Sicula.* Versione Italiana. Torino: Ermanno Loescher, 1880–81.

Amari, M., and C. Schiaparelli, eds. *L'Italia descritta nel "Libro del Re Ruggero" Compilato da Edrisi.* Roma: Salvucci, 1883.

Arezzo, F. G. *Sicilia Miscellanea di Studi Storici, Giuridici ed Economici sulla Sicilia. Glossario di Voci Siciliane Derivate dal Greco, Latino, Arabo, Spagnuolo, Francese, Tedesco, etc.* Palermo: Greco, 1950.

Ashtor, E. "Levantine Sugar Industry in the Late Middle Ages: A Case of Technological Decline." In A. L. Udovitch, ed., *The Islamic Middle East, 700–1900: Studies in Economic and Social History.* Princeton Studies on the Near East. Princeton: The Darwin Press, 1981.

Aymard, Maurice, and Henri Bresc. "Nourritures et Consommation en Sicile entre XIVe et XVIIIe Siècle." *Mélanges de L'Ecole Française de Rome—Moyen Age Temps Modernes* 87 (1975): 535–81.

Balfet, Helene. "Bread in Some Regions of the Mediterranean Area: A Contribution to the Studies of Eating Habits." In Margaret L. Arnott, ed., *Gastronomy: The Anthropology of Food and Food Habits.* The Hague: Mouton, 1975.

Beck-Bossard, Corinne. "L'Alimentazione in un villagio siciliano del XIV secolo, sulla scorta delle fonte archeologiche." *Archeologia Medievale* 8 (1981): 311–19.

Bellafiore, Guiseppe. *La Zisa di Palermo.* Palermo: S. F. Flaccovio, 1978.

Bellestri, Joseph. *Basic Sicilian-English Dictionary.* Ann Arbor: Joseph Bellestri, 1985.

Benjamin of Tudela. *The Itinerary of Rabbi Benjamin of Tudela.* Edited and translated by A. Asher. Vol. 1. New York: Hakesheth, n.d.

Bianchi-Giovani, A. *Sulla Dominazione Degli Arabi in Italia.* Milano: Civelli, 1846.

Boissonnade, P. *Life and Work in Medieval Europe: The Evolution of Medieval Economy from the Fifth to the Fifteenth Century.* Translated by Eileen Power. Westport: Greenwood, 1982.

Bosworth, Clifford Edmund. *The Islamic Dynasties: A Chronological and Genealogical Handbook.* Edinburgh: Edinburgh University Press, 1967.

Braudel, Fernand. *The Mediterranean and the Mediterranean World in the Age of Philip II.* Vols. 1 and 2. Translated by Siân Reynolds. New York: Harper & Row, 1972.

Bresc, Henri. "Les Jardins de Palerme (1290–1460)." *Mélanges de l'Ecole Française de Rome—Moyen Age Temps Modernes* 84 (1972): 55–127.

Bresc-Bautier, Geneviève, Henri Bresc, and Pascal Herbeth. "L'Équipement de la Cuisine et de la Table en Provence et en Sicile (XIVe–XVe Siècles) Étude Comparée." *Manger et Boir: Actes du Colloque de Nice,* October 15–17, 1982. Centre d' Etudes Médiévales de Nice no. 28 1ère serie. Nice: Les Belles Lettres, 1984. Vol. 2: *Cuisine, Manières de Table, Régimes Alimentaires.*

Brookes, John. *Gardens of Paradise: The History and Design of the Great Islamic Gardens.* London: Weidenfeld and Nicolson, 1987.

Brown, R. Allen. *The Normans.* Woodbridge: Boydell Press, 1984.

Brunschvig, Robert. *La Berbérie Orientale sous les Hafsides: Des origines à la fin du XVe siècle.* 2 vols. Publications de l'Institut d'Études Orientales d'Alger VIII. Paris: Adrien-Maisonneuve, 1940 and 1947.

Cahen, Claude. "L'Évolution de l'iqta' du IXe au XIIIe Siècle: Contribution à une histoire comparée des sociétés médiévales." *Annales Economies, Sociétés, Civilisations* 8 (1953): 25–52.

Camporesi, Piero. *Bread of Dreams: Food and Fantasy in Early Modern Europe.* Translated by David Gentilcore. Cambridge: Polity Press, 1989.

Canard, M. "Quelques Notes Relatives à la Sicile sous les Premiers Califes Fatimites." In *Studi Medievali in Onore di Antonino de Stefano.* Palermo: Società Siciliana per la Storia Patria, 1956.

Candolle, Alphonse de. *Origin of Cultivated Plants.* The International Scientific Series, vol. 48. New York: D. Appleton, 1885.

Carefoot, G. L., and E. R. Sprott. *Famine on the Wind: Man's Battle Against Plant Disease.* N.p.: Rand McNally, 1967.

Chalandon, Ferdinand. *Histoire de la Domination Normande en Italie et en Sicile.* Vols. 1 and 2. Paris: Alphonse Picard, 1907.

Chronicon Salernitanum: A Critical Edition with Studies on Literary and Historical Sources and on Language. Edited by Ulla Westerbergh. Studia Latina Stockholmiensia, vol. 3. Stockholm: Almqvist and Wiskell, 1956.

Ciccaglione, F. "La Vita Economia Siciliana nel Periodo Normanno-Svevo." *Archivo Storico per la Sicilia Orientale* 10 (1913): 321–45.

Colchie, Elizabeth Schneider. "Food." *Vogue,* April 1983, pp. 222–28.

Columella, Lucius Junius Moderatus. *De Re Rustica.* Cambridge: Harvard University Press; London: William Heinemann, 1955.

Consolo, Vincenzo. *La Pesca del Tonno in Sicilia.* Palermo: Sellerio, 1987.

Constantine Porphyogenitus. *De Administrato Imperio.* Edited and translated by Gy. Moravcsik and R.J.H. Jenkins. Dumbarton Oaks Texts I. Washington, D.C.: Dumbarton Oaks Center of Byzantine Studies, 1967.

———. *De Thematibus.* Edited by A. Pertusi, Studi e Testi, vol. 160. Vatican City: Biblioteca Apostolica Vaticana, 1952.

Cook, M. A. "Economic Developments." In Joseph Schacht, ed., with C. E. Bosworth, *The Legacy of Islam,* 2d ed. Oxford: Oxford University Press, 1979.

Cordaro, Bianca. *Giornale di Sicilia* (Palermo), October 6 and 10, 1968.

Correnti, Pino. *Pantelleria: La Perla Nera del Mediterraneo.* Milano: Mursia, 1982.

Correnti, Santi. *Storia di Sicilia come Storia del Popolo Siciliano dalla Preistoria all'Autonomia.* Catania: Niccolo Gianotta, 1956.

Cosman, Madeleine Pelner. *Fabulous Feasts: Medieval Cookery and Ceremony.* New York: George Braziller, 1976.

Crawford, Francis Marion. *Southern Italy and Sicily and the Rulers of the South.* New York: Macmillan, 1905.

Crespi, Gabriele. *The Arabs in Europe.* New York: Rizzoli, 1986.

Crino, Sebastiano. "Come si coltivava la canna da zucchero in Sicilia." *L'Agricoltura coloniale* 17 (1923): 81–89.

Curtis, Edmund. *Roger of Sicily and the Normans in Lower Italy 1016–1154.* New York: G. P. Putnam's, 1912.

d'Alba, Tommaso. "Sweet Sicily." *Sicilia Magazine,* no. 5 (Marzo 1989): 46–49.

Daniel, Norman. *The Arab Impact on Sicily and Southern Italy in the Middle Ages.* No. 4. Cairo: Istituto Italiano di Cultura per la R.A.E., 1975.

———. *The Arabs and Medieval Europe.* London and New York: Longman and Librairie du Liban, 1979.

Davidson, Alan. *North Atlantic Seafood.* New York: Viking, 1979.

———. *Mediterranean Seafood.* 2d ed. Baton Rouge: Louisiana State University Press, 1981.

De Gregorio, G., e Chr. F. Seybold. "Glossario delle voci siciliane di origine araba." In *Studi Glottologici Italiani* 3 (1903): 225–51.

Deerr, Noel. *The History of Sugar.* London: Chapman and Hall, 1949.

Di Gregorio, Pasquale. *Vicende Storiche dell'Agricoltura Siciliana.* Palermo: Priulla, 1904.

di Napoli Oliver, Fiammetta. *Invito alla Sicilia.* Milano: Mursia, 1984.

Dominione, Carlo. "Il 'Tesoro delle Paludi': Il Riso in Italia." In *Convegno di Studi sulla Civiltà della Tavola,* edited by Enrico Remondina. Atti dell'Accademia Italiana della Cucina, vol. 6. Milano: Accademia Italiana della Cucina, 1982.

Douglas, David C. *The Norman Achievement 1050–1100.* London: Eyre & Spottiswoode, 1969.

Duby, Georges. *The Early Growth of the European Economy: Warriors and Peasants from the Seventh to the Twelfth Century.* Translated by Howard B. Clarke. Ithaca: Cornell University Press, 1974.

Encyclopaedia of Islam II, entries "Ghida" and "Filaha."

Ettinghausen, Richard. *Arab Painting.* New York: Skira/Rizzoli, 1977.

Facaros, Dana, and Michael Pauls. *Italian Islands.* Chester: Globe Pequot, 1981.

Finley, M. I., Denis Mack Smith, and Christopher Duggan. *A History of Sicily.* New York: Viking, 1987.

Forbes, R. J. "Food and Drink." In Charles Singer et al., eds., *A History of Technology.* Oxford: Oxford University Press, 1956. Vol. 2: *The Mediterranean Civilization and the Middle Ages, c. 700 B.C. to c. A.D. 1500.*

———. Studies in Ancient Technology. Vol. 2. Leiden: E. J. Brill, 1955.

Gabrieli, Francesco. "Frederick II and Moslem Culture." *East and West.* N.s. 9 (1958): 53–61.

———. *Ibn Hamdis.* Mazara: Società Editrice Silicana, 1948.

———. "Arabi di Sicilia e Arabi di Spagna." *Al-Andalus* 15 (1950): 27–45.

———. "Greeks and Arabs in the Central Mediterranean Area." *Dumbarton Oaks Papers,* No. 18. Washington, D.C.: Dumbarton Oaks Center of Byzantine Studies, 1964.

———. "Islam in the Mediterranean World." In Joseph Schacht, ed., with C. E. Bosworth, *The Legacy of Islam,* 2d ed. Oxford: Oxford University Press, 1979.

Gallesio, Georges. *Traité du Citrus.* Paris: Chez Fantin, 1829.

Garufi, C. A. "Patti Agrari e Comuni Feudali di Nuova Fondazione in

Sicilia dallo Scorcio del Secolo XI agli albori del Settecento. Part I, Dal Gran Conte Ruggiero a Carlo V." *Archivio Storico Siciliano* 1 (1946): 39–111.

Gast, Marceau. *Alimentation des Populations de L'Ahaggar: Étude Ethnographique*. Mémoires du Centre de Recherches Anthropologiques Préhistoriques et Ethnographiques, Conseil de la Recherche Scientifique en Algérie, vol. 8. Paris: Art et Métiers, 1968.

Gibb, Sir Hamilton. "The Influence of Islamic Culture on Medieval Europe." In Sylvia L. Thrupp, ed., *Change in Medieval Society: Europe North of the Alps 1050–1500*. Toronto: University of Toronto and Medieval Academy of America, 1988.

Gibbon, Edward. *The History of the Decline and Fall of the Roman Empire*. Philadelphia: J. B. Lippincott, 1879. Vol. 5.

Gioeni, Giuseppe. *Saggio di Etimologie Siciliane*. Archivio Storico Siciliano, vol. 10. Palermo: Tipographia dello "Statuto," 1885.

Giudice, Pasqualino. "Arabi." Unpublished paper, 1989.

———. "Siracusa: culla di civiltà anche gastronomica." *Imprenditore Oggi* (Syracuse). January 1989, p. 56; March 1989, pp. 51–52.

Giuffrida, Antonino. "Considerazioni sul Consumo della Carne a Palermo nei Secoli XIV e XV." *Mélanges de L'Ecole Française de Rome— Moyen Age Temps Modernes* 87 (1975): 583–95.

Giunta, Francesco. *Bizantini e Bizantinismo nella Sicilia Normanna*. Palermo: G. Priulla, 1950.

Glick, Thomas F. *Irrigation and Society in Medieval Valencia*. Cambridge: Harvard University Press, 1970.

Gobert, Ernest G. "Les Références Historiques des Nourritures Tunisiennes." *Les Cahiers de Tunisie* 3 (1955): 501–42.

———. *Usages et Rites Alimentaires des Tunisiens*. Tunis: Bascone & Muscat, 1940.

Goethe, J. W. *Italian Journey (1786–1788)*. Translated by W. H. Auden and Elizabeth Mayer. San Francisco: North Point Press, 1982.

Goitein, Shelomo. "Sicily and Southern Italy in the Cairo Geniza Documents." *Archivio Storico per la Sicilia Orientale* 42 (1971): 9–33.

———. *A Mediterranean Society: The Jewish Communities of the Arab World as Portrayed in the Documents of the Cairo Geniza*. Berkeley: University of California Press, 1983. Vol. 4, *Daily Life*.

Golden, John. "Pantelleria." *Gourmet,* May 1981, pp. 28ff.

Gottschalk, Alfred. *Histoire de l'Alimentation et de la Gastronomie depuis la Préhistoire jusqu'à nos Jours*. Paris: Hippocrate, 1948.

Guercio, Francis M. *Sicily: The Garden of the Mediterranean, the Country and Its People*. London: Faber and Faber, 1954.

Guida d'Italia. *Sicilia*. 6th ed. Milano: Touring Club Italiano, 1989.

Hamdan, G. "Evolution of Irrigation Agriculture in Egypt." In L. Dudley Stamp, ed., *A History of Land Use in Arid Regions*. Arid Zone Research, vol. 17. Paris: UNESCO, 1961, pp. 119–42.

Harris, Valentina. *Traveller's Guide to the Food of Italy*. New York: Henry Holt, 1988.

Haskins, Charles Homer. *Studies in the History of Mediaeval Science*. Cambridge: Harvard University Press, 1924.

Hehn, Victor. *Cultivated Plants and Domestic Animals in Their Migration from Asia to Europe.* London: Swan Sonnenschein, 1891.

Henisch, Bridget Ann. *Fast and Feast: Food in Medieval Society.* University Park: Pennsylvania State University, 1976.

Herlihy, David. "The Agrarian Revolution in Southern France and Italy: 801–1150." *Speculum* 33 (1958): 23–41.

Hitti, Philip K. *History of the Arabs from the Earliest Times to the Present.* 10th ed. New York: St. Martin's, 1970.

Hodgson, Marshall G. S. *The Venture of Islam: Conscience and History in a World Civilization.* Chicago: University of Chicago, 1974. Vol 2, *The Expansion of Islam in the Middle Periods.*

Huillard-Bréholles, J. -L. -A., ed. *Historia Diplomatica Friderici Secundi.* Paris: Excudebant Plon Fratres, 1861–72. Vol. 1, pt. 1; vol. 2, pt. 1; vol. 5, pt. 1.

Hyams, Edward. *Dionysus: A Social History of the Wine Vine.* New York: Macmillan, 1965.

Hyde, J. K. *Society and Politics in Medieval Italy: The Evolution of Civil Life, 1000–1350.* London: Macmillan, 1973.

Ibn Jubayr. *The Travels of Ibn Jubayr.* Translated by R.J.C. Broadhurst. London: Jonathan Cape, 1952.

Jasny, Naum. *The Wheats of Classical Antiquity.* The Johns Hopkins University Studies in Historical and Political Science Series, vol. 42, no. 3. Baltimore: Johns Hopkins University Press, 1944.

Jones, Gwyn. *A History of the Vikings.* 2d ed. Oxford: Oxford University Press, 1987.

Kedar, Benjamin. *Crusade and Mission: European Approaches Towards the Muslims.* Princeton: Princeton University Press, 1984.

Kininmonth, Christopher. *Sicily.* London: Jonathan Cape, 1988.

Lane, Edward William. *The Manners and Customs of the Modern Egyptians.* London and Toronto: J. M. Dent; New York: E. P. Dutton, 1908.

Lévi-Provençal, E. "Une Héroïne de la Résistance Musulmane en Sicile au Début du XIIIe Siècle." *Oriente Moderno* 34 (1954): 283–88.

Lewis, Archibald R. *Naval Power and Trade in the Mediterranean, A.D. 500–1100.* Princeton: Princeton University Press, 1951.

Lewis, Bernard, ed. and trans. *Islam from the Prophet Muhammad to the Capture of Constantinople.* Vol. 2, *Religion and Society.* Oxford: Oxford University Press, 1987.

Lopez, Robert S. *The Commercial Revolution of the Middle Ages 950–1350.* Cambridge: Cambridge University Press, 1976.

Luzzatto, Gino. *An Economic History of Italy from the Fall of the Roman Empire to the Beginning of the Sixteenth Century.* Translated by Philip Jones. London: Routledge and Kegan Paul, 1961.

Macadam, Alta. *Blue Guide: Sicily.* London and Tonbridge: Ernest Benn; Chicago: Rand McNally, 1981.

Madan, C. L., B. M. Kapur, and U. S. Gupta. "Saffron." *Economic Botany* 20 (1966).

March, Lourdes. "The Valencian Paella—Its Origin, Tradition and Universality." *Oxford Symposium on Food and Cookery 1988: The Cooking Pot. Proceedings.* London: Prospect, 1989.

Ménager, Léon-Robert. "L'institution monarchique dans l'Etats normands d'Italie: Contribution à l'étude du pouvoir royal dans les principautés occidentales, aux XIe–XIIe siècles." *Cahiers de Civilisation Médiévale* 11 (1959): 303–31, 445–68.

Menocal, Maria Rosa. *The Arabic Role in Medieval Literary History: A Forgotten Heritage.* Philadelphia: University of Pennsylvania Press, 1987.

Mintz, Sidney W. *Sweetness and Power: The Place of Sugar in Modern History.* New York: Penguin, 1985.

Mortillaro, Vincenzo. *Dizionario Siciliano-Italiano.* Palermo: Vittorietti, 1983.

Mottahedeh, Roy P. *Loyalty and Leadership in an Early Islamic Society.* Princeton: Princeton University Press, 1980.

Norman, Barbara. *Tales of the Table: A History of Western Cuisine.* Englewood Cliffs: Prentice-Hall, 1972.

The Normans in Sicily and Southern Italy. Linei Lectures 1974. Oxford: Oxford University Press for the British Academy, 1977.

Norwich, John Julius. *The Kingdom in the Sun 1130–1194.* London: Longman, 1970.

———. *The Normans in the South 1016–1130.* London: Longman, 1967.

Ostrogorsky, George. *History of the Byzantine State.* Rev. ed. New Brunswick: Rutgers University Press, 1969.

Panetta, Rinaldo. *I Saraceni in Italia.* Milano: Mursia, 1973.

Parry, John W. *The Story of Spices.* New York: Chemical, 1953.

Pasqualino, Michele. *Vocabulario Siciliano, Etimologico, Italiano, e Latino.* Palermo: Dalle Reale Stamperia, 1785.

Pellegrini, Giovan Battista. *Contributo allo Studio dell'Elemento Arabo nei Dialetti Siciliani.* Istituto di Filologia Romanza 2. Trieste: Università degli Studi di Trieste, 1962.

———. *Gli Arabismi nelle Lingue Neolatine con speciale riguardo all'Italia.* 2 vols. Brescia: Paideia, 1972.

Petino, Gianni. "Per la Storia della Canna da Zucchero in Sicilia agli inizi dell'eta moderna." *Archivo Storico per la Sicilia Orientale* 45 (1969): 97–125.

Pitrè, Giuseppe. *La Famiglia, La Casa, La Vita del Popolo Siciliano.* Bologna: Forni, 1969.

———. *Bibilioteca delle Tradizioni Popolari Siciliane.* 15 vols. Palermo: Luigi Pedone Lauriel, 1887. Vol. 2, *Usi e Costumi Credenze e Pregiudizi.*

Postan, M. M. *The Cambridge Economic History of Europe.* 2d ed. Cambridge: Cambridge University Press, 1966. Vol. 2, *The Agrarian Life of the Middle Ages.*

Pryor, John H. " 'In Subsidium Terrae Sanctae': Exports of Foodstuffs and War Materials from the Kingdom of Sicily to the Kingdom of Jerusalem, 1265–1284." In B. Z. Kedar and A. L. Udovitch, eds., "The Medieval Levant: Studies in Memory of Eliyahu Ashtor (1914—1984)," *Asian and African Studies* 22 (1988): 127–46.

Revel, Jean-François. *Culture and Cuisine: A Journey Through the History of Food.* Translated by Helen R. Lane. New York: Da Capo, 1982.

Rice, David Talbot. *Islamic Art*. New York: Frederick A. Praeger, 1965.

Rizzitano, Umberto. *Storia e Cultura nella Sicilia Saracena*. Palermo: S. F. Flaccovio, 1975.

———. *La Cultura Araba nella Sicilia Saracena*. Vincenza: Società Edistampa, 1961.

Rodinson, Maxime. "*Romania* et Autres Mots Arabes en Italien." *Romania* 284 (1950): 233–48. Translated as "*Romania* and Other Arab Words in Italian"; *Petits Propos Culinaire*, no. 34 (March 1990): 31–44.

———. "Recherches sur les Documents Arabes Relatifs à la Cuisine." *Revue des Études Islamiques* 17–18 (1949): 95–165.

———. "Sur L'Etymologie de 'Losange.' " In *Studi Orientalistici in onore di Giorgio Levi Della Vida*. Istituto per l'Oriente 52. Roma: Istituto per l'Oriente, 1956. Vol. 2.

Root, Waverley. *The Food of Italy*. New York: Vintage, 1977.

Runciman, Steven. *The Sicilian Vespers: A History of the Mediterranean World in the Later Thirteenth Century*. Cambridge: Cambridge University Press, 1958.

Salomone-Marino, Salvatore. *Customs and Habits of the Sicilian Peasants*. Edited and translated by Rosalie N. Norris. London and Toronto: Associated University Presses, 1981.

Schimmel, Annemarie. "The Celestial Garden in Islam." In *The Islamic Garden*. Washington, D.C.: Dumbarton Oaks Center for Byzantine Studies, 1976.

Schnell, R. *Plantes alimentaires et vie agricole de l'Afrique Noire: Essai de Phytogéographie Alimentaire*. Paris: Larose, 1957.

Sciascia, Leonardo. "Sicily." *Vogue,* July 1985, pp. 178–79.

Sereni, Emilio. "Note di storia dell'alimentazione nel mezzogiorno: I Napoletani da 'Mangiafoglia' a 'Mangiamaccheroni.' " *Chronache meridionale* 5 (1958): 272–95, 353–77, 398–422.

———. *Storia del paesaggio agrario Italiana*. Bari: P. Laterza, 1961.

Sharman, Fay, and Brian Chadwick. *The Taste of Italy: A Dictionary of Italian Food and Wine*. London: Macmillan, 1985.

Simeti, Mary Taylor. *On Persephone's Island: A Sicilian Journal*. San Francisco: North Point, 1987.

Smith, Denis Mack. *A History of Sicily: Medieval Sicily, 800–1713*. New York: Dorset, 1968.

Solignac, Marcel. *Recherches sur les installations hydrauliques de Kairouan et des steppes tunisiennes du VIIe au XIe siècle (J. C.)*. L'Institut d'Etudes Orientales de la Faculté des Lettres d'Alger, vol. 13. Algers: La Typo-Litho et Jules Carbonel, 1953.

Spufford, Peter. *Money and Its Use in Medieval Europe*. Cambridge: Cambridge University Press, 1988.

Stobart, Tom. *Herbs, Spices and Flavorings*. New York: McGraw-Hill, 1970.

Sturlason, Store. *The Heimskringla: A History of the Norse Kings*. Translated by Samuel Laing. London: Norroena Society, 1907. Vol. 2.

Tacuinum Sanitatis (The Medieval Health Handbook). Edited by Luisa Cogliati Arano and translated by Oscar Ratti and Adele Westbrook. New York: George Braziller, 1976.

Talbi, Mohamed. "Law and Economy in Ifriqiya (Tunisia) in the Third Islamic Century: Agriculture and the Role of Slaves in the Country's Economy." In A. L. Udovitch, ed., *The Islamic Middle East, 700– 1900: Studies in Economic and Social History*. Princeton Studies on the Near East. Princeton: The Darwin Press, 1981.

Tannahill, Reay. *Food in History*. New York: Crown, 1989.

Targioni-Tozzetti, Antonio. *Cenni Storici sulla Introduzione de Varie Piante nell'Agricoltura ed Orticoltura Toscana*. Firenze: Tipografia M. Ricci, 1896.

"Ta'rikh Mansuri." In Francesco Gabrieli, ed., *Arab Historians of the Crusades*. Translated by E. J. Costello. Berkeley: University of California Press, 1969.

Tolkowsky, S. *Hesperides: A History of the Culture and Use of Citrus Fruits*. London: John Bale, Sons and Curnow, Ltd., 1938.

Traina, Antonino. *Nuovo Vocabolario Siciliano-Italiano*. Palermo: Lorenzo Finocchiaro e Fiorenza Orazio, 1890.

Trasselli, Carmelo. "Produzione e Commercio dello zucchero in Sicilia dal XIII al XIX secolo." *Economia e storia* 2 (1955): 325–42.

Treadgold, Warren. *The Byzantine Revival: 780–842*. Stanford: Stanford University Press, 1988.

Van Cleve, Thomas Curtis. *The Emperor Frederick II of Hohenstaufen Immutator Mundi*. Oxford: Oxford University Press, 1972.

Vasiliev, A. A. *Byzance et les Arabes*. Corpus Bruxellense Historiae Byzantinae 1. Bruxelles: Editions de l'Institut de Philologie et d'Histoire Orientales, 1935. Vol. 1, *La Dynastie d'Amorium*.

———. *History of the Byzantine Empire 324–1453*. Madison: University of Wisconsin Press, 1952.

Vavilov, N. I. *The Origin, Variation, Immunity and Breeding of Cultivated Plants*. Translated by K. Starr Chester. Chronica Botanica, vol. 13, nos. 1/6. Waltham: Chronica Botanica, 1951.

Visser, Margaret. *Much Depends on Dinner: The Extraordinary History and Mythology, Allure and Obsessions, Perils and Taboos of an Ordinary Meal*. New York: Collier Books, 1986.

Waern, Cecilia. *Medieval Sicily: Aspects of Life and Art in the Middle Ages*. London: Duckworth, 1910.

Waley, D. P. " 'Combined Operations' in Sicily, A.D. 1060–78." *Papers of the British School at Rome* 22 (1954): 118–25.

Watson, Andrew M. "A Medieval Green Revolution: New Crops and Farming Techniques in the Early Islamic World." In A. L. Udovitch, ed., *The Islamic Middle East, 700–1900: Studies in Economic and Social History*. Princeton Studies on the Near East. Princeton: The Darwin Press, 1981.

———. *Agricultural Innovation in the Early Islamic World: The Diffusion of Crops and Farming Techniques, 700–1100*. Cambridge: Cambridge University Press, 1983.

————. "The Arab Agricultural Revolution and Its Diffusion, 700–1100." *Journal of Economic History* 34 (1974): 8–35.

Watt, W. Montgomery. *The Influence of Islam on Medieval Europe*. Islamic Surveys 9. Edinburgh: Edinburgh University Press, 1972.

Wehr, Hans. *A Dictionary of Modern Written Arabic*. 3d ed. Ithaca: Spoken Language Services, 1976.

White, K. D. *Roman Farming*. London: Thames and Hudson, 1970.

White, Lynn, Jr. *Medieval Technology and Social Change*. Oxford: Oxford University Press, 1964.

White, Lynn Townsend. *Latin Monasticism in Norman Sicily*. Cambridge: The Medieval Academy of America, 1938.

Wilson, C. Anne. "The Saracen Connection: Arab Cuisine and the Medieval West: Parts 1 and 2." *Petits Propos Culinaires* 7 (March 1981): 13–22; 8 (June 1981): 19–28.

Wright, Clifford A. "Cuscusù: A Paradigm of Arab-Sicilian Cuisine." *Journal of Gastronomy* 5 (1990): 19–37.

Index

259

ABOUT THE AUTHOR

CLIFFORD WRIGHT was born in New York City in 1951. He graduated from Colorado State University and holds an M.A. degree in Philosophy from the Graduate Faculty of the New School for Social Research. He has worked as a foreign policy researcher at the Brookings Institution and most recently held the position of Executive Director of the American Middle East Peace Research Institute in Cambridge, Massachusetts.

An avid traveler and cook, Wright has toured Italy and Sicily, as well as the Arab world, researching not only the history and culture of each place, but the food as well. It was his interest in food and the Middle East that brought him to consider the notion of an Arab-Sicilian cuisine, culminating first in an article for *The Journal of Gastronomy,* then featured in an article in the *New York Times,* and finally, this book. Wright is also the author of *After the Palestine-Israel War: Limits to U.S. and Israeli Policy* and *Facts and Fables: The Arab-Israeli Conflict.* He lives in Arlington, Massachusetts, and is the father of three children.